YOU ENGLISH WORDS

You English words
I know you:
You are light as dreams,
Tough as oak,
Precious as gold,
As poppies and corn,
Or an old cloak . . .

EDWARD THOMAS: *Words*

YOU
ENGLISH
WORDS

BY JOHN MOORE

J. B. LIPPINCOTT COMPANY

Philadelphia and New York—1962

THIRD PRINTING

COPYRIGHT © 1961 BY JOHN MOORE

PRINTED IN THE UNITED STATES OF AMERICA

LIBRARY OF CONGRESS CATALOG CARD NUMBER 62-10535

Contents

Acknowledgments

ANYBODY WHO WRITES about English words inevitably refers his doubts and difficulties, puzzles and problems, to the great *Oxford English Dictionary*. Of its twelve noble volumes which have been my constant companions during the writing of this book I can only say that the more often a man consults them, the greater grows his respect for their urbane and impeccable scholarship.

Mr. Eric Partridge's *Origins* has shared a shelf with the *O.E.D.*, and borne likewise the wear and tear of continual use. So has his *Dictionary of English Slang*. These are books which one consults for information, and continues to read for enjoyment, long after the information is found.

Mr. Ivor Brown's series of "word-books" long ago quickened my interest and sharpened my curiosity concerning these tools of my trade. The first of them reached me at one of the grimmest periods of the late war; and the pleasure I had from reading it, in a warship at sea, still seems in retrospect like a warm glow against the cold and the dark.

Both to Ivor Brown and to Eric Partridge my debt is a double one: not only for their writings, but for their friendship as well.

I must express my thanks also to three more friends: Professor A. H. Smith, for his advice and help in many ways; Mr. W. Bridges Adams, for reading some of my chapters; and to Mr. A. L. Irvine, for his goodness in reading the proofs.

For permission to quote complete poems or longish passages, I am grateful to Mr. John Betjeman and his publishers, Messrs. John Murray and Houghton Mifflin Company; the Times Publishing Company; and the Exors. of Hilaire Belloc and James Elroy Flecker. I owe my special thanks to Mrs. Edward Thomas, for allowing me to quote from Edward Thomas' *Words* both in the book and on the dust-jacket.

J.M.

CHAPTER 1

An Amateur of Words

THIS IS A BOOK about the fun, the excitement, the wonder, and the sense of adventurous exploration among the minds of men, which as writer and reader I have found in my dealings with words. It is an amateur's book, and a personal one; being concerned with my own curiosity about the words I encounter or use in the practice of my craft, with my efforts to satisfy that curiosity by recourse to the works of real scholars, and with the entertainments and diverse pleasures which such quests have afforded me. Perhaps the best way to begin it is to give you some examples of those pleasures. I will start with a frivolous one, and confess that I am by nature an incorrigible collector. Like any bughunter, philatelist, or big-game-stalker on safari, I rejoice quite shamelessly in my occasional discovery of the rare, the unexpected, the freakish and the aberrant. Whenever in the course of my reading I come across a word I do not know or which I have never seen used in that particular sense, I go to the dictionaries and look it up. Very, very rarely I am unable to find it in the dictionaries; and then I experience in little the kind of triumph which Sir Henry Hamilton Johnston must have felt when, first of all mankind, he set eyes upon an okapi in the Congo forest in 1900.

I was reading, for instance, a biography of that foolish and unattractive person, the late Aleister Crowley. At one time he had a disciple called Victor Neuburg; and subsequently, according to his biographer, he was inclined to boast to his friends how he had turned Mr. Neuburg into a dromedary or a zebra by means of black magic. Hearing of this, Mr. Neuburg strongly denied it. Indeed the suggestion that his soul might have inhabited even briefly the body of such a beast seemed to make him very angry; for he declared that Crowley's story was "ostrobogulous piffle" from beginning to end. Utterly fascinated by "ostrobogulous," I sought it in all the dictionaries; but I could find no word bearing any resemblance to it. Dare I assume that it never ex-

isted before Mr. Neuburg's indignation proclaimed it to the world? It
is a splendid adjective, anyhow, though too powerful for everyday use.
No accusation lighter than that of having been turned into a dromedary ought to call it forth.

On another occasion I was glancing through William Cobbett's
Advice to Young Men, which is written in sturdy, opinionated and very
refreshing prose. In the very first of the "Letters" Cobbett expressed
his angry contempt for "the slavery of the tea and coffee and other slopkettle." He held these to be very un-English drinks compared with
beer; and I always think it sad that he was observed to drink a cup of
tea on the very day before he died,—"How are the mighty fallen!" exclaimed Mr. G. D. H. Cole, his biographer. Of course, I was not at all
surprised to find him riding his hobby-horse in *Advice to Young Men*:
but the word "slopkettle" caught my fancy as being just the right word
for Cobbett to use, a perfect expression of his bluff and blustering and
downright personality. I decided to look it up, and see who had used it
before him. To my surprise, it was not to be found even in the great
Oxford English Dictionary, so perhaps this is another word born of individual indignation? But what would Cobbett think of the tea-breaks
that occur nowadays in factories and offices? What would he *say* about
such a slopkettle tyranny?

While I was looking for this word in the *O.E.D.* I was diverted by
a definition of the word "slop." It has many meanings, among them
baggy breeches, a muddy hole, growing underwood, cheap clothing,
etc. sold in H.M. ships, a policeman (slang) and "the dirty water, etc."
of a household; but the first meaning given in the *O.E.D.* runs as follows:

A charmed bag employed to steal milk from cows. *obs. rare.*

The single example of its use is from an obscure work by one Robert
Brunne, *Handlyng Synne* (1303), and describes how a witch made a
bag for this naughty purpose. By the time I had speculated about this
oddity, wondered what kind of bag it was, and how she fixed it on to the
udder of the cow, I had wasted a good five minutes and had nearly
forgotten that I was seeking the word "slopkettle." This is the second
of the pleasures I find in words, and I will define it as the enjoyable
pursuit of red herrings.

I SUPPOSE it is almost impossible for anybody possessing the normal human allowance of curiosity to look up a word in the dictionary without being diverted once or twice by some other unfamiliar word. In my case such diversions are especially common, because I haven't got an alphabetical mind: despite years of practice I approach the word I am looking for rather as a moth approaches a flame, in a series of zigzags. If in the course of these manœuvres my eye happens to light upon such a word as—say—"soodle," "tohu-bohu" or "antisyzygy," my curiosity is aroused and my original quest is halted while I learn about "soodle," that it means "to stroll, saunter, to walk in a slow or leisurely manner"; about "antisyzygy," that it is Greek for a union of opposites, as it were of the Deity and the Devil; or about "tohu-bohu," a marvellous word which has been used by Mr. Gladstone and by Robert Browning, and which comes from a Hebrew phrase *Thōhū-wa-bhōhū*, which sounds like a lamentation and indeed turns out to be akin to one, for it means emptiness and desolation, utter confusion, ancient Chaos itself. In the Hebrew Bible, the dictionary tells me, *Thōhū-wa-bhōhū* appears in the second verse of the first chapter of the Book of Genesis; so I take down the Bible to see how it was translated and I read:

> And the earth was without form, and void; and darkness was upon the face of the deep.

Awe-struck by the splendour of those words, I cannot resist reading on; and what matter if this time I have altogether forgotten what purpose sent me to the dictionary in the first place!

SOME MORE ODDITIES which I have stumbled upon recently while seeking information about other words are "quockerwodger," "rumblegumption," "skilligolee," "calibogus," and "jobbernowl." He would be a strong-minded fellow who could pass them by without a second glance; and he would miss a lot of fun. A "quockerwodger" turns out to be a wooden articulated figure which, when pulled up by a string, jerks its limbs about. At least that is what the word used to signify. Our long-suffering citizens during the 1850's were struck by certain points of similarity between the behaviour of this toy and that of their Members of Parliament; so quockerwodger came to mean "a politician acting under an outsider's order." It is now obsolete; though the politician isn't.

"Rumblegumption" is a Scottish word for common sense. Skilligolee is sailors' or prisoners' soup made from many ingredients. Calibogus is a mixture of rum and spruce beer. A jobbernowl is a blockhead, and dates from the late 16th century when John Marston in his *Scourge of Villanie* wrote concerning a character of whom he did not think very highly:

His guts are in his braines, huge Jobbernoule, right Gurnetshead.

It is a good expressive word for a stupid oaf, and deserves I think to be revived.

DELIBERATE WORD-HUNTING in the dictionary—thumbing through it page by page in search of rarities—does not, however, much appeal to me. It is like looking at rare butterflies neatly arranged in the drawers of a cabinet in a museum, rather than finding them by chance at the wayside or in the wood. No dictionary discovery will give you so much pleasure as the finds you make for yourself in the course of your ordinary reading. Once again I can explain best by giving some examples. You are reading, let us suppose, Roper's *Life of Sir Thomas More*, and you have got to the point where Sir Thomas is confined in the Tower and his wife obtains permission to visit him. "Coming like a simple woman, and somewhat worldly too" she wastes no time upon commiserations or endearments, but "bluntly salutes him" as follows:

"What the good year, Mr. More," quoth she, "I marvel that you, that have been always hitherunto taken for so wise a man, will now so play the fool to lie here in this close filthy prison, and be content to be shut up among mice and rats, when you might be abroad with your liberty . . . if you would but do as all the bishops and best learned of this Realm have done. And seeing you have at Chelsea a right fair house, your library, your books, your gallery, your garden, your orchard and other necessaries so handsomely about you where you might, in the company of me your wife, your children and household be merry, I muse what a God's name you mean here still thus fondly to tarry." After he had a while quietly heard her, with a cheerful countenance he said unto her, "I pray thee, good Mrs. Alice, tell me, tell me one thing." "What is that?" (quoth she). "Is not this house as nigh heaven as mine own?" To whom she, after her accustomed fashion, not liking such talk, answered "*Tille valle, tille valle.*"

You can hear Lady More's voice upraised through the whole paragraph, but that *tilly-vally*—as it was usually spelt—fixes her in your mind for ever, epitomises her down-to-earthness, and sets you wondering how a woman with such devastating common sense ever came to marry a saint, and love him, and be loved by him. Tilly-vally means "nonsense" and it means "fiddlesticks," and goodness knows how many times her ladyship had occasion to say it to Sir Thomas before the King had his head cut off; but how it originated, nobody can tell me. Sir Toby Belch used it, when Maria warned him that his caterwauling with Sir Andrew might cause Olivia to turn him out of her house. "Am I not consanguineous? Am I not of her blood? Tilly-valley, lady!" cries Sir Toby, well in his cups. Whether you find it for the first time in *Twelfth Night* or in the *Life of Sir Thomas More* doesn't matter; tilly-valley (whichever way you spell it) is a prize that goes straight into your collection.

I DON'T SUPPOSE anybody cries tilly-valley nowadays. The fashion in exclamations seems very changeable; and out-of-date ones are apt to look most peculiar in print. In Webster's *White Devil* "pew-wew" appears as an expostulation. In Boswell's *Johnson* we frequently come across "Pho! Pho!" It is strange that the noises which the human animal utters to express its annoyance, agreement, excitement or indignation should differ from century to century, apparently they do so, for you can roughly date a novel by means of a careful study of the exclamations in it. If "Hallo!" is one of them, then the book was printed later than 1840; for the dictionary assures us that "Hallo!" was not used before that date, though a man might halloo his dogs—or his mistress' name to the reverberate hills—back in Shakespeare's day. "Hello!" first showed itself in 1850; "Hullo!" in 1857. People certainly have very different ideas about the way these exclamatory noises are to be spelt. An English grammar published in Paris in 1949 [1] asserts that when we are disgusted we are apt to say "Fie!" "Fudge!" "Whew!" or "Harrow!"; when we are impatient we say "Whip!" "Buzz!" or "Pop!" Pleasure is expressed by "He!" "Heyday!" "Aha!" And lastly, "On

---

[1] Cestre and Dubois: *Grammaire Complète de la Langue Anglaise.*

pleure: *uh, uh!*" I notice that in tough American novels the girls are apt to exclaim "Uh-uh," without the accompaniment of tears.

Some exclamations, however, seem to be untouched by time or fashion. As modern today as when it was written nearly 600 years ago is the squeak of laughing mockery uttered by Chaucer's Alisoun:

> *Tehee, quod she, and clapte the window to.*[1]

I CAME ACROSS a very rare word, "refocillate," meaning "to warm into life again, to revive," when I was reading John Aubrey's *Brief Lives*. The passage, concerning one William Prynne, has a special interest for authors and others whose work entails the long loneliness of solitary study:

> His manner of studie was thus: he wore a long quilt cap, which came, two or three, at least, inches, over his eies, which served him as an umbrella to defend his eies from the light. About every three houres his man was to bring him a roll and a pott of ale to refocillate his wasted spirits. So he studied and dranke, and munched some bread; and this maintained him till night; and then he made a good supper.

Aubrey's writings are a happy hunting ground for the rare-word collector (Mr. Ivor Brown found "scobberlotcher" there);[2] but we take pleasure in *Brief Lives* mainly for its presentation of a gallery of individualists, who act according to their beliefs and inclinations without regard for what other people may think of them. Thomas Hobbes, for instance, "when he was abed, and doors made fast . . . he sang aloud (not that he had a very good voice) but for his health's sake; he did believe it did his lungs good, and conduced much to prolong life." A namesake of mine, Sir Jonas Moore, preserved his health by more daring means. "Sciatica he cured it, by boyling his buttock."

THE WORKS of Sir Thomas Urquhart, especially his translations of Rabelais, are another fruitful source of out-of-the-way words and oddities of language. Sir Thomas was a Scot possessing labyrinthine learn-

---

[1] *The Miller's Tale.*
[2] See his *Just Another Word.* It was a term of abuse invented by a Dr. Kettle, President of Trinity College, Oxford, for boys who "went idleing about with their hands in their pockets."

ing, a cranky and contentious mind, and a vast unconventional vocabulary. For variety of invective he would be hard to beat. Here are some of the rude names which he gave to the "beastly looking fellows" who were warned on no account to set foot within the Abbey at Thélème. He began by calling them *Puft up, wry-necked beasts, worse than the Huns or Ostrogoths, forerunners of baboons,* and from that good start he went on to describe them as base snites, curst snakes, seeming Sancts, pelf-lickers, slipshod caffards, smell-feast knockers, doltish gulls, out-strouting cluster-fists, coin-gripers, niggish deformed sots, Pluto's bastards, chichie sneakbill rogues and fat chuff-cats. You will not find many of these expressions defined in the dictionary; but I understand "chichie" means stingy, and as for "chuff-cat," the word seems to have had the sense of churlish and miserly, but also fat-cheeked. I see a chuff-cat as both plump and mean: a horrible combination.

THESE CURIOSITIES of course are simply collectors' pieces, of interest chiefly for their scarcity, or because they are old and obsolete, like those queer triangular stamps of the Cape of Good Hope. I find a peculiar pleasure nevertheless in archaic words, which when you meet them unexpectedly seem to stand up like old oaks left by the town-planners in the midst of new housing-estates, splendid, sombre, and doomed. The Bible keeps some of them alive for us: "damsel" and "raiment" would perhaps be hardly known today but for the fact that they appear so often in the Authorised Version. Shakespeare's greatness perpetuates some stranger words; I shall have something to say about them later. Meanwhile let us take a brief look at one typical archaism, which remains familiar to us through the twin agencies of *Hamlet* and of heraldry:

> *Head to foot,*
> *Now is he total gules.*

The more ham our Hamlet, the more he is likely to enjoy reciting the Player's speech:

> *Horridly trick'd*
> *With blood of fathers, mothers, daughters, sons . . .*
> *And thus o'er-sized* [1] *with coagulate gore,*
> *With eyes like carbuncles, the hellish Pyrrhus . . .*

[1] "Covered as with size": invented by, and used only by, Shakespeare.

"Gules" may derive from a Mediaeval Latin word meaning "ermine dyed red," or it may come from *gula*, the throat, because of the red colour of the open mouths of the beasts which appear in heraldry. It is one of the conventional heraldic colours; the others are or, argent, jaune, blanc, sable, vert and purpure.

"Gore," by the way, long before it signified blood, meant dung, filth, or the plum-tree-gum, as Hamlet put it, of old men's eyes. Its use nowadays in the sense of "blood" is always whimsical; though in Victorian times I suppose people like Simon Tappertit employed it seriously; "Something will come of this; I hope it mayn't be human gore." [1] I have hated this word ever since I was a child, when a dentist practised in my native town, whose brass plate I always looked at in terror, called Mr. Gore-Boodle.

IT IS NOT ONLY the unfamiliar word that will send you searching through the dictionaries; it is the common word popping up unexpectedly, out of period, keeping the wrong company, or bearing a strange meaning, like a person in disguise,—for instance "The silly buckets on the deck" in *The Ancient Mariner*, where "silly" means "plain and homely." To come across an apparently "modern" word in an old context is even more surprising. When do you imagine "spliced" was fashionable slang for married? Certainly it has a rather shabby and dated appearance nowadays; and if I had tried to guess what period it belonged to, I should have put it between 1890 and 1910, the heyday of facetiousness, when Jerome K. Jerome's *Three Men in a Boat* was thought very funny, and Gilbert the Filbert was Colonel of the Knuts. I should have been wrong; for you may find it in Charlotte Brontë's *Villette*:

> Alfred and I intended to be married in this way almost from the first; we never meant to be spliced in the humdrum way of other people.

Smollett used it a hundred years earlier, in *Peregrine Pickle*; but I obtained that piece of information from the dictionary, and so it did not please me so much as my accidental stumbling upon the word in Charlotte Brontë's novel, where it seemed quite out of character, and as anachronistic as "What the dickens" does in *The Merry Wives of*

[1] Dickens: *Barnaby Rudge*.

Windsor. "I cannot tell what the dickens his name is," says Mistress Page,—a line which troubles those members of the audience who have always associated such a use of "dickens" with the novelist. In fact it is one of the many polite pseudonyms for the Devil, used by Shakespeare in exactly the same way as "the deuce" was used by the Victorians.

THE OTHER DAY I was reading Philip Stubbes' account of the Maypole dance in his *Anatomie of Abuses*:

> Their cheefest jewell is their Maie poole, which they bring home from the woods with great veneration. They have 20 or 40 yoke of oxen, every Oxe having a sweete Nosegaie of flowers tyed on the tippe of the hornes and these Oxen draw home this Maie pool (this stinckyng Idol rather) which is covered all over with Flowers and Hearbes . . . And thus being reared up with handkerchiefs and flagges streaming on the toppe, they . . . set up sommer haules and arbors hard by it. Then fall they to banquet and feaste, to leape and daunce about it, as Ye Heathen peoples did . . .

Indignation winged the words of the puritans whenever they wrote of the May-day goings-on; but I certainly did not expect to find "stinking" used in 1585 in the manner of Smith Minor's prep-school slang. Crabbed old Stubbes' spiteful aside sent me to the *O.E.D.*, where I learned that the Mass had been called "most vile and stinking" in 1564 (these godly fellows were pretty free with their language), that Wycliffe in 1380 had condemned "stynkynge pryde," and that the first known use of the word in this sense occurred as long ago as 1225!

YOU WILL GET many surprises of this nature if you read fairly widely among the older authors. The "affable Archangel" in *Paradise Lost* really startled me the first time I met him. This was because I associated the epithet with the kind of easy-going friendliness of manner which you would expect of what Dr. Johnson called a clubable man; but to imagine the Archangel Raphael splendid and shining in the context of a club was impossible, if not downright blasphemous. In truth, however, "affable" means no more than "easy to speak to," and if you look at it hard you will see how it is related to "confabulate" (talk together) and to "fable" (a tale).

Another word that looks very odd without the associations in which we dress it up is "engine." "Rais'd by that curious engine, your right hand." The line is from *The Duchess of Malfi*, and we who all our lives have thought of engines in connexion with cars, ships, aeroplanes and railway-trains are brought up sharp by the word and made to consider it afresh. Where does it come from? The people in my native town when they speak of an *ingin*-driver unwittingly echo its origin; for an engine is a product of "ingenuity," from Latin *ingenium*, an inborn quality, mother wit. (A related Latin word is *Genius*, the god who presided over birth, especially that of the talented.) It is easy to see how "inherited ability" got itself identified with cleverness, hence inventiveness, so that "engine" became the word for a contrivance or device,—at one time even for an artful trick: for "mal engyn" in Malory's *Morte d'Arthur* means "evil craft, low cunning." And Richard Franck, an authority on angling contemporary with Izaak Walton, wrote in his florid fashion of poachers who caught salmon at night by the aid of torches and spears:

What, are these canabals, or murdering moss-troopers, to surprize fish by the engine of firelight? [1]

An engine was also a machine or instrument of war, such as the "petard," for example, which was employed to blow in a gate or wall. That word too is a bit of a curiosity, for it came to us from French *peter*, to break wind! This does not suggest a very great explosion; nevertheless it was advisable to use a long fuse—

> For 'tis the sport to have the enginer
> Hoist with his own petar. [2]

The idea of somebody blowing himself up with his own fireworks got a laugh from the Elizabethans as it still does from ourselves today.

You see how the inquiries we were prompted to make by happening to find "engine" used so strangely have given us a glimpse of the word's ancestry and relations and of its "life-history" in the minds of Englishmen? Possibly until now we have used it a score of times every week without ever giving it a thought; henceforth we shall see it not merely as a disregarded passer-by but at least as a nodding acquaintance, of

[1] *Northern Memoirs.*
[2] *Hamlet.*

whose background we know a smattering. And so in the case of any word, however familiar,—if we are only a little aware of the implications lying behind it, by that much our reading, our writing, even our speaking and our listening will be the richer.

BUT MOST OF US hardly ever have occasion to examine critically the words that slip so glibly off our tongues and our pen-nibs. It is astonishing to what an extent we take them for granted, using all kinds of peculiar expressions without considering what they really mean or why they have become current in the language. Because we have been "brought up with them," we accept them without question; but if for any reason we *do* stop and look at them, observe them from a fresh angle, hold them up to the light, we are sometimes amazed by their strangeness, and puzzled why it has never struck us before. People who are not naturally good spellers, when they look closely at a doubtful word to make sure they have spelt it correctly, often find its appearance so outlandish that they almost persuade themselves it has no existence outside their own imagination. And I must confess that there are certain words and phrases which make the same kind of impact upon me, if I allow myself to take a critical view of them. "Burglariously," which the police are so fond of, strikes me as a most ludicrous word belonging perhaps to Gilbert and Sullivan, but not to a court of law; whenever I read or hear it I wonder whether somebody is making a joke. "Jeopardy" seems unaccountably archaic, as if it had strayed out of the 15th century, where it surely belongs. Oddly enough, Dr. Johnson had this feeling too. In his dictionary he describes jeopardy as "a word not now in use"; which is strange, because it was in continuous use during the whole of the 18th century. It comes, by the way, from Old French *jeu parti*, which meant "a divided game," hence "an uncertain chance," in chess and similar games. There is a verb, "to jeopard," but it is rarely seen; and journalists, especially, take great delight in using "jeopardize" instead. I can never get accustomed to it, and whenever I see it on a printed page it is as if I glimpsed a spotted hippogriff grazing among the domestic kine.

Two common expressions, if I ever really *think* about them, have a similar effect on me: "foul play" and "taking umbrage." The former surprises me every time I encounter it in a newspaper. I read, let us say, that the body of a "partially clad" young woman has been found in a lonely quarry, and that she has "apparently died from strangulation" after having been "interfered with" (one of the most horrible euphemisms in the English language today). The report concludes: "Foul play is suspected." How very odd—or perhaps how very English—to equate rape and murder with cheating in a game! Surely there must be some other interpretation of the phrase,—perhaps it came about through some corruption or misunderstanding, perhaps the scholars can explain it away? Nothing of the kind. Shakespeare as far as is known was the first person to use it, and he meant by it—plain murder. "It is apparent foul play," said Salisbury in *King John,* suspecting wrongly that Hubert had killed the young Prince Arthur. Clearly the metaphor does refer to cheating at some kind of game, probably cards; I doubt if the rough-and-tumble outdoor games of the Elizabethans made much more distinction between fair and foul than the witches in *Macbeth* did. The phrase "foul play," by my guess, originated in a gamblers' den, though Shakespeare first attached it to murder. That we should continue to use it in this sense still seems to me rather peculiar.

"Taking umbrage" is a phrase I can never regard seriously. Like "burglariously," it makes me want to laugh; and indeed by doing so I have sometimes discomfited the takers of umbrage themselves. When the word first appeared in English, nobody dreamed of "taking" it; umbrage was the shade of trees, or of anything that got in the way of the light (from Latin *umbra,* a shadow). Drummond of Hawthornden wrote of a woman whose

> *Deare amber Lockes gave Umbrage to her face.*

Clouds were umbrageous when they threw their fleeting shadows on the grass; and so were doubts and suspicions when they darkened men's thoughts. The first person to be recorded as *taking* umbrage was a bishop in 1680; the occasion was a sermon by another clergyman! Since then all manner of princes and prelates, ministers and monarchs, despots and demagogues, have taken umbrage at each other's behaviour, an attitude which has sometimes led to war. Clearly the world would be a better place if umbrage were once again limited to some such grateful shade as that of the great oak-tree which Plot describes in his *Natural History of Oxfordshire:*

Under the umbrage of which tree . . . no less than 324 horses or
4,374 men, may sufficiently be sheltered.

"DISGRUNTLE" is another of these words which have a vague, inexplicable air of absurdity. The verb with the opposite meaning *does* exist,
though few people know of it and hardly any use it nowadays. A gruntle means the snout of a pig, and has done so since 1535. To gruntle is
to utter a not very loud grunt, as a swine or other animal. Nowadays
we think of a grunt as an expression of annoyance; the human grunt is
certainly so. But when men lived closer to the soil than most of us do,
gruntling was recognised as indicative of a pig's pleasure; indeed, my
own pigs gruntle happily when I feed them, and as they submerge their
snouts in the swill they continue to do so, often blowing bubbles and
gurgling and choking in consequence. Because I keep pigs, "disgruntle," meaning "to put into sulky dissatisfaction or ill-humour,"
makes more sense to me than it does to most people.

   A few years ago at Oxford University a fashionable slang was built
upon the foundation of words like "gruntle." "Gusting" and "pellent"
expressed enthusiastic approval, being the opposites of disgusting and
repellent. Some women undergraduates started a magazine, *Couth,* so
called because it was intended to express Oxford's "exquisite approach
to life," the opposite of "uncouth." In fact, however, "couth" is a
very old English word, pre-Chaucerian, and its original sense was
merely "known," "familiar." Our English dislike of the unfamiliar
probably got "uncouth" its present meaning: foreigners seem uncouth
because they don't speak our language and are apt to prefer *sole bonne
femme* to fish and chips!

A WORD which struck me as particularly queer popped up the other day
during a talk I had with an angler who was trying to catch roach in our
River Avon. You must understand that this hobby of word-collecting
and word-observing goes with a man everywhere; it is by no means confined to the study and the Reading Room. You can learn about words
wherever there are people, at parties, races, political meetings, auction
sales, in trains, buses, shops, markets, pubs! Now my angler was fishing
with maggots, that is to say, blowfly grubs which he'd fattened on a bit
of rotten meat; but although he spoke the rough speech of the Black
Country, he practised the greatest refinement in describing these little

creatures that wriggled in his bait-tin. He called them "gentles"—as indeed fishermen have been doing since the 16th century; but his, perhaps, had a special qualification to be called so, for he had dyed them with aniline dye, bright red and yellow, that they might tempt the appetites of the (probably colour-blind) fishes. They were very refined gentles.

I was curious to know how maggots had managed to earn themselves such a name; so when I got home I looked the word up and found that an old use of the word "gentle," now obsolete, was for anything "not harsh, soft, tender, pliant, supple, yielding to the touch." For instance we have a plant called the Gentle Thistle because it is smooth, and lacks prickles. If you can ever bring yourself to handle a maggot, you will be impressed both by the pliancy of its body, and by the silky texture of its skin.

Dipping into the dictionary set me thinking of the word in its more usual sense—of Chaucer's "Verray parfit gentil knight," [1] of Sir Ector's mourning for Launcelot at the end of the *Morte d'Arthur*, "Thou was the meekest man and the gentlest that ever ate in hall among ladies," —and I thought what a long way it had come down in the world since then; for if a girl nowadays were to say that a gentleman was taking her to the pictures, it would be very Non-U indeed! A vast amount of social history is wrapped up in this word "gentleman" and in its various relations, such as "genteel." Dr. Johnson, writing in 1775 "Most vices may be committed very genteelly; a man may debauch his friend's wife genteelly; he may cheat at cards genteelly" presumably used the word in the sense of "stylishly, in a polished manner." But when people began to concern themselves too much with the business of being "genteel," making gentility into an affectation, the word changed its meaning altogether and its usage became, about the middle of the 19th century, sarcastic and contemptuous. To employ it now in any other sense is a vulgarity. So is the language a mirror of our moods and our manners; and so do the dictionaries record our fads and our foibles, perhaps more accurately than the history books.

But the word "gentle" set me off on all kinds of investigations before I had done with it.—These are the sort of "entertainments and delights" which I had in mind when I wrote the first paragraph of this

[1] *Canterbury Tales.*

book: we are tempted down unexpected by-ways, where often we make for ourselves fascinating discoveries.—I recollected, for instance, a charming phrase "the small gentrice" which occurs in that *Ballade of the Lords of Old Times* which C. K. Scott-Moncrieff translated from François Villon. I went back to my books, and soon I found the quotation I wanted:

> *Where, from Vienne and from Greno'les,*
>   *Are the proud Dauphins, I not wis;*
> *From Dijon, from Salins, from Doles*
>   *Lords and their eldest sons we miss,*
>   *And where is each of the small gentrice,*
> *Herald, trumpeter, pursuivant;*
>   *Have they drunk indeed of the last deep dish?*
> *The wind alone wist whither they went.*

Now "the small gentrice" sparked off another memory (there is no end to such a quest as this) and I went a-hunting once more, this time for a quaint use of the word "gent" in a fragment of an old, anonymous, untitled verse that had somehow stuck in my mind for twenty years. I wasted half an hour looking for it but I found it at last and copied it out: as you see, its old spelling suits it:

> *There was a mayde cam out of Kent,*
>   *Deintie love, deintie love;*
> *There was a mayde cam out of Kent,*
>   *Daungerous be;*
> *There was a mayde cam out of Kent,*
>   *Fayre, propre, small and gent,*
> *As ever upon the ground went,*
>   *For so should it be . . .*[1]

Did I say "wasted" half an hour? It would have been worth twice as long to remind myself of that Kentish maid, "fayre, propre, small and gent,"—but why was she "daungerous"? Here a fresh hare starts up before us, and it leads (for hares are very apt to double back suddenly) to the *Oxford English Dictionary* once again. I knew, of course, that this maid was not dangerous in the sense of being a *femme fatale*;

---

[1] From W. Wager: *The longer thou livest the more fool thou art.* 1575.

she was difficult to please, particular, ticklish, fastidious, delicate or nice. That use of the word is now obsolete; but the O.E.D. gave me a quotation from Roger Ascham (who was Queen Elizabeth's school-master when she was a girl) which perfectly exemplified the old sense of "dangerous": "Great shippes require costlie tackling, and afterwards dangerous Government." [1]—which I daresay was exactly what our Kentish maid required, a sailor's hand both light and firm upon the helm of her headstrong spirit, daungerous be. I hope she married one.

But see how far we have wandered. This digression began with mag-gots genteelly called gentles!

YOU NEVER CAN TELL where your curiosity about words is going to lead you. A man remarked to me at a party: "Of course, the chap's a roar-ing pansy," and I was immediately diverted by a lively picture in my mind of this chap roaring away like Snug's Lion in *A Midsummer Night's Dream*,—for I am afflicted with an absurd visual imagination, by means of which the road-sign BEAR LEFT, for example, conjures up the image of a grizzly growling behind the hedge.

I still do not know why we persistently attach the epithet "roaring" to those who might more reasonably be supposed to squeak; nor have I any idea why crooks habitually thump, whereas cads stink. These are rather like the recurrent epithets which we find in ancient Greek, where dogs are always noisy, ships fast, the Achaeans great-hearted, a lyre is tuneful, the dawn rosy-fingered, and the sea is either fishy or wine-dark. In the same way these modern English epithets, roaring, thumping, stinking, hang on to the backs of their victims like Old Men of the Sea. Here are a couple of Homeric examples from the works of Mr. John Betjeman:

> "*Let us not speak, for the love we bear one another—*
> *Let us hold hands and look.*"
> *She, such a very ordinary little woman;*
> *He, such a thumping crook;*
> *But both, for a moment, little lower than the angels*
> *In the teashop's ingle-nook.*[2]

Less compassionately, in the second example, Mr. Betjeman invokes

[1] *Scholemaster* I.
[2] *In a Bath Teashop.*

the enemy to drop his bombs on Slough and in particular upon an
odious business-man who lives there:

> *And smash his desk of polished oak*
> *And smash his hands so used to stroke*
> *And stop his boring dirty joke*
> *And make him yell.*
>
> *But spare the bald young clerks who add*
> *The profits of the stinking cad;*
> *It's not their fault that they are mad,*
> *They've tasted Hell.*[1]

Epithet and noun are practically inseparable. If you swopped them
round the effect would be as odd as if you were to speak of a roaring
wilderness, or a howling pansy. But you *can* speak of a howling cad.

ASKING QUESTIONS about words counts as one of my "pleasures," then;
looking up the answers is certainly another. But sometimes there is no
need to involve the dictionaries: a word encountered by chance may
set off a whole train of personal mnemonics, as "sally" did in my mind
the other day when a country boy of whom I'd asked the way used it
in his directions:

"You turns left at the corner by the old pond with the sally-bushes
round it."

We always call the pussy-willows "sallies," our country version of
"sallow," which in turn is related to the willow's Latin name *salix*.
(Properly, of course, they are only pussy-willows in the spring, when
their unopened catkins are soft and grey and feel like a kitten's fur if
you stroke them: catkin, a little cat.) The *colour* sallow, reddish-yellow
or dirty-yellow, derives from the name of the bush, its shoots are reddish-yellow in early spring.

But isn't "sally" a word of innumerable happy associations? I
thought, as I walked along the lane towards the old pond, of Yeats'
poem: "Down by the sally gardens my love and I did meet," and that
led me on to Gerard Manley Hopkins' phrase about the "palms" when
they have the gold-dust on them, "mealed-with-yellow sallows"; and
then I thought of the charming girl's name, my favourite of all girls'

[1] *Slough.*

names, the one that straightway brings an old song to mind, for everybody knows about that Sally whose "father he makes cabbage-nets and
through the streets doth cry 'em,"—

> *Of all the girls that are so smart*
> *There's none like pretty Sally.*
> *She is the darling of my heart*
> *And she lives in our alley.*

Isn't it surprising that Henry Carey, who wrote *Sally in Our Alley*,
should also have written *God Save the King*? At least, it is generally
ascribed to him; though I think he took an old Stuart song and neatly
turned its coat for it, so that it might praise the Hanoverians. By an
irony of chance it was first sung at the Drury Lane Theatre in September, 1745, amid great emotion; for at that time it seemed still uncertain whether God would save King George the Second from Prince
Charles Edward and his Jacobite invasion.

Henry Carey was a versatile fellow, for he also wrote

> *Aldiborontiphoscophornio!*
> *Where left you Chrononhotonthologos?*

though this, I assure you, was perpetrated in sport. The lines occur in
a burlesque subtitled "The Most Tragical Tragedy that ever was
Tragediz'd by a Company of Tragedians."

But it is his song that has kept his name alive; and it was that song
of a poor prentice-lad in love which was running in my head when I
came to the old pond and saw the twigs of the sallies glowing pink and
yellow in the light of a sinking February sun:

> *But when my seven long years are out,*
> *O, then I'll marry Sally;*
> *O, then we'll wed, and then we'll bed—*
> *But not in our alley!*

Nor did my pursuit of the word's associations end there; for I remembered Belloc's poem called *Hannaker Mill*:

> *Sally is gone that was so kindly;*
> *Sally is gone from Hannaker Hill,*
> *And the briar grows ever since then so blindly;*

And ever since then the clapper is still . . .
And the sweeps have fallen from Hannaker Mill.

Hannaker Hill is in desolation;
Ruin a-top and a field unploughed.
And Spirits that call on a falling nation,
Spirits that loved her calling aloud,
Spirits abroad in a windy cloud.

Spirits that call and no one answers—
Hannaker's down and England's done.
Wind and thistle for pipe and dancers,
And never a ploughman under the sun:
Never a ploughman, never a one.

I have special reason to feel affection for this poem and for the unknown Sally it commemorates. One morning in September, 1940, I
came back from a flight across the Channel, and over the coast of
Sussex looked at my map to see exactly where I was. I glanced down,
and beneath me was Hannaker Hill, with its mill yet standing. I dived
low over it, and shouted to myself the verses, so loud that I could hear
them above the scream of the engine; and as I banked round the hill
with my starboard wing pointing straight down at the field where
Belloc had seen the thistles dancing to the wind's tune, there lay in
my sight the broken skeletons of three German aeroplanes shot down
the previous day, but looking already like the Archaeopteryx partially
reconstructed from fossil-fragments. And as I intoned to myself "Hannaker's down and England's done" I knew suddenly that it wasn't true:
Hannaker stood and so did England, in angry defiance; and so would
Sally have done, I felt sure, pitchfork in hand against any invader, had
she still been there!

THE STUDY of derivations and etymologies, in however amateur a way,
is another of the enjoyments to be had out of words,—perhaps a less
idle one than my chasing of quotations to and fro across the centuries,
or my magpie acquisition of the curious and the rare. It is just as fascinating. Take "assassin," for example: a word which looks as if it originally belonged to the dark alley-mouths and the shadowy backstreets of
Paris, boon-companion perhaps of *apache, garrotteur* and *sans-culotte.*

This time we will refuse to be led away into devious pursuits; even so pretty a hare as this must not tempt us:

> An intelligent Russian once remarked, "Every country has its own constitution; ours is absolutism moderated by assassination." [1]

(Is it still?)—But let us stick to the derivation of the word. We may indeed have had it through French, but the original source is Arabic: *hashshāshīn* as a general term means "eaters of hashish," but in particular it describes a sect of Moslem fanatics, which at the time of the Crusades dedicated itself to the purpose of killing Christians. Their sheikh was called The Old Man of the Mountains; and before he sent his men forth on their missions of murder he permitted them to acquire some Dutch, or Arab, courage by means of the drug. I can well believe this would have transformed peaceable cowards into fiends entirely without fear; for I once met a mad hashish-eater in the public gardens at Tetuan, who in pursuit of some phantom which troubled his mind took a running jump at a hedge of sword cactus, landed in the middle of it, with what horrible consequences I can only imagine, plunged through it heedless, and then for good measure hurled himself into a thicket of prickly pear from which he eventually emerged, dripping with blood, frothing at the lips, rolling his eyes and mouthing dreadful imprecations. He rushed past my wife and me without seeing us, so possessed was he by the image of his phantasmal enemy. For all I know it may have been a Christian! Through him we got a glimpse, I am sure, of what a member of the Order of Assassins looked like, as he rushed forth mad-drunk from his den, in the early eleven-hundreds.

Another word with a queer history is "tawdry," which is really short for "tawdry lace," cheap but showy stuff with which the country girls would doll themselves up during the 17th century. The story goes back much farther than that, however,—right back to the late six-hundreds when Etheldreda, the virtuous daughter of a King of East Anglia, was painfully dying of a tumour in her throat. She believed that this was an affliction sent by God to punish the follies of her girlhood, when she had taken pleasure in wearing pretty necklaces; the throat they had once adorned must now pay the price of its vanity. This poor demented creature, whose name was anglicised as Audrey, was later

---

[1] Georg Herbert, Court Minister, *Political Sketches of the State of Europe.*

sanctified and became patron saint of Ely; and at the annual fair held on St. Audrey's day "necklaces of fine silk" were sold in her memory. These "Saint Audrey's laces" gave their name to the poor-quality stuff which was soon manufactured all over England; until by 1700 "tawdry" was a name for any cheap finery or trumpery thing.

We shall come across many more such oddities of derivation in the course of this book; meanwhile for a word of simpler origins, the homely sandwich springs to mind. It got its name from John Montague, fourth Earl of Sandwich, who was so addicted to the gaming-table that he once played cards for twenty-four hours on end, without breaking off for a meal. Instead he called for food to be brought to him; and it took the form of slices of cold beef placed between pieces of toast. This happened about 1760. Such snacks became popular, and were named after his lordship; by 1765 the word was firmly established in the English language. This same Lord Sandwich, by the way, was a disreputable politician as well as a gamester, and of his twelve-year spell as First Lord of the Admiralty it is recorded that "For corruption and incapacity Sandwich's administration is unique in the history of the British Navy." At so sweeping a claim the mind boggles. He was one of the wild crew who performed peculiar rites at Medmenham Abbey; and he was a close friend, and later a bitter enemy, of John Wilkes, who once addressed to him the most devastating repartee in social history:

LORD SANDWICH: I am convinced, Mr. Wilkes, that you will die either of a pox or on the gallows.

WILKES: That depends, my lord, whether I embrace your mistress or your principles.

CHAPTER 2

Strange and Sweet Equally

ETYMOLOGY WOULD BE a simple science if it involved no more than the unravelling of such straightforward word-histories as those of sandwich or assassin. But of course it is concerned also with the remote ancestries and complex relationships of words, not only within a language, but branching out through many different tongues. Amateurs rarely possess a wide enough scholarship to be much use at this game; all we can do is to accept the authority of the experts and enjoy the fruits of their labours. The derivations and condensed histories can generally be found in the *O.E.D.* or in Skeat's *Etymological Dictionary*; but if we want to learn about the inter-relation of words we cannot do better than consult Mr. Eric Partridge's *Origins*, where the words are arranged according to their elements: that is to say, they are placed in family-groups which demonstrate their common ancestry and present relationship. For instance carnivore, carnal, carnage, incarnate, carnival (originally perhaps a festival of flesh) and carnation (named because of its flesh-colour) are all obviously descendants of the same Latin word *caro*,[1] genitive *carnis*. It happens that these all look alike. So do vermicelli, vermilion, varmint and vermin, though their common ancestry is not immediately clear. You can guess that the thin, worm-like pasta gets its name from Latin *vermis*, a worm; but to understand about "vermilion" you have to know that the colour scarlet was originally obtained from the cochineal insect, in Latin *vermiculus*, a little worm. "Varmint" is of course a corruption of "vermin"—I've heard a keeper speak of "they troublesome varmints," the stoats and the jays; and "vermin" itself, which so shocked Aneurin Bevan's Tory opponents when he used it to describe them in 1945, derives from *vermis* by reason of the horror which worms generally evoke. Expres-

[1] Flesh.

sive of disgust, it has become attached to any small, objectionable creature.

For an example of the great complexity of these word-relationships, we may look up "poach" in Mr. Partridge's book, where we learn that to poach (e.g. the squire's pheasants) derives from an Old French verb *pocher*, to thrust, wherefore to encroach; poker, the utensil, has a similar ancestry, and poker, the game, comes from a related Dutch word, meaning to boast or bluff, whence also the wild duck called pochard gets its name, because of its loud quacking. But what about poaching an egg? This kind of "poach" has a completely different origin, and a different set of relations, some of them rather unpleasant ones,—pock (a pustule), and the pox. The general sense is "to make swell like pouches," hence to cook an egg so that the yolk is enclosed in a white "pocket." There is yet one more complexity, for it happens that you can poach a man's ground *without* stealing his game: the word also bears a meaning "to tread or tramp into miry holes." Farmers say that their ground is poached by the hunting-folk in wet seasons; and here of course the word clearly belongs to the second group and is related to pock and pucker, pouch and pocket, and the poke in which you should not buy a pig.

Often enough the relationship between words is only apparent to a scholar's eye,—as that of woman, viper, vibrant and whip, which words share a complicated cousinship. Another group of cousins includes such a surprising assortment as welterweight, evolution, walk, convolvulus, waltz, revolver, well, revolting, welder, wallow, willow, and the mollusc whelk, all of which derive from related words in Latin and Germanic which share the basic idea of "roll, roll around." Thus "welter" means a rolling, tossing, tumbling (as of waves), hence a state of turmoil, hence also a surging and confused mass. I suppose the welterweight boxer gets his name through his likeness to a surging mass?

But as I said, one has got to know a lot about language to recognise relationships such as these. You and I, perhaps, might reasonably hazard that there was some connexion between "time" and "tide," if only because *tides* occur at regular *times*; but we should never have guessed that "tiddlywinks" belonged to the same family. It seems to do so, for its "tiddly" part is said to derive from the smallness of the discs which "wink" when they turn over, "tiddley" (little) coming from "tidy," which nowadays means neat but originally implied "seasonable," as the tides are.[1]

AS AN INSTANCE of the diversity of words which may come from a common source, here are nine picked at random from a hundred or so which Mr. Partridge groups together under the heading "rex":

Royal	Adroit	Incorrigible
Rector	Direct	Dirigible
Right	Raja	Rectum

What they have in common is an Indo-European root *reg-*, "to set straight, to lead or guide straight"—as a king should do, or a rector, or a raja. The root has become obscured in "adroit"[2] but in most of the words you can easily recognise it. An incor*rig*ible person is one who cannot be cor*rect*ed (i.e. made to go straight), a di*rig*ible is an airship capable of being guided (as compared with a balloon that has to go where the wind listeth), the *rect*um is a "straight" part of the intestine, and so on.

So do the etymological dictionaries present a picture of ramifying relationships, of widely branching family trees of words, which can sometimes be traced back from the present generation to remote Latin, Greek, even Sanskrit ancestors. Dozens of languages, living and dead, may be involved in such a history. The Latin word *regina* on Queen Elizabeth's coinage and the Hindi word *maharani* are sisters under the skin; both come from that ancient root signifying "to lead or guide straight"—as do the German *reich*, the French *roi*, the Romany *rye* (gentleman) beloved of George Borrow, and hundreds, maybe thousands, of other words connected with "straightness," in all the tongues that are spoken from India to Iceland.

ON THE OTHER HAND there are some common words which have no known parentage and no living relations: lone wolves of words, mysteries, indicated in the dictionaries by the initials o.o.o.—"of obscure origin." "Curse" is such a one; and in the etymological dictionary it stands alone. It appeared, as it were from nowhere, in Old English

---

[1] *Origins.*
[2] French *à droit* comes from Latin *directus*, in which you can see the root plain enough.

as *curs*; "No word of similar form and sense," says the *O.E.D.* "is known in Teutonic, Romanic or Celtic." But wherever it came from, we find it very useful; and as it snarls its lonely way through the poetry and the prose and the speech of Englishmen, it bears the whole burden of "an utterance consigning, or supposed or intended to consign, a person or thing to spiritual or temporal evil, the vengeance of the deity, the blasting of malignant fate etc." [1]—a sizeable achievement, for one little syllable. But words are like coinage, where a small piece of metal may stand for a large bulk of goods. Francis Bacon put it very neatly when he said they were "tokens current and accepted for conceits (concepts) as moneys are for values." [2] They are a means of exchange between minds.

IT IS NOT always a fair exchange, because words have an emotional content as well as an intellectual one; and this emotional "charge" which any given word carries has by no means the same effect upon different individuals. There are a few words which still give me something like a small electric shock every time I hear them; yet some people seem to be utterly unmoved by both the sound and the associations, and would never be able to understand why I, as a boy of twelve or so, went about saying "tatterdemalion" and "flibbertigibbet" aloud to myself (which words I had just acquired) because I had so much delight in the sound of them. A year later "t'gallants'ls" (top-gallant-sails) and "mandragora" were two words which caught my young imagination in the same way. I pronounced the latter incorrectly, putting the accent on the penultimate syllable; it sounded fine that way. I often mispronounced; for I must have been very much like the young Mr. Polly in H. G. Wells' novel: "New words had terror and fascination for him. He could not avoid them, and so he plunged into them." He was "curiously attracted" by "words rich in splendour, words rich in suggestions." So was I; and how often, in my case, were they proper names of people I had scarcely heard of,—

> O lang will his Lady
> Look owre the Castle Downe,

[1] *O.E.D.*
[2] *The Advancement of Learning.*

> *Ere she see the Earl of Murray*
> *Come sounding through the town!* [1]

The last two lines were the ones which I used to shout aloud. Then there was a line in *Lepanto* which seemed to summon up the splendours:

> *It is Richard, it is Raymond, it is Godfrey at the gate!* [2]

I sang it in the bath, and even believed amid the steam that my schoolboy treble thundered those names. But not all the glory belonged to martial sounds. I came under the spell of two lines from *Lycidas*:

> *To sport with Amaryllis in the shade,*
> *Or with the tangles of Neæra's hair.*

My inclination, however, was strongly towards Amaryllis. I may have been a little put off by the idea of Neæra's elf-locks; and I had my customary pronunciation-trouble in the case of her name. But Amaryllis! Amaryllis! I was fourteen, and just awakening to an awareness of girls—also to an awareness of Swinburne, who is surely the Poet Laureate of puberty:

> *O daughters of dreams and of stories*
> *That life is not wearied of yet,*
> *Faustine, Fragoletta, Dolores,*
> *Félise and Yolande and Juliette!* [3]

These were the names that had put their enchantments upon me by the time my fifteenth birthday came round; but a fortunate birthday-present of Macaulay's ballads acted as a useful corrective, and saved me from becoming soppy-sick with Swinburne, as adolescents often are. I had not, however, grown out of my childish delight in saying the words that pleased me aloud to myself at all sorts of odd times. This was believed among my relations to be evidence of a weakness of mind. Nevertheless it persisted; and one day, walking along the edge of a wood,

---

[1] *The Bonny Earl of Murray.*
[2] G. K. Chesterton.
[3] Dedication, *Poems and Ballads.*

I was in full cry, the newly-discovered word being "oriflamme" and the context Macaulay's *Ivry:*

> *Press where ye see my white plume shine, amidst the*
> *ranks of war,*
> *And be your oriflamme today the helmet of Navarre.*

Suddenly there emerged from the wood within a few yards of me my House Master, a desiccated mathematician we called Tweaker. Had I met at that moment the man who taught me History and Classics, he would have laughed and I should have laughed, and it would have seemed natural to want to speak a word like oriflamme to the winds and the woodlands. But Tweaker looked at me as if I were a madman; and I in terror pretended not to see him, and blundered on, head down, red-faced, shambling, so that later I was called to his study and punished for not taking my cap off to him. This cured me of talking to myself for the sake of the sound of the words; though when I wrote that word "oriflamme" a few minutes ago, I caught myself breathing its syllables. Words connected with "flame" have always warmed my imagination—"The chestnut casts his flambeaux" in the Housman poem,[1] and flamboyant, which we made out of that French word *flambeau,* and flamingo, a name as lovely as the bird. Oriflamme, of course, means a golden flame, and was the name given to the sacred banner of Saint Denis, "the great and holy standard of France." [2]

NOW A WORD about the "wonder" which I promised at the very beginning of this book. A poet, W. J. Turner, has expressed it far better than I can, in a poem called *Talking With Soldiers:*

> *It is strange that a little mud*
> *Should echo with sounds, syllables, and letters,*
> *Should rise up and call a mountain Popocatepetl,*
> *And a green-leafed wood Oleander.*[3]

I got to know the poet a little time before he died; and he was less like a poet than a small farmer, stocky, with a red face, and a red waistcoat

---

[1] *Last Poems.*

[2] Cotgrave, *Dictionary of the French and English Tongues.*

[3] It is surprising that neither Shakespeare nor Marlowe used this lovely word Oleander, though it was theirs for the having,—it's been in English since 1548.

matching it like a cock robin's. A sort of homely earthiness about him seemed to reflect the theme of his poem; for secretly this ordinary-looking chap was altogether possessed and bewitched by words, names, "sounds, syllables and letters," the more outlandish they were the more they captivated him, a map of South America set his wits into a whirl:

> *Chimborazo, Cotopaxi,*
> *They had stolen my soul away.*[1]

The wonder of language was ever-present with him; and I think it troubled him, as it sometimes troubles me, to contemplate the vast vocabulary of man. It is one of those marvels that one shrinks away from in awe, this naming of everything that walks or flies or runs or crawls or swims beneath the sea, of all the stars our telescopes can count, of minute bacilli and invisible viruses, of every concept that happens in our heads, colours, measurements of time and space, ideas of heaven, hell, infinity, eternity, God. That a piece of valiant dust should do all this!—or a handful of mud, as Turner saw the mind of man. You can sense his wonder and terror and awe again and again in the poem:

> *It has called a far-off glow Arcturus,*
> *And some pale weeds, lilies of the valley.*

"WHAT WORDS DO," and how they do it, makes an even more tantalising study than that of "what words are." It is fun, as I said, to collect and dissect them, to watch the experts placing them in order to show their ancestry and relationships; and this leads in the end towards some philosophical profundities concerning the fundamental nature of man's thought. But as soon as we begin to take a look at words in action we come up against the *poetic* mysteries; and they are even more bewildering because they can be demonstrated but not explained. Othello saying goodbye to all the glories cries out:

> *Farewell the plumed troop and the big wars!*

and of course it is the joining-up of "big" and "wars" which makes us catch our breath. But we cannot tell why this particular pair of words being placed together have their power suddenly raised, as it were, to

---

[1] *Romance.*

the *n*th. We only know that if we substitute "great" for "big," it doesn't happen.

Sometimes a single word, itself quite ordinary, seems to act as a catalyst upon several others, giving to the whole mixture an explosive force. Cleopatra has watched Antony die before her eyes:

> *O, wither'd is the garland of the war,*
> *The soldier's pole is fallen; young boys and girls*
> *Are level now with men: the odds is gone,*
> *And there is nothing left remarkable*
> *Beneath the visiting moon.*

It is "visiting" that does the trick there; and by showing us the moon that comes and goes uncaring month by month for ever and ever—yet never again to shine upon an Antony—it sets Cleopatra's despair in the cold light of eternity.

Now let us take two of the simplest words in English and see what unexpected and extraordinary things happen to them in the context of great poetry. They are words which make a beautiful contrast in the language: "bright" and "dark"; so the poets delight in them.

> *Beauty is but a flower*
> *Which wrinkles will devour;*
> *Brightness falls from the air;*
> *Queens have died young and fair;*
> *Dust hath closed Helen's eye;*
> *I am sick, I must die—*
> > *Lord, have mercy on us!*

So Thomas Nashe makes a marvellous use of "brightness" in that magical poem, *In Time of Pestilence*. But now see how Shakespeare, handling "bright" with his supernatural skill, lets its brief shine fall momentarily upon an unsheathed weapon or a head of hair. "Keep up your bright swords, for the dew will rust them," Othello tells the nobles of Venice. And Clarence dreaming ghastly dreams in his cell at the Tower sees

> *A shadow like an Angel, with bright hair*
> *Dabbled in blood; and he shriek'd out aloud,*

"Clarence is come—false, fleeting, perjur'd Clarence,—
That stabb'd me in the field by Tewksbury." [1]

And in *Macbeth:*

Angels are bright still, though the brightest fell;

and in *All's Well,* "a bright particular star," three words most wonderfully joined together; and again in that fiery speech by Hotspur, impatient as an over-corned thoroughbred:

By heaven, methinks it were an easy leap
To pluck bright honour from the pale-fac'd moon. [2]

—Always "bright" is the catalyst. And so is "dark" in that extraordinary sentence which Edgar, feigning to be poor Tom, speaks in *King Lear:*

Child Rowland to the dark tower came.

The line itself is altogether a mystery: Shakespeare did not invent it; it seems to be a fragment of a long-lost Scottish ballad. It has no associations to aid its impact upon us: we do not know who Child Rowland was nor why he came to the dark tower; and yet the power of those seven words, arranged in that particular order, is truly hair-raising; every time we hear them they evoke afresh the fear, the excitement and the wonder.

"Dark" is one of those words with which poets can do almost anything—conjure awe, horror, pity, fear. It has a kind of wild beauty in *Adonais:* "The massy earth and spherèd skies are riven! I am borne darkly, fearfully afar." [3] But hear how hollowly it echoes in the vault where Romeo looks his last on Juliet:

Shall I believe
That unsubstantial Death is amorous;
And that the lean abhorred monster keeps
Thee here in dark to be his paramour?

—And hear the dreadful cry of despair which the repeated word makes

[1] *King Richard III.*
[2] *King Henry IV, Part I.*
[3] P. B. Shelley.

in Milton's description of Samson, eyeless in Gaza; remember that
Milton himself knew all about the dark,—

> O dark, dark, dark, amid the blaze of noon,
> Irrecoverably dark, total eclipse . . .[1]

Now there is a sentence in *Antony and Cleopatra* where Shakespeare sets at opposite ends these two words, bright and dark, so that
we see in contrast the noonday sun and the everlasting night. It is
fashioned with consummate craftsmanship out of ten common syllables, all familiar to any child; and as well as being one of the most
beautiful, by reason of its shape and cadences, it is possibly the most
moving sentence in the whole English language. It is given, oddly
enough, to one who has only a little part in the play, to Iras, one of
Cleopatra's gentlewomen. Antony is dead, Cæsar has entered Alexandria, and Cleopatra believes that he means to take her to Rome and
lead her in triumph through the streets. That is unthinkable. Finish,
good lady, Iras says:

> Finish, good lady; the bright day is done,
> And we are for the dark.

CONSIDER THE RICHNESS of a language in which two of the *commonest*
words can achieve all that! Of course it is true that there was never
such a poet; but the language was wonderfully matched to Shakespeare,
who needed a choice of some 17,000 words to say what he had to say,
and found most of them ready for use in his native tongue. Those
which he lacked he adapted or invented, and left to us as an extra
heritage. English is always hungry for new words, anyhow. Though it
is so deep-rooted in history and tradition, it has a flexibility of structure
in which words from all kinds of remote sources settle down and find
themselves at home. Indeed, almost every language under the sun at
one time or another has made its contribution large or small; even
those of the Babylonian and the Blackfellow. The former gave us
"babel," after the Tower where the confusion of languages occurred,
and the latter gave us "billycan" from *billa*, meaning "water" in
Aboriginal Australian.

[1] *Samson Agonistes.*

I think English may also be the most versatile of languages, because it has such immense resources to draw upon. You cannot fail to be aware of them if you are the kind of talker or writer who does not always use "the first word that comes into his head." As you search for the right one, you will realise that for every word in the forefront of your thoughts there are powerful reserves in the rear, nicely graduated in meaning and infinitely various in their associations, their rhythms and their sounds. Even the most fastidious of word-users can find whatever he needs to match the quirks of his individual style; moreover a great number of the words are themselves Jacks-of-all-trades, as happy and efficient in the blank verse of *Paradise Lost* as they are in the light operas of W. S. Gilbert; in the majestical verses of the *Book of Isaiah* as in the "fine brushwork" of *Sense and Sensibility*. They work equally well on any level, whether in terms of what Sir Osbert Sitwell called "those overtones and echoes, those matchless rhythms and transcendental glimpses" [1] or in the plainest prose imaginable; as we shall see if we take an example of each and set them side by side.

Here then are some words spoken in an hour of dire peril: stark, short, urgent, imperative, no frills, no trimmings, no tricks. The British Prime Minister, speaking for all Englishmen, addresses the House of Commons, the country and the world:

> We shall not flag or fail. We shall go on to the end. We shall fight in France, we shall fight on the seas and oceans, we shall fight with growing confidence and strength in the air; we shall defend our island, whatever the cost may be. We shall fight on the beaches, we shall fight on the landing-grounds, we shall fight in the fields and in the streets, we shall fight in the hills; we shall never surrender.

(Sir Winston Churchill, 4th June, 1940.)

And here is a learned physician gravely concerned, during the 1640's, with a Christian's attitude towards mortality:

> If the nearness of our last necessity, brought a nearer conformity unto it, there were a happiness in hoary hairs, and no calamity in half senses. But the long habit of living indisposeth us for dying . . .

(Sir Thomas Browne: *Urn-Burial*)

---

[1] *Laughter in the Next Room.*

In each case, because his choice was such a wide one, the writer was able to lay hands upon the very word he happened to need at that particular moment to do that particular job: the words which were "light as dreams" or those which were "tough as oak," as Edward Thomas described them in his poem,—those which were "Strange as the races Of dead and unborn" or those which were

> *Familiar,*
> *To the eye,*
> *As the dearest faces*
> *That a man knows,*
> *And as lost homes are.*[1]

Elsewhere in the poem he speaks of the English words as "strange and sweet equally," and I am sure it is this aptitude for fusing together the homely and the outlandish, the new and the old, the native and the foreign, which is one of the splendours and marvels of the language. It may beg and borrow and filch and copy all manner of weird words from other tongues; the more the merrier indeed; for in no time their rhythms will be matched to its own, and their sounds (however uncouth at first) will become part of its harmonies. This process has been going on for nearly a thousand years now; and what we call "English" is in fact made up of a beautiful blending of Anglo-Saxon and Latin and Norman French, with a sprinkling of Greek and a sea-salt tang of Viking, a smack of the Mediterranean (many-flavoured as that indescribable whiff you get in all the ports from Alexandretta to Algiers!)—plus a garnishing and spicing of strange and savoury words from all the far places of the globe.

Because of this miraculous hotchpotch which is contained within its covers, I can never look upon even the humblest English dictionary as merely a tool of my trade.

[1] *Words.*

CHAPTER 3

"The Harmless Drudgery"

A s FOR the great Dictionary which stands upon my shelves, and which I still regard with awe, nobody could think of that one as a mere tool! The life-work of four devoted editors went into it; the work of editing took 70 years; and publication was spread over 45.

The story of the *Oxford English Dictionary* begins in 1857, when a learned Divine, Richard Chenevix Trench, of whom you will hear much more in the course of this book, delivered an address to the Philological Society complaining of "The Deficiencies of English Dictionaries." This started a lively debate, out of which emerged the bold idea of making a new comprehensive dictionary that would be concerned with the life-histories of words as well as their origins and definitions. Trench was one of those energetic Victorians who managed to get through much more work in the absence of telephones, aeroplanes, cars, Dictaphones, typewriters, elaborate filing-systems, and highly trained secretaries than we do with the aid of these amenities. He was Dean of Westminster (later Archbishop of Dublin), a considerable philologist, a prolific though uninspired poet, a heavyweight theologian, a lecturer on Church history and, of course, the moving spirit in this ambitious project for a new dictionary. It went ahead in a typically English way. A Committee was formed, which shortly divided itself into two Committees. Sub-committees were born.

An able young man called Herbert Coleridge was appointed Editor, but he died after four years' work on the dictionary,—"In its service he caught the cold which resulted in his death," we are surprisingly told in the *Supplement*. His successor, F. J. Furnivall, lived long, worked hard, and even in his retirement continued to contribute information and quotations, so that it was said of him: "If the Dictionary at one period quotes the *Daily News* and at another the *Daily*

Chronicle, it is because Furnivall had changed his paper in the meanwhile."

Volunteers had been called for to read between them some 4500 carefully-chosen books in search of uncommon words and usages. The Victorians being great collectors of all manner of objects from seashells to pressed ferns, they undertook with enthusiasm the amassing of quotations. Their industry was astonishing; a Mr. Austin is credited with sending in 165,000 quotations, a Mr. Douglas with 136,000, while a devoted Dr. Helwich of Vienna made a noble contribution of 50,000. Before long nearly a thousand of these volunteers were committed to reading the appointed works and recording their discovery of any words which might strike them as "rare, obsolete, old-fashioned, new, peculiar or used in a peculiar way." They had to copy out the relevant passages on specially designed "slips" and send them to the editors. It is a measure of their industry that in 1879, when J. A. H. Murray succeeded Furnivall, he took over from him 1¾ *tons* of material which had accumulated under his roof; and Murray, whose house was perhaps less capacious, had to put up an iron building, which he called a *Scriptorium,* to house and safeguard all these ponderable words. He fitted it up with blocks of pigeon-holes, "1029 in number," for the reception of the alphabetically-arranged slips which came in from the volunteer readers. In the event, *five million* quotations were collected, of which 1,800,000 eventually appeared in the dictionary. Sorting them out alone presented a formidable task. It took forty days to deal with the single word "set," which is as a problem-child to lexicographers, and in the *O.E.D.* occupies 18 pages on its own. Devoted sub-editors undertook such jobs as these; and probably considered themselves highly rewarded by the (generally unread) acknowledgment in the Preface, e.g. "W. Gee Esquire, sub-editor of B words."

Z was reached at last, and the V-Z section published in 1928. The great Dictionary was done, in so far as any such work is done, and for the first time all the known words in the English language had been alphabetically arranged, critically examined, and derived where possible; their biographies told, and their changing uses exemplified. The work was much more than a dictionary, as the word had been previously understood; for if all the other books in the world had been destroyed, a scholar could have read, in those twelve fat volumes, the whole story of the English people, their literature, science, social and political history; their inventions, discoveries, explorations; their economics, hobbies, pastimes, fashions, domesticity, follies and faiths; their varying fortunes in war; their conquests, commerce and colonisations all over the globe.

As to the number of words defined and discussed in the *Oxford English Dictionary*, I am told they amount to 414,825: which is ten times as many as in Dr. Johnson's. But new words had been accumulating fast during the seventy years which it took to edit and print the twelve volumes. About 30,000 of these were included in a *Supplement* which came out in 1933. Another will soon be needed for the words which have been minted since then to meet the changing needs of science and technology, to communicate new ideas in philosophy and physics, and to serve the ends of extreme individualists and eccentrics who could not find what they wanted among our existing four-hundred-thousand.

WHAT KIND of devoted creatures, I ask myself, have dedicated themselves to this slow, patient, ill-rewarded toil of making dictionaries? I am not thinking so much of the *O.E.D.* as of the earlier ones; the *O.E.D.*, after all, was backed by large resources and a sound organization, was served well in its first stages by eager young scholars and subsequently became the life-work of one great man, Sir James Murray, who worked on it for 38 years, editing 7027 of its 15,487 pages. But what of the lesser dictionaries that were published before it, and without which perhaps it could never have been undertaken: dictionaries made with inadequate means by men who were often hacks, sometimes cranks, and generally poor? I see them as human moles, burrowing among learning, purposive, persistent, but working mainly in the dark,—for in their day the "authorities" on words were few and far between, and over any given question were as likely to differ as to agree. I see them as single-minded and (what goes with single-mindedness always) rather humourless; it would be difficult, I think, to perform the hack-work on a dictionary if you had a lively sense of the absurd. In the definition of words, for instance, the pursuit of precision, which is all-important, would be sure to lead you sometimes to the brink of the ridiculous; but the single-minded person is not aware of the ridiculous, he carries on. So we find Dr. Johnson defining "network" as "anything reticulated or decussated, at equal distances, with interstices between the intersections"; and the O.E.D. defining one sense of the word "bosom" as "the enclosure formed by the breast and the arms."

You smile? Then you lack the right attitude towards lexicography. Try to define those two words as clearly and precisely but in a less pedantic way. You can't? I doubt if anybody can.

PICTURE THEM, then, in their habitats of garret or college library, these lesser servants of learning whose work long ago makes our work easier, though we probably do not know their names. I see them bent short-sightedly over old badly printed pages in stuffy, ill-lit rooms where books for want of space are piled in heaps on the floor; or perhaps they have more space but less comfort, and shiver in great draughty libraries where the shelves go as high as the ceiling and ladders must be used to reach the books on them. Old musty dons, who since long-ago bumping races have never taken any exercise but this, clamber up and down the ladders, shuffle along round-shouldered as they bear a pile of books from the shelves to their desks, from their desks back to the shelves, day after day in term or vacation, for all that's left of a lifetime . . . In those early days it was mainly a labour of old men, I think; the young ones would have insufficient learning and too much ambition; whereas, in these consecrated hacks I am thinking of, ambition (which once was high for professorships or even the writing of poetry) became gradually shrunken, until at last it was so little that it could be expressed in some such terms as this: "I should dearly like to see the letter H finished before I die."

Someone else would finish it, if that one didn't! Habituated, industrious, anonymous, remote, building like coral-insects always upon each other: I see these unknown men who worked upon words as a sort of apostolic succession; and if you trace it back for two hundred years or so you may suddenly imagine that you hear, out of a dusty book-lined corner in a house in Gough Square, the great grumbling voice of a word-weary man defining in irony his own status:

Lexicographer: A writer of dictionaries, a harmless drudge.

DR. JOHNSON began the huge work in which that definition appears because he needed some money, and wanted some fame, in the year 1746. He had been toying with the idea of editing Shakespeare's plays, which he knew would get him some money; and of writing a Life of Alfred the Great, which for no good reason he thought might earn him fame. Both propositions had come to nothing, and now a consortium of booksellers,[1] joining together their resources, were reluctantly offering him £1575 for the first real dictionary of the English language, to be completed in three years. The enormous indolence of Dr. Johnson was at odds with his perpetual nagging need; necessity won, on the 18th of July, 1746, when he signed a contract over breakfast, to which he invited the booksellers and for which he may even have paid. Three years, for one man to make a great dictionary! Someone pointed out that it had taken forty members of the French Academy forty years to finish the equivalent work in French. Dr. Johnson's reply suggests that he may have been a little drunk when he made it. "Sir," said he, "thus it is. This is the proportion. Let me see. Forty times forty is 1600. As three to 1600 so is the proportion of an Englishman to a Frenchman."

At this stage he was actually looking forward to the task. Disillusion came later. At the outset he had resolved, as he wrote in his Preface long afterwards, "to leave neither words nor things unexamined," and he pleased himself

with a prospect of the hours which I should revel away in feasts of literature, with the obscure recesses of northern learning which I should enter and ransack, the treasures with which I expected every search into those neglected mines to reward my labour, and the triumph with which I should display my acquisitions to mankind . . . I resolved to show likewise, my attention to things; to pierce deep into every science, to inquire the nature of every substance of which I inserted the name, to limit every idea by a definition strictly logical, and exhibit every production of art or nature in an accurate description . . . But these were the dreams of a poet, doomed at last to wake a lexicographer. I soon found that it is too late to look for instruments, when the work calls for execution; and that whatever abilities I had brought to my task, with those I must finally perform it. To deliberate whenever I doubted, to inquire whenever I was ignorant, would have protracted the undertaking without end . . . I saw that one inquiry only gave occasion to another, that book referred to book, that to search was not always to find, and to find was not al-

---

[1] They were what we should call "publishers" today.

ways to be informed; and thus to pursue perfection, was, like the first inhabitants of Arcadia, to chase the sun, which, when they had reached the hill where he seemed to rest, was still beheld at the same distance from them.

CONSIDERABLE EXPENSES had to come out of the £1575. You need a lot of room for making a dictionary; so Dr. Johnson took a large house specially for the job, in which he accommodated the six "amanuenses" whom he had engaged to do the donkey-work. Five of these were Scots, whom he chose presumably for their industry, despite all the hard things he had said against their nation. And indeed I daresay the Scots, with their tenacity and single-mindedness, their love of learning for its own sake and their slightly pedantic turn of mind, may well make the best lexicographer's assistants in the world. Dr. Johnson treated them with courtesy and compassion. For one, who wrote a book on geography, he contributed a Preface; for another, who died of consumption, he "showed much tenderness," according to Boswell; for a third he obtained a job, that of librarian to a Duke; and for a fourth, who was "reduced to penury," he paid the cost of burying both him and his wife.

These amanuenses, without doubt, worked much longer hours than their master. He liked to get up late, eat a large breakfast in an absent-minded way, potter off to a coffee-house, meet his friends, and talk, talk, talk. Thus he spent most of the day "in the brown coat with the metal buttons and the shirt which ought to be at wash, blinking, puffing, rolling his head, drumming with his fingers, tearing his meat like a tiger, and swallowing his tea in oceans." [1] It would take more than the writing of a dictionary to make him alter the habits of a lifetime; though he was certainly aware of the formidable nature of his task. He was rather proud of its vastness, which matched his own intellectual stature. He despised trivialities always. "No, Sir," he once declared. "A man would never undertake great things could he be amused by small. I once tried knotting [2] . . . but I could not learn it." The truth of the matter was that he was too lazy even to learn to "knot."

[1] Macaulay, *Life of Johnson.*
[2] I thought this meant simply knitting; but the O.E.D. confuses me by saying that "it means the knitting of knots"! In fact it seems to have been a sort of "tatting," making lace out of sewing thread with the aid of a shuttle.

He would certainly have been too lazy to finish the dictionary if he hadn't been in desperate need of the cash; but the booksellers, with their usual low cunning, had avoided paying him the £1575 in one lump sum. They doled it out bit by bit, as the sheets of the dictionary were handed over to them. It was always a tug of war between Dr. Johnson's idleness and Dr. Johnson's poverty. When his needs became desperate, he worked very hard indeed; the moment they were alleviated he stopped work. A consequence of this was that what had looked like a well-paid job became a rather unprofitable one. He took seven years to write his Dictionary—the better part of two having been spent in planning and thinking about it. Therefore out of the £1575 he had to keep not only himself but the six amanuenses for seven or eight years instead of three. Three-quarters of the way through he became desperately weary. Who could fail to be touched by this entry in his diary?

> *April* 3rd 1753—I began the second vol. of my "Dictionary" room being left in the first for Preface, Grammar and History none of them yet begun.
>
> o GOD, who hast hitherto supported me, enable me to proceed in this labour, and in the whole task of my present state; that when I shall render up, at the last day, an account of the talent committed to me, I may receive pardon, for the sake of JESUS CHRIST *Amen*.

Early in 1755, however, the very last of the sheets were sent off to the bookseller, Andrew Millar. When the messenger came back to Gough Square Dr. Johnson asked him: "Well, what did he say?"

"Sir, he said, 'Thank God I have done with him!' "

Dr. Johnson smiled. "I am glad that he thanks God for anything."

The printers must have worked fast in those days. The two folio volumes, containing definitions of more than 41,000 words, came out in April, 1755, price £4. 10. 0; and they could have appeared even sooner if Dr. Johnson had not been so desirous that the letters "M.A." should appear after his name on the title page. Since he possessed no M.A., he must set about getting one; and publication was held up while he went down to Oxford and put the matter right.

Meanwhile the famous dispute with the Earl of Chesterfield had been running its course. At the very start of the project, His Lordship had become in a rather vague way "patron" of the dictionary; he had invited Dr. Johnson to his house, and graciously given him £10. Possibly the Doctor's appearance, which was never smart, often uncouth, and almost always dirty, may not have found favour in the eyes of one who considered himself so refined that he could assert, "In my mind, there is nothing so illiberal and so ill-bred, as audible laughter." It is on the cards that Dr. Johnson so far forgot himself as to laugh aloud! Anyhow, the Earl of Chesterfield seems to have lost interest both in the man and in his dictionary, until he heard it was about to come out. He then became very anxious about the dedication, which he felt he deserved; and he wrote two articles for a journal, *The World*, in which he gave Dr. Johnson the most extravagant praise. Reading them, the Doctor remarked to Garrick: "I have sailed a long and painful voyage round the world of the English language, and does he now send out two cockboats to tow me into harbour?" He proceeded to elaborate this theme in that terrible letter of protest which he addressed to the man of whose own published *Letters* he was later to declare, that they taught "the morals of a whore, and the manners of a dancing master."

> Seven years, my Lord, have now past since I waited in your outward rooms or was repulsed from your door; during which time I have been pushing on with my work through difficulties of which it is useless to complain, and have brought it, at last, to the verge of publication without one act of assistance, one word of encouragement, or one smile of favour . . .

The sentences move in majestical procession, so that Lord Chesterfield, to do him justice, when he recovered from the first hurt and showed the letter to a friend, was compelled to admit almost in awe: "This man has great powers."

> —Is not a Patron, my Lord, one who looks with unconcern on a man struggling for life in the water, and when he has reached ground, encumbers him with help? The notice which you have been pleased to take of my labours, had it been early, had been kind; but it has been delayed till I am indifferent, and cannot enjoy it; till I am solitary, and cannot impart it; till I am known, and do not want it . . .

Posthumous fame is a chancy business altogether; but it seems likely that Philip Dormer Stanhope, fourth Earl of Chesterfield, owes his to

Dr. Johnson's attack on him, rather than to his own writings, however elegant and witty.[1] His name, however, has got itself a kind of immortality on its own account, for it appears in many English dictionaries subsequent to Dr. Johnson's:

> *Chesterfield* (f. the name of an Earl of Chesterfield) 1. A kind of overcoat. 2. A stuffed-over couch or sofa with a back and two ends, one of which is sometimes made adjustable.

NOW THAT the dictionary was published Dr. Johnson seemed indifferent to its fate and unaware of its importance. He remarked airily that he could have finished it in two years if he had been fortunate enough to possess diligence and good health! In fact, his achievement was unique in the history of literature. His was the first English dictionary, in the sense in which we understand the word; most of the previous ones had been "glossaries," lists with definitions of unusual or selected words only. Moreover Johnson's work was done so admirably, and based on so sound a plan, that it has served as a model for all the dictionaries which have been made since,—and so it stands as undisputed ancestor of the great *Oxford English Dictionary* itself.

Again, it is remarkable in being the work of one man,[2]—for the six amanuenses were little more than copyists or clerks. Certainly it took him seven years to compile it; but the brothers Grimm, who began a Dictionary of the German language in 1854, took twice as long to finish the letter A, and this work, on which various scholars have been working for the last 106 years, has only just been published. The Swedish Academy's dictionary and the *Woordenboek der Nederlandsche Taal* are not completed yet.

Lastly, Dr. Johnson's is the only Dictionary of any importance which bears the stamp of its maker's idiosyncrasies. One of these was that he would never quote examples from those he considered to be "ungodly writers" lest his readers should be led by the references to

---

[1] Dr. Johnson had once thought him a lord among wits: after their quarrel he decided he was only a wit among lords!

[2] Noah Webster also worked single-handed to produce his *American Dictionary of the English Language* in 1828. Moreover, he learned 20 languages in order to equip himself for the task, and unlike Dr. Johnson seems to have done without the aid of copyists. We are told he wrote every word of the manuscript in his own hand. There were 70,000 entries!

read them! For the sake of the idiosyncrasies the Dictionary can be read for fun. You can hear the tone of his voice in most of the definitions: "*Booklearned.* Versed in books, or literature: a term of some contempt." Nor was he afraid to display his personal prejudice and bias: "*Excise.* A hateful tax levied upon commodities, and adjudged not by the common judges of property, but wretches hired by those to whom Excise is paid" . . . "*Pension.* An allowance made to anyone without an equivalent. In England it is generally understood to mean pay given to a state hireling for treason to his country." The former drew an angry protest from the excisemen, who naturally objected to being called wretches; the latter served as a sharp weapon in the hands of Johnson's enemies, when he himself accepted a pension from George III.

Such *jeux d'esprit*, when we come across them in so learned a work, are as surprising as the gambols of an elephant. "*Oats.* A grain which in England is generally given to horses," wrote the Doctor; and in high delight at scoring another point in his lifelong argument against the Scots, he added contemptuously, "but in Scotland supports the people."

But although he permitted himself such jests in the body of the work now and then, the magnificent Preface was written in a mood of gloomy resignation, after the rest of the book had been done:

Though no book was ever spared out of tenderness to the author, and the world is little solicitous to know whence proceeded the faults of that which it condemns; yet it may gratify curiosity to inform it, that the *English Dictionary* was written with little assistance of the learned, and without any patronage of the great; not in the soft obscurities of retirement, or under the shelter of academick bowers, but amid inconvenience and distraction, in sickness and in sorrow.[1] It may repress the triumph of malignant criticism to observe, that if our language is not here fully displayed, I have only failed in an attempt which no human powers have hitherto completed. If the lexicons of ancient tongues, now immutably fixed, and comprised in a few volumes, be yet, after the toil of successive ages, inadequate and delusive . . . I may surely be contented without the praise of perfection, which, if I could obtain, in this gloom of solitude, what

---

[1] His wife had died, after a long and wretched illness, in 1752.

would it avail me? I have protracted my work till most of those whom I wished to please have sunk into the grave, and success and miscarriage are empty sounds; I therefore dismiss it with frigid tranquillity, having little to fear or hope from censure or from praise.

OF COURSE Dr. Johnson knew well that his dictionary began to be outdated even while the proofs were on their way back to the printer. It is the despair and delight of lexicographers, that in language they are dealing with a living thing; and none of them must be so foolish as to think "that his dictionary can embalm his language, and secure it from corruption and decay; that it is his power to change sublunary nature, and clear the world from folly, vanity, and affectation . . ."

I quote again from Dr. Johnson's Preface. It is well worth quoting. Concerning the French and Italian academies, which tried to fix their languages in a "classical" changeless mould, he thunders gloriously: "Academies have been instituted to guard the avenues of their language, to retain fugitives, and repulse intruders; but their vigilance and activity have hitherto been vain; sounds are too volatile and subtile for legal restraints; to enchain syllables, and to lash the wind, are equally the undertakings of pride." [1]

Language, inevitably, is in a state of continual flux. In ancient times conquests and migrations were often the cause: words were the imponderable luggage which Anglo-Saxons and Norsemen brought to England, whether they came to settle or to slay; but nowadays "total and sudden transformations seldom happen." In another of his tremendous sentences, Dr. Johnson refers to some other causes of change "which, though slow in their operation, and invisible in their progress, are perhaps as much superior to human resistance, as the revolutions of the sky, or intumescence of the tides." He gave among his examples commerce with foreign parts; the "enlarging stock of ideas"; each increase in knowledge "real or fancied"; the cultivation of sciences; "the tropes of poetry"; vulgar corruption through misunderstanding; and, of course, manners and snobbery. He showed that the quaint business

[1] The Fellows of the American Society of Languages sought "to lash the wind" in 1780. Believing that "The highest perfection of English, with every other branch of human knowledge," was reserved for what they called "this land of light and freedom" they dedicated themselves "to correct, enrich and refine it" until perfection should "stop their progress and end their labours."

of "U and Non-U" was operating in his day just as it is now, and indeed as it must have done ever since language first began.

Such processes never cease; and all the time, in every tongue, new words are budding, old ones are dying away. You can think of words as creatures whose environment is man's thought, as reflected in all that he speaks or writes. Every trifling change in the environment—in the climate of social opinion, for example—acts upon these "creatures" of words, just as in the field of nature climatic changes act upon the multitudinous living organisms. Some wither away like plants lacking rain; some multiply like butterflies in a hot summer; some adapt themselves to the new climate—take on new forms or acquire new meanings. Moreover, a kind of Darwinian process of natural selection comes into play: the outmoded, like the dinosaur, cannot survive—and we find it fossilised in the dictionary, labelled "Archaic" or "Obsolete." On the other hand new forms are born to match new necessities, or old forms burgeon afresh to surprise us with their renewed beauty, strangeness, aptitude, or practicality.

This process goes on all the time, in language as it does in nature. You and I can think of many words that have altered their meanings during our lifetimes; of many born within the last few years, such as antibiotic, spaceman,[1] radar, television, wireless; of others that were fashionable in our youth and are out of favour today—a few years hence they may be dead as the dodo. More often these processes are too slow for us to perceive them; during several score of years a word may gradually enlarge or contract the boundaries of its meaning, or change by some shade or nuance its significance, pronunciation, spelling or usage. But we cannot watch the change happening, any more than we can watch an oak-tree growing, or one of its branches withering away, in the context of a vast woodland.

[1] After all this may not be a new word, though it certainly has a new and urgent meaning; for the other day upon an advertisement hoarding I saw a notice SPACE-MEN WANTED, which clearly was not asking for volunteers to go to the moon. Perhaps it means "people who let space on hoardings," or who stick bills on them.

CHAPTER 4

Some Bees in Some Bonnets

SEEING THAT WORDS are obviously products of evolution, and that every living European language is demonstrably built upon the structure of yet earlier tongues which themselves derived from older ones, I never cease to marvel at the courage and cool cheek of the people who have taken it upon themselves to invent *new* languages. It is an ambition comparable with Frankenstein's, who sought to manufacture in his laboratory the creature which nature had taken millions of years to evolve; yet a great many extraordinary fellows have attempted it, and some very extraordinary monsters have been produced. The appearance of some of them suggests that their inventors had fallen upon the English language in a fury and dismembered it with a blunt hacksaw. Their names alone are alarming. Volapuk was invented in 1880 by Father Schleyer. Someone called Elias Molee invented a jabberwocky named Tutonish. A Mr. Foster, from America, produced the quaintly named Ro, which is all his own work in the sense that it bears no resemblance whatever to any known tongue; truly a "special creation"—as was another queer philosophical language invented by a Bishop Wilkins, of which I read somewhere, and the fact unaccountably stuck in my mind, that its word for "fire" was "deb."

There were other monsters called Idiom Neutral, Isotype, Occidental, and Novial.

Esperanto was invented by a Polish Jew [1] in 1887, and consists of French, English and German elements grafted on to Latin roots. It seems to have a curious effect upon the people who go to the trouble of learning it; they soon begin to regard it not so much as a language as a Cause. They carry banners for Esperanto; and they speak in Hyde Park. In this way it has a considerable vogue, and individuals from many nations attend International Congresses at which, I daresay, it is

[1] Dr. L. L. Zamenhof.

as heinous an offence to speak any language other than Esperanto, as it is to utter a word of English at an Eisteddfod. This game makes a lot of people happy, and I can do no more than confess my humble opinion that those people are all rather odd.

But then I cannot see any point or purpose whatever in an artificial language. It must surely be a great bore, and a most unrewarding labour, to learn a language that possesses neither a literature nor any historical associations. If an international language were really needed, then we have one ready to hand in Latin, which once served as the *lingua franca* of almost all the civilised peoples, and which is still a means of communication between the doctors and the natural scientists of almost every nation. A man who learns Latin acquires much more than the knowledge of a dead language; he has a key to the wisdom of the ancient world, with the poetry of Virgil, Horace, Catullus, Ovid chucked in as a bonus. Latin also makes the learning of a whole family of other languages very much easier. Therefore it would seem much more sensible for these woolly internationalists to bear their banners for Latin, and to cry Hurray for Horace in Hyde Park, than to proselytise on behalf of its bastard descendant, this bloodless, backboneless, witless deformity called Esperanto.

However, I am not at all sure that we need an international language; it is good for us to learn each other's. If a Spaniard takes the trouble to acquire English, then Shakespeare and Milton and all the other glories are showered into his lap as an extra; if I take the trouble to learn Spanish, I can read *Don Quixote* in Cervantes' original and, through it, partake of the very spirit of Spain.

Meanwhile, because of various historical accidents, and by reason of its vigour and versatility, English widens its influence every year. American servicemen, and later the enormous generosities of American aid, have carried the U.S. version of our common tongue all over the world during the post-war years; in south-east Asia and Japan particularly has English become a second language for millions. Indeed, if we think in terms of a "world language" we may perhaps look for it among the various mutations of ours. For paradoxically, as the British Empire contracts, so does the English language extend its dominion. It is difficult to see how the new nations emerging out of our old African colonies will speak to each other save in English; for they have no common language of their own. As for India, she pays a pleasant compliment to those who once ruled her, by taking over the Parliamentary democracy, the legal system, the game of cricket and the English language which they left behind. But of these I daresay cricket is the only one which won't have its rules altered in the course of time. The language is bound to change, and may acquire different rhythms and pronunciations, even perhaps different constructions, from those of the parent tongue. I should be surprised if it hasn't already given birth to some new words of its own. In a hundred years, this "Indian English" may be as different from B.B.C. English as the slang speech of Sydney, or the American of Damon Runyon's New York; and who knows what variations of "the tongue that Shakespeare spake" may emerge and find fresh vigour among the free nations now rising up between Freetown and Zanzibar?

This new-flowering of English seems to me a very happy prospect; but of course the spread of a living, evolving language throughout the world is exactly the opposite of what the adherents of Esperanto want. For they are dedicated to the idea of a fixed, immutable, universal tongue; and that is as silly a proposition as if they looked for a standstill in what Dr. Johnson called "the revolutions of the sky and the intumescence of the tides."

THE SUBJECT of language is one that breeds bees in bonnets more freely, I think, than any other; and not only cranks, but rational men, and sometimes great men, are especially troubled by them. George Bernard Shaw didn't invent a new language, though the temptation must have been strong. Instead he wanted above all things to impose a new spelling upon the existing English language, by means of adding fourteen more letters to the alphabet; and he directed in his Will that a portion of his estate should be devoted to this end.

The ambition which possessed him was simply to save time. He saw clearly that the spelling of words could be rationalised and shortened by the addition of some new phonetic symbols. He therefore directed his Trustee

To institute and finance a series of inquiries to ascertain or estimate as far as possible the following statistics (a) the number of extant persons who speak the English language and write it by the established and official alphabet of 26 letters (hereinafter called Dr. Johnson's Alphabet) (b) how much time could be saved per individual scribe by the substitution for the said Alphabet of an Alphabet containing at least 40 letters . . . (c) how many of these persons are engaged in writing or printing English at any and every moment in the world; (d) on these factors to estimate the time and labour wasted . . . (e) to add where possible to the estimates of time lost or saved . . . estimates of the loss of income in British and American currency . . .

He wished also that a phonetic expert should be employed to transliterate *Androcles and the Lion* into a 40-letter alphabet "assuming the pronunciation to resemble that recorded of His Majesty our late King George V."

The bees had swarmed, alas, and settled in his old mind as in a hollow tree, setting up a ceaseless and intolerable buzzing there. His own large intellect was so fully engaged during every waking minute that the matter of time-saving seemed all-important to him; indeed he had learned both shorthand and speedwriting with the idea of "saving time" while writing his plays—though it would be astonishing if even Shaw were able to compose his beautiful sentences more quickly than the hand could write them down. For this reason I think the whole "time-saving" argument is a fallacy. Any author who can compose 500 words in an hour is thinking very fast indeed: at that rate his hand is mostly idle, as it waits for further orders from the mind. We don't write *better* if we write quicker; we almost always write worse. As for reading, most of us go too fast as it is, and if the 40-letter alphabet should enable me to read *Hamlet* in less than two hours, then the worse for me, and the worse for Shakespeare.

But the whole business was part and parcel of Shaw's curiously calculating attitude to matters which he ought to have known were outside calculation; and it is quite extraordinary that a man whose prose at its best matches that of the Collects could solemnly propose to do violence to the English language on a stupendous scale, simply for the sake of saving x million hours per annum which very few people would know what to do with when they had saved them. And make no mistake, a new Alphabet would rob the written language at one fell swoop of its history, its tradition, and most of its beauty. In such "New Spellings" as I have seen, the sentences look as if they were trying to record the chatterings of a baboon; a Shakespeare sonnet becomes sheer gibberish. You may say that this is because I have not been brought up on the new spelling and I shy away from it simply as an old horse shies away from some new sort of vehicle which he has never seen before. Even if this is true, it is only one of the reasons why the new spelling makes the words meaningless to me. I can no longer get a glimpse of their lineage; I lose my awareness of their antecedents; the new phonetic symbols have the effect of uprooting them clean out of the past. Nor is this a loss which only matters to the few who know a bit of Greek and Latin,—who when they read *anemone* are reminded of the *wind* that tosses the frail white blossoms in March, or when they come across such a phrase as "the *circumambient* dark" can imagine the darkness *walking round*, like a wolf about a camp-fire, as the dangerous dark deepens. There are many more such people than is often supposed; and obviously they are the ones who get the most out of reading poetry and great prose. But in fact, I think that almost everybody who reads seriously is conscious that words have associations, histories, and meanings-behind-their-meanings which are tied up with the way they are spelt. We cannot thoroughly enjoy a poem unless we are aware of these overtones and echoes. I do not deny that a new spelling, once we had learned it, might prove an even more efficient vehicle than our present one for such a communication as, say, *There has been a further reduction in the price of pork*; but I am quite sure it would fail lamentably to convey the full meaning of *Charm'd magic casements opening on the foam Of perilous seas, in faery lands forlorn.*

Shaw, almost alone of great writers, was little moved by poetry; and although he wrote some of the noblest prose written in our time—the Inquisitor's speech at Saint Joan's trial, for instance—he did not cherish words for their own sake, he was only concerned that they should serve him well in the presentation of his argument. It is in character with the man who wrote part of *Saint Joan* in shorthand that he didn't care tuppence about the overtones of language and he had no real respect for the words which were his raw material. But it is strange that Shaw the internationalist did not see what a barrier any new spelling would set up against the foreigner who seeks to learn English. At present most Europeans recognise a good many of our words because they have roots in common with their own tongues—just as I can get the sense of an article in a Portuguese newspaper, although I don't know

Portuguese. This recognition of a common ancestry and acknowledgment of cousinship is a great help in learning a language, both psychologically and practically. Mark Twain observed that "foreigners spell better than they pronounce" [1] which of course is profoundly true: in the spelling of foreign words we can see their bare anatomies, their skeletal selves, which are often the same as the skeletons of our *own* words, though our different pronunciations make them seem, in speech, to be absolutely different. A new spelling would conceal these relationships; and would probably cause a great many foreigners to view the English language with the same sort of bewilderment and alarm that affects me when I contemplate Magyar!

Fortunately, there is not the slightest danger of any new alphabet coming into general use. We shall of course carry out the terms of Shaw's senile Will, and spend a moiety of the tremendous royalties earned by *My Fair Lady* in trying to make these futile inquiries concerning the number of people writing and printing English at any and every moment: and the "amateur phoneticians etymologists Spelling Reformers patentees of universal languages inventors of shorthand codes or rival alphabets . . . disputants about pronunciation" and all the other wrangling irreconcilables as the old man described them in the Will, hating each other as only like-minded cranks can do, will continue to fight like cats about how to carry out this fatuous proposition, while the majority of us happily forget all about it.

[1] *Innocents Abroad.*

CHAPTER 5

The Sound and the Sense

I SAID that Shaw "did not cherish words for their own sake"; he looked upon them as tools, or more often as weapons, when he was concerned only that their impact should be sharp. Neither in his plays nor, I think, in his conversation, did he ever seem to dwell with delight upon a word; and unlike most writers (including Shakespeare) he had no special favourites which it gave him a peculiar pleasure to speak or write. Shaw would never have fallen into the cardinal error and dreadful heresy (as modern writers on language hold it to be) of speaking of a word as "beautiful" or "ugly," or significant by reason of its sound and appearance alone. This is described as naïvety. "Certain words are reputed," writes Mr. John Press in his excellent book about poetry called *The Fire and the Fountain*, "to have an elemental significance incapsulated in their sound . . ." Mr. Press holds this notion up to ridicule, telling us of a Russian who affirmed that for him the most beautiful word in the English language was "coal-scuttle," and parodying *Kubla Khan* to demonstrate that the sound of the words has no æsthetic value when divorced from their sense. And of course in a way it is all too easy, by these and other such ingenuities, to demonstrate that when we call the sound of a word repulsive or its form beautiful we are really bemused by the *associations* of the word and the images it calls up in our minds. You have only to point out that the very sublime and beautiful word "celestial" has but one exact rhyme in the English language, which is the very base and hideous word "bestial." Or you can suggest, as Mr. Ivor Brown has done, that the refined and exquisite word "philomel," which for two or three centuries our poets preferred to the plain English "nightingale," makes much the same music in our ears as the name of that homely purge, calomel. And you can sum up by quoting old Rowley, the farm-labourer in Mr. Aldous Huxley's *Crome Yellow*, who remarked of some swine which were happily wallowing in the mud: "Look at them, sir. Rightly is they called pigs."

No doubt in many cases it *is* simply a word's associations which deceive us into the fancy that it possesses a "character" of its own. "Swastika" is to some of us "an evil word." Yet its meaning, in Sanskrit whence it comes, was "fortune, well-being, good luck." The primitive symbol associated with this good luck was quite unfamiliar to Englishmen until it began to appear on the covers of Rudyard Kipling's books. It was there I saw it first, when I was very young and was just beginning to read the *Jungle Books*. Hence I came to associate it, erroneously, with elephants. The image which the word "swastika" would conjure up in my mind remained a confused one of India and elephants until the late nineteen-thirties. But now, of course, I no longer see the elephants. I see that little man with the black lovelock and the Charlie Chaplin moustache, and behind him I see the barbed wire, the gas chambers, murdered Jews, Anne Frank.

"HONOUR" is a very good example of an emotive word; more than a hundred entries in the *Oxford Dictionary of Quotations* testify to its power. From time to time it moves anybody capable of being moved by a word. I was first affected by it at the age of seven, when the word broke out like a rash all over the papers in connexion with the beginning of World War I. Grown-ups, about the same time I suppose, were shedding tears over a young poet's latest sonnet: "Honour has come back as a king to earth And paid his subjects with a royal wage." [1] Even in the light of all that has happened since, and all the dishonour done in honour's name, I should hate the man who sneered at Rupert Brooke for writing those lines. Nevertheless one has to admit that "honour" is a word that shines less bright than it did; it has become tarnished through being bandied about by time-servers and sycophants, lackeys, sentimentalists and stooges. We need not be ashamed therefore if we enjoy the spectacle of Falstaff stripping the frills and the falsities from it, in *Henry IV, Part I*:

Well, 'tis no matter; honour pricks me on. Yes, but how if honour pricks me off when I come on? how then? Can honour set-to a leg? no: or an arm? no: or take away the grief of a wound? no. Honour

[1] *The Dead.*

hath no skill in surgery, then? No. What is honour? a word . . . Who
hath it? he that died o'Wednesday. Doth he feel it? no. Is it insen-
sible, then? Yea, to the dead. But will it not live with the living? no.
Why? Detraction will not suffer it:—therefore I'll none of it; honour
is a mere scutcheon: and so ends my catechism.

Shortly afterwards, upon this "Plain near Shrewsbury," Falstaff
stumbles upon the fresh-slain corpse of brave Sir Walter Blunt. He
studies it thoughtfully.

"I like not such grinning honour as Sir Walter hath," says he.
"Give me life."

MR. ALDOUS HUXLEY observed that Tennyson's lovely line

And after many a summer dies the swan

lost all its radiance if for "swan" was substituted the word "duck." Mr.
John Press, expanding this, makes some interesting comments on the
association of the two words:

> *Swan* conjures up a visual image of exquisite whiteness, luminosity
> and grace, whereas the vision produced by the word *duck* is of a
> small, waddling creature devoid of dignity and of pathos. But over
> and above the purely visual representation of the swan and of the
> duck, we are conscious of a host of associations which influence our
> responses to these words. Out for a duck, a dying duck in a thunder-
> storm, a man with duck's disease . . . The swan brings with it an
> aura of mystery and of beauty as it sails down the reaches of the
> mind, recalling the silver-throated swans of the madrigalists and of
> Spenser, the swan which caressed Leda, the swans which haunt some
> of Yeats' finest poems, and those living birds which still glide un-
> ruffled on the Backs at Cambridge. Tennyson's swan dies against the
> traditional background of English poetry, amid the lamenting music
> of five centuries.

Of course a word's associations depend largely on the range of your
reading; and I know some people who when they meet with "swan" are
less likely to think of the madrigalists than of the bar of a notable pub
in my native town. Sometimes, on the other hand, the associations
which a word has for us are extremely remote and subtle; it may even,

as the psychiatrists know well, act upon us through our subconscious minds, and so produce responses that are personal, puzzling and peculiar. For most of us, as for Mad Margaret in *Ruddigore*, there is "some word that teems with hidden meaning—like Basingstoke"; and the odds are that we don't know why. Consider, for instance, the strange case of the word "Mesopotamia." An old lady, according to Brewer's *Dictionary of Phrase and Fable*, confided to her pastor that "she found great support in that comfortable word Mesopotamia." This quaint anecdote ties up with a remark which David Garrick is said to have made concerning the Methodist preacher George Whitefield. Garrick, who naturally knew all about audiences, was greatly impressed by the power and the modulations of the preacher's voice. "He could make men either laugh or cry by pronouncing the word Mesopotamia."

Our soldiers in the First World War were not, however, bemused by it; they associated it with discomfort, disease and flies, and shortened it to "Messpot."

But was not Messpot very expressive of what they felt about it? Can you imagine an apter pair of syllables? In a very short time not only the soldiers, but most of the people on the Home Front, were speaking of Messpot. They liked the little joke wrapped up in the name; and it matched their mood. Now this is where I begin to have some doubts about the modern view, that it is naïve to suppose words sometimes possess "a significance incapsulated in their sounds." For we know they are subject to a process of natural selection. In their environment of man's thought some thrive, some survive only narrowly, some wither away and die. Why? The main factor must surely be human choice. Writers and speakers by the million, generation after generation, have unendingly sought for the right words to match their thoughts; often devotedly, sometimes desperately, they have looked for the aptest, rejecting a dozen, at last selecting one. Is it not likely that they chose, other things being equal, the word which had the most *expressive sound*—and that if they were writers they may even have been influenced a little by the appearance of the word on the page, when written or printed? For the "shape" of a word, as well as its sound, may surely possess a significance for some people. "With a name like yours," said Alice to Humpty-Dumpty, "you might be any shape almost."

There was a river in Phrygia, called by the Greeks *Maiandros*, which

became proverbial for its winding course; and so through Latin we got
the verb "meander," meaning to wind or turn in this sinuous, aimless
and devious way: as the Sacred River does in *Kubla Khan*, "Five miles
meandering with a mazy motion." Why has this particular word survived in English, and indeed flourished? Not very many people who
use it today have ever heard of Phrygia, which is now called Anatolia,
or of the river, now called Menderes, or know of that river's famous
windings to the sea. But speakers and writers still use "meander" in
connexion with a devious stream because—surely—the sound-sequence
of its syllables seems to fit the idea of such a course. There is an inevitable slight pause after the first syllable which is suggestive of a
lazy progress; and the latter part of the word is reminiscent of "wander," perhaps. I believe this is why the classical word "meander" is
alive today, and not "obsolete."

Now say to yourself "forlorn." It has been described as the loneliest
word in the English language, and by reason of its sound it is one of
the saddest. "Forlorn! the very word is like a bell!" [1] I suppose I am
liable to be accused of naïvety; but I still maintain that "forlorn" possesses an incapsulated loneliness, such as that, for instance, of a bell
tolling slowly on a slowly-heaving buoy, in a cold grey fog at sea.

MAN IS a very different animal from what I believe him to be if the
sound and the meaning, in such words as this, are *not* closely related.
It is almost a game with him, to match syllables to ideas in such a way
that the idea is strengthened and enlarged by them. Children do it in
their nursery rhymes; poets do it all the time; and very often ordinary
and unlearned men show such an aptitude for it that in giving, say, a
pet name to a creature they surprise themselves and everybody
else by conjuring up ideas and images which they had not intended or
even thought of. A very good example is the name of a little polar bear
that was born in the London Zoo, and greatly endeared itself to the
public, a few years ago. It was called Brumas: a high-faluting name
compared with that of its mother, which was Ivy. But it was not intended to be high-faluting; for it was made, by two of Ivy's keepers,
out of their own Christian names, Bruce and Sam, with Sam spelt
backwards. But what a name for a polar bear, Brumas!—the sea sighs,

[1] Keats: *Ode to a Nightingale.*

the north wind moans in it; the bitter brume of the polar regions seeps through it. Most likely Bruce and Sam were not consciously aware of these associations. Their lively fancy told them that the name "sounded right"; and during the cubhood of the creature millions of people who visited the Zoo agreed that it "sounded right," recognised the aptness and chose it with acclaim; so that "Brumas" was on everybody's lips, and even made headlines in the papers.

NOW THIS PROCESS of "choosing words because they sound right" has been going on, I imagine, since the beginning of speech; and it would be very odd indeed, it would argue some lack of both a sense of poetry and a sense of the fitness of things, if the generations of Englishmen had *not*, on the whole, selected words which make swifter the communication between minds, by reason of the sounds reinforcing the meaning. Yet this is doubted by some of the experts in linguistics. They readily allow that certain words are echoic or imitative—cuckoo, titter, howl, splash—but they would deny that there were such things as essentially prim words, solemn words, fat words (pudding?), soft words, hard words, ominous words, sad words (willow?), proud words etc., and would accuse me of being emotional in my belief that they exist. Let me nevertheless suggest a few for their learned consideration. Does not the *sound* of "prim" carry the meaning of a particular attitude or expression of demureness, precision and formality? Indeed we can scarcely make the sound without presenting such a face to the world. It is a prunes-and-prisms word. "Father is rather vulgar, my dear," said Mrs. General in *Little Dorrit*. "The word Papa, besides, gives a pretty form to the lips. Papa, potatoes, poultry, prunes and prism are all very good words for the lips, specially prunes and prism." Again, "You have only, when before your glass, to keep pronouncing to yourself nimini-pimini —the lips cannot fail of taking their plie." [1] Now consider the word "pomp." It always seems to me to have a splendid solemnity; which perhaps it may have got from the formality which is generally imparted by the letter "p," plus the drum-sound of the whole word—*pomp, pomp, pomp!* We acquired it from Latin *pompa*, a transliteration of Greek *pompē*, meaning a solemn or sumptuous procession, parade, or display. It brings its drums with it into English poetry and prose: "Soon

[1] John Burgoyne: *The Heiress*.

will the high Midsummer pomps come on" [1]—"Pride, pomp, and circumstance of glorious war!" [2]—"The pomps and vanity of this wicked
world, and all the sinful lusts of the flesh." [3]

UNLESS you are Scottish you are not very likely to know the meaning
of the word "sonsie," so you can judge without prejudice whether you
think that it looks and sounds a "fat" word or not. Burns addressed
the haggis:

> *Fair fa' your honest sonsie face,*
> *Great chieftain o' the puddin'-race!*

The original meaning of the word was "bringing good luck," whence it
acquired the sense of "thriving," "plump," "comfortable-looking," as
Burns used it of the bulging haggis, and also of girls—he wrote of "My
sonsie, smirking, dear-bought Bess." "Buxom" is its southern equivalent; and a bouncing, blooming, bonnie pair of words they make together. Buxom, however, did not always carry a sense of cheerful come-
liness. It is a Germanic word which used to mean bendable, pliable,
obedient. Foxe in his *Book of Martyrs* could write of being "buxom
and obedient to the Church of Christ," and a Monk of Gloucester,
in a Christmas sermon, reproved his congregation for being "covetous
of unbuxomness." Slimming girls are so today; but we use the word
differently.

I SUGGESTED there were soft words and hard words. "Agate" seems to
me a hard one for a hard thing; and it would be very difficult for anybody to maintain that "sillabub" does not carry an implication of the
luscious softness of the delicacy which was made as follows:

> Take a pint of Verjuice in a Bowl, milk the Cow to it, then take
> the curd off, and take sweet cream, and beat them together with a
> little Sack and Sugar, put it into your sillabub-pot, strew sugar on it
> and serve.[4]

I imagine a sillabub was the unfrozen Elizabethan equivalent of a

[1] Matthew Arnold, beginning his list of the scented and showy flowers, in
Thyrsis.
[2] *Othello.*
[3] The Catechism: *Book of Common Prayer.*
[4] *The Accomplish't Lady's Delight.*

very superior sundae, with sherry taking the place of the fruit. "Sundae," by the way, apparently comes from "Sunday," improbable though this may seem. Mr. H. L. Mencken, the great authority on the American language, says it does, and the cautious *O.E.D.* agrees. Mr. Partridge suggests pleasantly: "Whereas an ordinary ice-cream was good enough for a week-day, this special kind was good enough for a Sunday." [1]

The sillabub too was for special occasions. Sir Henry Wotton associates it with the spring:

> *JONE takes her neat-rub'd Pail, and now*
> *She trips to milk the Sand-red Cow*
> *Where, for some sturdy foot-ball SWAIN,*
> *JONE stroaks a sillibub or twain.*

"Foot-ball" is quaintly used as an adjective, implying "pretty tough and healthy." I like "stroaks," which suggests the practised ease of Joan's milking. But "sillabub"—is not its sound replete with meaning, and was not it obviously chosen long ago, by an electorate composed of cooks and dairymaids and football swains and poets, as just the right word to do that particular job of suggesting whipped cream and sugar?

IN THE SAME WAY, "slimy" seems to me suggestive of viscosity, and I cannot help feeling its currency demonstrates that "natural selection" among words does result in the survival of the fittest. It's an old word in English, akin to Latin *limus*, mud, mire, and possessing a lot of slimy relations, for example Greek *leimax*, a snail, and *limnē*, a marsh, Old English *lim*, glue, birdlime, Old English *sliw*, a fish, Norwegian *slo*, a blindworm (whence our slow-worm) and the English words slick (whence the American "slicker" and Mr. Osborne's Paul Slickey), sleek, loam (sticky earth) and liniment (something smeared on). The slight revulsion which most of us experience when we encounter this word *may* be due to its associations with, say, snails, or eels or slugs,— of which a whole genus bears the scientific name *Limax*. It may; or is there also some viscous suggestion in the sound?—

> *The very deep did rot: O Christ!*
> *That ever this should be!*

[1] *Origins.*

*Yea, slimy things did crawl with legs
Upon the slimy sea.*[1]

"DOOM" is another word in which it seems to me sound and sense match so well that pure chance is unlikely to have been responsible. Incidentally its rhyme-fellow "gloom" also has ominous implications. The original meanings of "doom" in English were "a law or decree, justice, verdict," etc. It is a word which drops from the lips with a fearful finality. It is stronger even than "love," in that most steadfast of Shakespeare's sonnets:

*Love's not Time's fool, though rosy lips and cheeks
Within his bending sickle's compass come;
Love alters not with his brief hours and weeks,
But bears it out even to the edge of doom.*

The Great *Domesday Book* was so-called, not by those clerks who compiled it, but in awe and wonder, possibly tempered with a shade of mockery, by the people themselves; because it set out to be the final and conclusive authority concerning every matter that came within its scope; like those scrupulous tomes of the Recording Angel. Doomsday itself was of course the occasion of ultimate judgment:

HAMLET: What news?
ROSENCRANTZ: None, my lord, but that the world's grown honest.
HAMLET: Then is doomsday near.

I HAVE ALWAYS THOUGHT "Catherine of Aragon" to be the proudest-sounding title in English history, saving perhaps "Harry of Hereford, Lancaster and Derby"; I remember how my imagination leaped every time I heard it at school. In fact, I have read that Catherine was a rather colourless person, though she suffered with dignity and resignation the insults put on her in connexion with the divorce. But isn't Aragon a splendid word, as proud as Spain herself, where indeed most of the place-names are like battle-cries: Salamanca, Saragossa, Guadalajara, Santander! Hear this word Aragon ring out like a shout from a hill-top, in Belloc's *Tarantella*:

[1] Coleridge: *The Ancient Mariner.*

Never more;
Miranda,
Never more.
Only the high peaks hoar:
And Aragon a torrent at the door.

And so in English is "arrogant" a word which seems to me as proud
as Lucifer: as soon imagine Uriah Heep saying "We are so very
'umble" [1] with his head thrown back, as a man muttering "arrogant"
into his beard!

I daresay if they read that sentence the sad scientists of words will
shake their heads. "Purely emotional," they will say.

BUT IS NOT all language a product of human emotion? Were not all the
pickers-and-choosers of words, the poets, the preachers, the politicians,
the story-tellers, the love-letter-writers, and all the casual users, ranging
from him who only talks about the weather to her who berates her
husband for coming in with dirty boots,—were they not all "emotional"
in the exercise of their choice, selecting this word because it tickled
their fancy, this one because it sounded angry, this one because it
seemed persuasive, this one because its dramatic harshness might startle
an inattentive listener, and this one because the arrangement of its
syllables was in some way suggestive of pride? If so, then it seems
natural and inevitable that, being themselves so charged with emotion,
words should produce an emotional response in us; and I find it quite
impossible to regard them simply as arbitrary symbols, in the way that
H_2O is a symbol indicating oxide of hydrogen, commonly called water.
The chemical formula means nothing more than that; but the *word*
"water," whenever you or I encounter it, is liable to trigger off in our
minds certain currents of thought, which may lead us, say, from *King*
over the to *fish out of*, from teetotalism to Minnehaha, from *blood*
thicker than to *Wellington at Waterloo*. For a word possesses not only
its one or many meanings, and numberless shades of meaning, but carries with it the whole sum of its past usage in prose and poetry, proverb
and pun. Moreover, it is accompanied, you might almost say haunted,
wherever it goes in the language by the murmurous and unruly echoes
of all the similar and connected and associated words. And lastly it is

[1] *David Copperfield.*

burdened by a vast imponderable luggage made up of hints, inklings, reverberations, reflections all related to various facets of human action and behaviour. The word "bauble," for example, bears upon its back forever, with all the other images, one of Oliver Cromwell, warts and all; and the word "expects" will wear, as long as English lasts, the bunting which Nelson hoisted about it at Trafalgar.

So though we cannot by any stretch of the imagination describe these phantoms as living things, yet do they take on a kind of life from ourselves; they are like faithful and ceaseless reflections in a looking-glass held up to the multitudinous minds of men; and in their histories we can trace the whole course of our history, our thought, our bewilderment and our speculation,—as I shall try to show you, with the help of the learned philologists, in the chapters that follow.

CHAPTER 6

Light as Dreams, Tough as Oak

A SOLITARY CELT, one of the last surviving Ancient Britons, goes lumbering through our language in the form of brock the badger. He is called "badger" in English simply because he wears a badge, the white mark on his forehead; but the earlier Celtic name for him, "brock," is still preferred by country people, and when they say it they are using a word which Boadicea may have spoken 1900 years ago. Only a few stray fragments of her tongue have got into English: among them, the experts think, are "crock" (the pot or jar, not the broken-down horse or person) and "dun" (the colour, not the debt-collector). But for the most part the Celtic words have survived only as components of place-names. The Somerset "coombes" are Celtic—compare the Welsh *cwm*—and so are the Devon "tors."

THE BRONZE AGE people who carried huge splinters of granite down off these tors, and set them up on Dartmoor in circles and rows, had no written language; and so they seem utterly remote from us. We can lay our hands where their rough hands once gripped the great Beardown Man, as they heaved that solitary stone into place three or four thousand years ago; but we do not know what it was for—whether it marked a chieftain's grave or a boundary between territories, a victory in battle or the place appointed for worship, ritual or sacrifice. The words which could have told us about it have vanished into limbo unrecorded.

If only writing had gone side by side with speaking, through the prehistory of man! Then we should know how language first evolved; and we might even find the answer to the most tantalising and tormenting question of all: *How did it begin?* If we knew that, we should know how beasts became men.

We can imagine the physical evolution easily enough: a tail diminishes and disappears, a brain-pan grows more spacious, a forefoot becomes prehensile, a foreleg turns into an arm. It is much more difficult to visualise a transition from the state of having "no language but a cry" [1] to that of using words. For words are sounds representing thoughts, and it is very doubtful indeed if thoughts can exist without them. The transition, then, was from animals which, because they lacked words, could not "think," into men who, having words, were thereby enabled to store memories and formulate ideas. It was the possession of these words and ideas which gave mankind his dominion over the whole of nature.

Old skulls and jawbones, ulnas and femurs, can show how the body changed. There is no evidence at all concerning the changes from word-less and thought-less into speaking and thinking beings. No new organs were needed, nor were any made redundant; nature with ingenious parsimony made use of the tongue, teeth, lungs and throat originally designed for other jobs, and they provided the physical means of speech. What happened within the brain-pan nobody knows. It seems likely that while physical speech tentatively explored its potentialities, thought crept like a dawn millions of years long upon the awakening mind. And so, simply because of this marvellous acquisition of words, a creature something like an ape became the glory, jest and riddle of the world.

BUT THIS is guesswork. The very earliest picture writing is only five or six thousand years old; the Chinese ideographs go back to 1800 B.C.; the strange undeciphered script of ancient Crete, called Minoan, is said to date from 1900 B.C., which was about the time, I suppose, when our Bronze Age people were expressing themselves more clumsily by erecting those stones that loom up through Dartmoor's mists like threatening giants. But these tribesmen, alas, had not learned that a thought could be made to last much longer if some symbol representing it were carved upon a rock; and of their speech not a syllable remains,—not their names nor their gods' names, nor their battle-cries nor their ballads nor their prayers.

Not a syllable, unless—who knows?—by a fluke of survival some echo of their language, as it might be the gaunt word "tor" itself, became caught up in the speech of the Celtic tribesmen who came after

[1] Tennyson: *In Memoriam.*

them and who were grazing their flocks of sheep on the moorlands when Caesar and his legions arrived in Britain.

THE ROMANS came and went; their hearts were never in this land, and the legionaries in their garrisons at Caerleon, York and Chester must have felt themselves expatriate and forgotten, as they dreamed of the southern vineyards and the olive-trees. In time the legions were withdrawn, or simply rotted away. But when the Angles, Saxons and Jutes came streaming across the narrow sea it was a very different matter. They built byres instead of barracks, and cultivated the soil. They had no homesickness for a kindlier land; for they knew none kindlier than this one, and they meant to settle down in it for ever! In the face of such purposefulness the usually warlike Britons, who were "of horrible aspect in battle" according to Caesar, but who nevertheless gently worshipped rivers and the nymphs of the bubbling springs, withdrew and took their language with them into the mountains where the rivers rose. There, under the names of Gaelic and Welsh, it is vigorous still. In Ireland, however, it has to be kept alive by artificial respiration; while in Cornwall it died out during the 18th century, and in the Isle of Man, within living memory.

THE GERMANIC INVADERS did not take over any appreciable part of their victims' vocabulary, as conquerors often do. They had a lively and adequate language of their own, though it was not, if we are to believe the Romans, very pleasing to the ear. Julian the Apostate, who had the misfortune during one of his campaigns to hear it sung by some soldiers, could only compare it with "the croaking and shrill screeching of birds." Others described the Germanic place-names as sounding like "a noisy war trumpet," and declared that a Roman could not possibly be expected to pronounce them. Of course the Roman attitude to "barbarians" was much the same as that of our own vintage colonels who believed that niggers began at Calais and thought it tiresome of the Frogs to say "pang" and "vang" instead of "bread" and "wine."

There were doubtless many dialects of this—to refined southern ears —displeasing and guttural tongue, which incidentally had already picked up some Latin words from the legions stationed in the outposts of the Empire. Among them were *strata* (a straight paved road), *molina*, and *caseus*, which, being mispronounced, ultimately became "street," "mill" and "cheese." For the most part the Germanic language was so utterly unlike Latin that no one could have suspected it had sprung originally from the same stock. Yet it was, in fact, a kind of "distant cousin" of Latin; and we shall not see the English language in perspective unless we pause here for a moment and take a glance at its family tree.

PHILOLOGISTS are the natural historians of words, who study their behaviour in the living languages and trace their ancestries back through the dead ones. William Cowper, in some half-mocking, half-admiring lines which Mr. Eric Partridge quotes on the fly-leaf of his *Origins*, describes the untiring pursuit:

> *Philologists who chase*
> *A panting syllable through time and space,*
> *Start it at home, and hunt it in the dark,*
> *To Gaul, to Greece, and into Noah's Ark.*[1]

In the course of such a chase, they may cross the frontiers of many different languages; and of course they need to know the relationship of these languages to each other so that they may group together those which have a common source. This study was hardly begun before the early eighteen-hundreds, since when, I have read, 3076 distinct languages (not counting dialects) have been catalogued and scientifically examined.

Only about a dozen of these need concern us: the family of languages, of which English is a member, that had its origin long ago in a culture which had grown up somewhere on the borders of Europe and Asia. The family is called Indo-European, sometimes "Aryan," after the fair-skinned people whose old civilization was identified with its spread. *Arya* is Sanskrit for "noble." The term is discredited because a generation of German professors, mixing anthropometry with self-delusion, persuaded themselves and many of their countrymen that the Germans (with the Scandinavians and the blonder specimens among the British) were the direct descendants of this superior race. This piece of Teutonic silliness, involving head-measurements, skin charts showing 36 different shades, and boxes of 20 glass eyes for matching with real ones, was funny while it remained academic; it became tire-

[1] *Retirement.*

some when it was used as an excuse for despising Italians, Frenchmen, Spaniards and Greeks, and monstrous when it served as a pretext for murdering Russians and Jews.

It has put most people off using the word "Aryan."

INDO-EUROPEAN, then, is the ancestor of a whole complexity of languages which have roots in common, though you and I would not readily recognise these likenesses owing to changes in spelling and pronunciation. The philologists divide them into two groups. The eastern group comprises Russian and the other Slavonic tongues, Indian languages including Sanskrit, Iranian and modern Persian, Armenian and Albanian. The western group consists of Greek, ancient and modern; Latin with its derivatives—Italian, French, Spanish, etc.; the little that's left of Celtic; and the "Germanic" languages, German, Dutch, Scandinavian, Flemish and English.

The various members of the family have grown very far apart, through early contact with other languages and because they have evolved separately, during thousands of years, in the minds and in the mouths of diverse races. For of course there are physical as well as mental factors concerned: different people make different sounds. Prod a German, an Italian, an Indian in the stomach; each will react with a different noise!

Therefore the Persians and the Greeks, when they were fighting each other so bitterly during the fifth century B.C., had no idea that they spoke a related language. They probably each thought their opponents croaked like frogs and screeched like birds, which gave them an added reason for enmity! And likewise, in our own time, a native of what a Birmingham man would call Pearsher (Pershore in Worcestershire) could make no communication whatever with him whom the Brummie would differentiate as coming from Pearsher (in Aysher). Their respective languages would impress each other as sheer gibberish, spoken ten times too fast. Nevertheless both sprang (eight—nine—ten thousand years ago?) from the same source; and in many of their words the expert philologist would find more likeness than dissimilarity.

ENGLISH HAD its beginnings, then, in the various dialects of "Germanic" which the Jutes, Angles, Frisians and Saxons brought with them across the sea. It emerged as a written language towards the end of the 7th

century, and in a very short time began to demonstrate its vigour
and individuality. Word-making became a game with the Anglo-
Saxons,—partly, perhaps, because their alliterative poetry had great
need of synonyms. The author of *Beowulf* used a dozen different words
for "battle," and the Old English poets between them played about
with no less than 30 words for "sea" and 27 for "ship" or "boat." Although they had become landsmen, these Anglo-Saxons had a seafaring
past, which they liked to romanticise; and a language always sprouts a
rich crop around the subject which its speakers are particularly interested in. The Arabs have a lot of words relating to camels. The most
moving and pitiful story I know about this aspect of language concerns
the Araucanian Indians, whose "language distinguishes nicely between
a great many shades of hunger." [1]

The Anglo-Saxons increased their stock of words in Nature's old-
fashioned way, by joining two together to make a third,—e.g. leech +
craft for the science of medicine. By adding various suffixes to "God"
they invented no less than a score of words expressing ideas which
ranged from "divine majesty" through "gospel" to "impiety."

Having such an inventive quality, English did not need to borrow
much from other languages at this stage; though as the country became
Christianized various words from Church-Latin naturally crept in:
"monk" from *monachus*, "bishop" from *episcopus*, "priest" from *pres-
byter*,[2] "Mass" from *Missa*, "minister" from *monasterium*. It also took
some useful grammatical elements (e.g. the personal pronouns "they,"
"them") as well as many common words (sky, week, both, take, same)
from the Vikings who came to raid, and often decided to stay. The
pundits all point out that these Norse influences upon the language
were very slow in appearing; but it seems to me that if some great,
hairy, helmeted strangers come out of the sea in the middle of the
night, set fire to your thatches, rape your wives, cleave in twain the
skulls of all your friends, devour your cattle, and carry off your daughters, you—being perhaps the sole survivor—are unlikely to add to your
language any words you may have heard the fearful fellows speak.
"Fellow," as it happens, is one we *did* borrow: *felaga* in Norse. We took
it over with many others when the Viking settlements were established

---

[1] O. Jespersen, *The Growth and Structure of the English Language*, quoting
from Gabelentz, *Sprachwissenschaft*.
[2] The foregoing three words were originally Greek.

and the Norsemen were living more or less at peace with us. Among them were *wrang* (wrong) *utlaga* (outlaw) *husting* (meeting-in-a-house—compare our modern "hustings") and *husbonda* (house-dweller, which we turned into "husband"). A rather odd one was *eggian*, to urge, "to egg on"—nothing whatever to do with the "spheroidal body produced by the female of birds"! "Snare" and "net" are Norse words which suggest that our visitors may have been able to teach us a thing or two in the poaching line. "Ransack" is another which might be described as in character. "Ugly" is a most expressive one, which comes from the Norse verb *ugga*, to fear. We might have acquired many more such words but for King Alfred's brave defence of Wessex, which kept the Norseman out of the lands of the White Horse and his words out of the West-Saxon dialect, which became the literary language of England.

But another reason why we did not take more from the Vikings may have been that our language was in any case very similar to theirs; and you don't borrow your neighbour's lawn-mower if you have a serviceable one of your own. A well-read Anglo-Saxon could talk to a cultivated Norseman—indeed it has been said that "Serpent-tongue" Gunnlaug, the Icelandic poet, being invited to the court of King Ethelred the Unready, recited a poem to him which the King was able to understand. This says much for Ethelred: many of our kings since his day haven't been able to understand poems written in their own language, let alone anybody else's.

DESPITE those occasional acquisitions from Latin and Norse, until the 11th century English remained "pure" and uncorrupted by contact with any other language. Russian is in this situation even today. I should have thought it a disadvantage,—languages, like peoples, require a little miscegenation now and then lest they become weak through interbreeding. But at various periods English writers have sadly bewailed her lost "purity" as if it were a quality as desirable in language as it is supposed to be in daughters. As long ago as 1450 a somewhat eccentric theologian called Reginald Pecock tried to get rid of the Latin element by popularising words like "ungothroughsome" for "impenetrable." He even invented the monstrosity "not-to-be-thought-upon-able," but far from becoming fashionable it sent the already Latinised Englishmen into fits of laughter. Again in the 19th century Wil-

liam Morris started a cult of "pure Anglo-Saxon" without much
success, and the Dorset poet William Barnes tried to produce an English grammar without any foreign words at all—indeed he had to title
it *Speech-craft of the English Tongue* because he was sworn not to use
the "Latin" words "grammar" or "language"! Like most ideas carried
to their logical conclusion, this one became merely silly, when Barnes
was compelled to invent the phrase "mark-word for suchness" for
"adjective" and to use "folkwain" for "omnibus." However, the be-
lievers in "pure English" did have one small success during the
19th century. The word "hand-book" came back into the language,
and after a time replaced the Latinate "manual." For this it got itself
a severe reproof from none other than the Very Reverend Richard
Chenevix Trench, D.D., begetter of the *Oxford English Dictionary*.
He called it "that very ugly and very unnecessary word . . . which is
scarcely, I should suppose, ten or fifteen years old." Although he was
one of the greatest philologists of his day, he supposed wrong. *Handboc*
had been invented by the Anglo-Saxons and used by King Alfred. The
handy little word took as much notice of the Dean of Westminster's
strictures as a mouse in the Abbey would have taken of his sermons;
it scuttled back into its rightful place.

BUT if there is one thing we know for sure about the behaviour of
words, it is that they are not obedient to pedagogues. A language
has behind it the dynamic, the daemonic power of a whole people; Dr.
Johnson did well to compare its momentum with that of the tempest
and the tide. Barnes, Morris, Pecock and others who sought to change
the course of English should have learned a lesson from Canute. They
made themselves look silly; but they had no influence at all upon the
progress of events.

English had thrown aside her "purity" about 1100. Norman French
was the ravisher.

> The fine French kings came over in a flutter of
>   flags and dames.
> We liked their smiles and battles, but we never
>   could say their names.[1]

[1] G. K. Chesterton: *The Secret People.*

We tried hard nevertheless. It was a big step towards the acquisition of Frenchified manners when we permitted our oxen, calves, sheep, deer and swine to become beef, veal, mutton, vension, and pork as soon as they appeared on the table—another French word, by the way! How comfortably at home in our language are these French words now— table and chair, honour, reason, mercy, grace, peace, lake, virtue, favour —compared with the words we have borrowed from French more recently and which haven't yet had time to settle down: connoisseur, chef, valet, amateur, bizarre, façade.

It is not surprising that many of the Norman French words in our language are those concerned with food. The Normans doubtless did themselves well, for they came from a lush land and must have learned the ways of high living. For instance it was they who hit upon the discovery that a cock could be "made as it were female by kernynge of the gendringe stones"[1]—"capon" was one of the very first words we learned from them. By the time Chaucer wrote his *Canterbury Tales* our cooks had become almost as French chefs, by the sound of it:

> A Cook they hadde with hem for the nones,
> To boille the chiknes with the marybones,
> And poudre-marchant tart, and galingale . . .
> He coude roste, and sethe, and broille, and frye,
> Maken mortreux, and wel bake a pye . . .
> For blankmanger, that made he with the beste.

I don't know what poudre-marchant tart was made of. Galingale was a gingery root used for flavouring; we got the word through French but originally it came from Chinese, *Ko-liang-kiang!* Mortreux we are told was "a kind of milk soup." Most of these delicacies are unknown to English cooks today, and we are left with the revolting "blankmanger," which indeed they make with the beste still.

Other than terms of cooking, some of the earlier words that came into English from French were those which you would expect the inhabitants of a land to learn from the occupying power. Prison was one of the first, with rent, tower, war,[2]—and forest, which had a dark meaning for Englishmen. The Norman king was hunting-mad, he "loved the red deer as if he had been their father," he took large areas

---

[1] Trevisa, tr. *Bartholomeus, De Proprietatibus Rerum.*
[2] Old Norman French *werre,* which became *guerre* later.

of land to make his chases, and hedged them about with savage laws.
Where many of the people could not read, these had to be proclaimed:
and the proclamation was preceded by the injunction OYEZ! Give ear,
listen. Our Town Criers however pronounced it exactly as it was spelt,
in which form it has been ringing in our ears for seven centuries; it has
become as familiar as the cry of a man selling cockles and winkles at
the seaside.

Legal terms became important to us, since we were often in trouble
with our conquerors; in a short time we had not only learned but had
taken into our language such words as plaintiff, defendant and dis-
traint, while the lawyers sought to impress us with tongue-twisters like
malfeasance and lèse-majesté. We also added to our growing collection
of Latin words—which we'd been picking up ever since the 10th century from travellers, traders and priests—an assortment of scholarly
new ones passed on to us by the Normans: proviso, legitimate, index,
simile, memento, mediator, were among these; with pauper, a heartless
cold word for a poor man.

BY 1386, in which year the *Canterbury Tales* were begun, English had
changed so profoundly that on an average *one word in every line* of
the seventeen thousand lines that make up that great poem was a
French one,—that is to say, about one word in eight. These French
words, plus clerkly ones from Latin, classical ones from Greek (ecstasy,
nymph, harmony, tyrant, diphthong, theatre) and romantic ones from
the Italian whence Chaucer got many of his tales, were prodigally
thrown together with the Old English words, which despite the foreign
fashions we still used and cherished. It made a sizzling hotchpotch,—
here, for instance, is our sturdy old Norse word "fellow," grown more
convivial with age, and fallen into some French and Latin company!
Chaucer is writing of that good-humoured and most accommodating
drunk, the Somnour:

> *A bettre felawe sholde men noght finde.*
> *He wolde suffre, for a quart of wyn,*
> *A good felawe to have his concubyn*
> *A twelf-month, and excuse him atte fulle . . .*

English had been too long the drudge of clerks and chroniclers; it
took a poet to bring out her natural gift of laughter. Chaucer was her

first great poet; and upon that April morning when the pilgrims set out for Canterbury, and the sun shone and the birds were singing, it must have seemed to him that each fad or foible of his companions was none other than an affectionate jest on the part of God their maker. Often in *The Canterbury Tales* a simple statement of fact seems to have a small but happy joke hidden away in it:

> *Up-roos the sonne, and up roose Emilye.*

Perfectly matching his mood, the words laughed in their couplets however demurely he arranged them:

> *No-wher so bisy a man as he ther nas,*
> *And yet he seemed bisier than he was,—*

That was the Sergeant-at-Law, self-important. Here is the jolly Friar:

> *His eyen twinkled in his heed aright,*
> *As doon the sterres in the frosty night.*

And here is the Monk who loved hunting better than books of learning:

> *And, when he rood, men mighte his bridel here*
> *Ginglen in a whistling wind as clere,*
> *And eek as loude as dooth the chapel-belle.*

Sometimes for fun the poet would introduce the great words in among the simple ones, words such as "nigromanciens" for black magicians, or "Nebuchadnezzar" which he happily spelt Nabugodonosor, or he would suddenly dress up a line or two with many-syllabled pomposities from the Latin or the Greek. Then the English language would wear these fancy foreign words not as if they were unaccustomed fineries, but as if they were hers by right, a trousseau designed for her especially. For this was her youth and springtime when nothing came amiss to her; the true splendour and the great glory were still in store; but meanwhile she stood upon the brink of fulfilment,

> *And she fair as is the rose in May.*

THE LATIN WORDS in Chaucer mostly came through Norman French, though some had been carried here earlier by the two or three ripples of Mediterranean culture which reached our shores. It wasn't until the beginning of the 16th century that the great waves of the Renaissance, breaking over England, threw up the many-coloured words like spray that has the sun behind it. They would surely have submerged and overwhelmed any language less tough and individualistic. English took them as the flowers take a summer shower.

Greek came hard in the wake of Latin, bringing some words so useful that it's difficult to see how we had managed so long without them: alphabet, irony, drama, chorus, basis, epic, theory, and that dilemma [1] upon whose horns we so often impale ourselves. Greek was now taught in the schools; and soon in the printed books which were still as new as toys, Roger Ascham at Hatfield was teaching the young Elizabeth to read the old brave tales which before long her sailors with their lives would write again: the *Iliad* and *Odyssey* in Homer's Greek. As for Latin, by the time she was Queen it had become as a second language to her; and she used it, with great majesty, for the purpose of reproving the Spanish Ambassador when his King displeased her. Learning was in the very air; and the quickening imagination raced to keep up with the poets as the map-makers strove to keep pace with the explorers. Words, as you may imagine, proliferated as never before, and all the processes of word-making and word-changing were speeded up so that the budding, the blossoming, the withering away and the budding-again often took but a tenth of the time they take when the spirits of men are quiescent.

Out of this hubble-bubble and confusion, these exuberances and excitements, the consummate English language emerged in her prime and her perfection at more or less the same time as her predestined poet left Stratford-on-Avon and came to town with the taffeta phrases already singing in his head.

[1] Literally a double assumption; hence an ambiguous proposition.

CHAPTER 7

"Of Learned Length and Thundering Sound"

"TAFFETA PHRASES": Shakespeare was fascinated by that word, I think. At any rate he used it five times,—once most strikingly: "And the blessed sun himself a fair hot wench in flame-coloured taffeta." [1] The bright stuffs from abroad, with their eye-taking sheen and skin-smooth texture, were peddled in the markets all over the land, and homespun went out of fashion as the foreign gladrags took its place. And so did the language which clothed men's thoughts dress itself in the new words that came out of the south,—words warm as Italy and sweet as France, wonderful as the West Indies; bizarre as the new-fangled striped gillyvors in the Elizabethan gardens, luxurious as orchids, gaudy as parrakeets. No wonder the young poets fell upon them as eagerly as the country wenches buying lengths of taffeta at the fairs.

Nobody's memory could store more than a fraction of these new-found and newly-invented words; so that one Elizabethan [2] complained in desperation after reading a theological treatise: "Maister Heskins fareth as if he were half-madde, sending us to the vocabularies, calepines and dictionaries." A calepin, by the way, was a polyglot dictionary, named after an Italian, Friar Calepino, who made one.

For a time, indeed, England seemed to go crazy about words. Philosophers were splitting hairs with them, actors were gloriously ranting them, poets were doing conjuring-tricks with them, and prose-writers such as Lyly were so bemused by the sound of them that they let the sense go hang. Mountebanks at street-corners invented new words for

[1] *King Henry IV, Part I.*
[2] William Fulke.

old ills whenever they felt the lack of them,[1] and thus provided themselves with vocabularies as vast as Dr. Donne's, preaching at St. Paul's.
Frenchified formalities, extravagances from Italy, fantastications from
Spain, were in turn the fashions of a season, all the rage while they
lasted. Sonneteering was a popular game played with words—as we do
crossword puzzles. Antithesis became an addiction, and punsters a pest.
Meanwhile the learned and the would-be-learned vied with each other
in the employment of very *long* words, reaching at last the limit of
absurdity with

HONORIFICABILITUDINITY

which Shakespeare contrived to stretch out still farther when he made
fun of it in *Love's Labour's Lost*, because he used the original Latin
word in its ablative plural. "I marvel thy master hath not eaten thee for
a word," says Costard to Don Armado's servant, Moth, "for thou art
not so long by the head as *honorificabilitudinitatibus*." It is a word to
frighten the horses indeed; but it means no more than "honourable-
ness" after all!

SHAKESPEARE, who had himself toyed with the new extravagances,
seems to have decided that the nonsense had gone far enough; he not
only ridiculed the foolish fashions in *Love's Labour's Lost*, but put
into the mouth of Biron a stern renunciation of all "Three-pil'd hyper-
boles, spruce affectation, Figures pedantical." It almost looks as if
Shakespeare himself was making a bow of verbal puritanism. If so, it
is lucky for us that he broke it, or we should be the poorer by some
of his greatest poetry. On the other hand, what a lot of bad writing
we should have been spared if some of our later writers had made and
kept Biron's resolve!

THE TRUTH of the matter is, of course, that the influence of Latin upon
English has been both glorious and degrading. Long words are not always the best words; and whoever puts several of them together in a
row is liable to write a horrible sentence. Disraeli doubtless had his
tongue in his cheek when he described Mr. Gladstone as "a sophistical

---

[1] The Wambling Trot, the Strong Fives, the Marthambles, the Moon-Pall and
the Hockogrockle were among the diseases they claimed to cure, according to
Dame Edith Sitwell in *The English Eccentrics*.

rhetorician, inebriated with the exuberance of his own verbosity"; [1] the *tour de force* is amusing, but you cannot hold it up as an example of decent prose. And when the infant Macaulay spilt some hot coffee over his legs and replied to a lady's solicitous inquiry, "Thank you, Madam, the agony is abated," he wasn't speaking good English, even for a four year old: he was speaking as an odious little prodigy and prig. Whenever an unqualified or untaught person has used the big "Latin" words to bolster up his self-importance, the consequences have either been disastrous or absurd, as Shakespeare showed in the characters of Holofernes and that ass Armado,—who spoke of "the posteriors of this day; which the rude multitude calls the afternoon." But when a writer really knows how to handle them, these stiff, formal words become obedient and pliable, they slip sonorously into his prose and may even be seen to gambol in his lighthearted poetry,—here is a lovely one in a verse by Herrick:

> A *winning wave* (*deserving note*)
> In the tempestuous petticoat.[2]

And here's another; the good clergyman had a frank and lively appreciation of girls' dresses and what lay beneath them:

> *Whenas in silks my Julia goes,*
> *Then, then (methinks) how sweetly flows*
> *That liquefaction of her clothes.*[3]

"Liquefaction" is the last word you would expect to find at home in a love poem. It is happy there because Herrick knew his Latin as well as he knew his English, and was dexterous in matching them together in his poetry. More superbly, his contemporary Sir Thomas Browne was doing the same thing in his prose. "When the funeral pyre was out, and the last valediction over . . ." goes the tremendous opening sentence of the "Epistle Dedicatory" to his *Urn-Burial*. "Valediction" is the word that does the trick, of course; and when we call to mind how often such powerful words have lent their majesty to our poetry and prose, we can almost persuade ourselves that English owes her loveliest

[1] Speech at Banquet in the Riding School, Knightsbridge, July 27th, 1878.
[2] *Delight in Disorder.*
[3] *Upon Julia's Clothes.*

rhythms to the words she has taken from Latin; though, alas, the following owes almost everything to Latin too:

> Dear Sir: Reference your communication of the 31st ult. I anticipate immediate receipt of your remittance in order that the transaction may be finalized.

There you have an assortment of longish words, all derived ultimately from Latin, handled by someone who does not know how to use them. The old authors could handle such words because Latin was a second language to them. Indeed it was so for every cultured Englishman during the four centuries 1400-1800; most could converse in Latin as easily as they could read or write. Whether a boy went to Eton or to a Grammar School or to a private tutor, his education was sure to be founded on Virgil and Ovid. Grammar School boys *even out of school hours* were not allowed to speak anything but Latin; a spy aptly named *lupus* was sometimes paid to report whether they used English words while at play. If they did, they were flogged! [1]

For learned communications Latin was always preferred. Francis Bacon, though he had a limpid style in English, chose to write all his profounder works in Latin. Indeed it would have been very unconventional in his time to publish a philosophical work in English. A hundred years later Milton used Latin as "a living language," wrote some of his poetry in it, and found it more effective than English for purposes of controversy.[2] In 1686 Newton published his great work on the theory of universal gravitation, his *Principia*; once again Latin was the chosen tongue.

Foreign correspondence and most diplomatic exchanges were naturally conducted in Latin,—though back in 1553, when Sir Hugh Willoughby's expedition set off in search of a North-east Passage, it carried a letter of goodwill from the young King Edward VI to any Prince of Cathay or elsewhere who might be able to understand it, written in *Greek*.[3] Both Greek and Latin were drummed into the head, or beaten into the behind, of every small boy who was thought fit to be given a secondary education; and one familiar English word, though originally a Law Courts term, carries a rather pathetic echo from the

---

[1] G. M. Trevelyan: *English Social History*.
[2] E.g. in his *Defensio Secunda*.
[3] Hakluyt's *Voyages*.

16th century schoolroom in which, I suspect, it first gained a wider currency. The word is *"ignoramus,"* Latin for "We do not know."

Because the classical languages were taught at such an early age, and probably because they were inculcated with such severity, the puns and the tags and the old words of wisdom remained as it were the background of a man's thinking, and bore him company all his days. However far he rode, the hexameters running through his mind were apt to keep time with his horse's hoof-beats. There was no escape from them, not even for a drunken foxhunting squire. So we find madcap John Mytton, though suffering from D.T.s and from the agonising after-effects of setting his nightgown on fire to cure a hiccup, quoting from Sophocles and the New Testament in Greek, and punning on a line of Horace to make a joke about port. The Regency sportsmen whom we read of in the pages of "Nimrod" even took Latin into the hunting-field with them. One of them, jumping a tall thick hedge in Leicestershire, nearly fell into a sawpit on the other side of it. A companion galloping beside him asked: "Why did you not look before you leapt?" and got the answer: *"Nemo mortalium omnibus horis sawpit."* [1] A generation later, our soldier-administrators in India were exchanging Latin puns about their victories:

"Peccavi—I've Scinde" wrote Lord Ellen so proud.
More briefly Dalhousie wrote *"Vovi*—I've Oude." [2]

THAT WAS more than 100 years ago. Since then the Classics have died out of the thoughts of all but a tiny percentage of Englishmen; but the immense ponderous vocabulary remains, which was built up in the years when the Latinate word came as readily as the Anglo-Saxon one to the writer who paused in search of a forceful phrase. You might liken this vocabulary to a magnificent cellar of vintage port, inherited by a generation that knows nothing about wine. Indeed I think Latinity is remarkably like port in its effect upon the English. Good and great Englishmen often thrive wonderfully upon such vintages, which prove the undoing of lesser ones. Both by port and by Latinity pompous men are made more pompous, little men are puffed up unwarrantably, the vulgar and corruptible are vulgarized and corrupted, while in the

[1] The pun is on *"sapit."*
[2] *Punch*, 1856.

case of those unaccustomed to such stuff both the words and the wine are apt to go to the head.

Of the splendour of "Latin in English" I shall have much to say later; let us first take a look at what overindulgence in the heady stuff has done to bad poets, half-educated journalists, uneducated business-men, pompous lawyers and policemen, smug civil servants, and cor-ruptible politicians.

PART OF THE TROUBLE, of course, lies in the very power of the words. This potency makes them unfitted to be the playthings of every Tom, Dick and Harry. See what happened to "conflagration" when the penny-a-line journalists of the 19th century began to use it every time they wrote about a fire. What might have sounded awesome in an ac-count—by Gibbon, let us say—of Nero's Rome engulfed by flames, became ludicrous when it described the trifling consequences of a cat knocking over a clothes horse on which her mistress' combinations were drying before the stove.

"Floods, see Inundations," says the index to a historical account of my native town, published in 1850. "Flood" had become a colloquial, almost a vulgar word; and so "inundation," once grandly used to de-scribe the vast outflowings of "Nilus in Ægypt," was dragged down to the scale of the petty floods which every winter creep over Tewkes-bury's river-meadows.

These journalists, using words derived from Latin and Greek at a time when a smattering of the Classics was thought to be the mark of a gentleman, invented a weird and wonderful English all their own, rather like Mr. Micawber's: a walk was a "peregrination," a traveller was a "peripatetic," a fox was "the vulpine quarry" and a fieldsman at cricket was "expeditious in pursuit of the leathern spheroid." This half-jocular style became fossilized in small provincial newspapers, where you can find traces of it still,—only the other day I read of a "beverage" being "partaken of" in the course of some village outing. On this occasion the horrible word *may* have been used to keep the teetotallers guessing; even if it wasn't, the reporter could have quoted no less than a Poet Laureate for his precedent. Wordsworth wrote:

And sitting on the grass partook
The fragrant beverage drawn from China's herb,—

upon which another Poet Laureate, Tennyson, sensibly commented: "Why couldn't he say 'And sitting on the grass had tea'?"

THE JOURNALISTS who loved the long words have given place to those who love short ones because they are handy for the headlines,—"bid" (meaning attempt), "drama" and "wed," for instance, the latter now being *Obs.* and *Vulg.* save in the daily papers. The philomel-eglantine-harbinger-halcyon school of poetry has died out too; and in the absence of those poets I think the police, oddly enough, are the most determined Latinists of all. When you think of the pace at which the average bobby's sputtering pen takes down a statement, you would suppose that he would thank his lucky stars for the brevity of such a common English verb as "to go." Not a bit of it. I once had to make a statement about a minor motor accident. I began:

"I was going towards Worcester——"

"Proceeding," said the constable firmly.

"No. Going."

"Excuse me, sir," he said, "but it is usual to put proceeding."

I told him I had spent a great many years trying to learn how best to say what I meant in English, and he reluctantly accepted "going," though I noticed that he put it between quotation marks. He would have much preferred the verb that comes from Latin *procedere*, to advance or progress. I should have thought it worthwhile to teach policemen to use plain English, which after all is much easier, and comes more naturally to them, than lawyer's jargon; for their misunderstanding of a word could cost a man his liberty. I read of a case the other day in which a constable said on oath that when he looked at the pupils of a man's eyes he noticed they were "dilated." Counsel for the Defence asked him what he meant by that word. His reply was "Pinpointed." The Judge dismissed the case with costs, and we can assume that the man whose pupils were like pinpoints was not guilty of driving "under the influence"—another word from Latin, which used to mean in astrology an emanation from the stars.

"Inebriated" was the Latin word which our bad poets used for this condition, e.g. *Lines Written for a Friend on the Death of his Brother, caused by a Railway Train running over him whilst he was in a State of Inebriation,* by James Henry Powell.[1] It means literally one who has

[1] *Phases of Thought and Feeling,* 1857.

drunk too much from a wine-jar. The police prefer "intoxicated"; this indeed is the word of all words which slips most glibly from a policeman's tongue. Obviously the Law cannot charge a man with being bosko absoluto, and most of the other fanciful synonyms in Roget's *Thesaurus* are unsuited to a court of law; but it is sad that official English couldn't find a better word than this dreary one, which comes from Latin *toxicum*, a poison, and so pleases our puritans, who tell us "That is precisely what alcohol is." Mr. John Steinbeck's answer was that unlike strawberries and oysters and lobsters, which also poison some people now and then, the poison that is alcohol has sometimes "given courage to cowards and made very ugly people attractive"; and he told a story of a tramp lying in a ditch, somewhere in Sweden on a Midsummer Night:

> He was ragged and dirty and drunk, and he said to himself softly in wonder, "I am rich and happy and perhaps a little beautiful." [1]

THE POLICEMAN, then, "proceeds to the location of the accident, renders what assistance he can to the pedestrian, and forms the opinion that the driver of the vehicle is intoxicated." The doctor describes his patient as "edentulous" when he simply means "toothless." The auctioneer advertises his sale to "commence"—never to begin. The civil servant wastes his own time and his secretary's by saying "the majority" for most, "in isolation" for by itself, "materialize" or "eventuate" for happen, and "transmit," "terminate" and "purchase" for send, end, buy. The Rodent Operator, as he calls himself, may even advise the deratization of your premises. The more petty the person, the larger the proportion of Latin or pseudo-Latin words in his vocabulary, the greater his devotion to rehabilitation, redundant, residence and reaction, the more frequent his recourse to such terrible verbs as "dehospitalize." "There seems to be a notion," wrote Sir Alan Herbert,[2] "that any British or American subject is entitled to take any noun or adjective, add *ize* to it, and say 'I have made a new verb. What a good boy am I.'—This notion must be finalized." I entirely agree with Sir Alan, though I must point out that Shakespeare was one of the worst offenders in this particular direction,—"No place, indeed, should murder

[1] *The Log of the Sea of Cortez.*
[2] *What a Word!*

sanctuarize," [1]—"To monarchize, be fear'd, and kill with looks." [2]
Shakespeare's great genius enabled him to get away with almost anything, but "sanctuarize" seems to me horrible even though the greatest
poet that ever lived invented it. So does "finalize," which apparently
has been coined since 1933: the *O.E.D. Supplement* knows nothing of
it. I have noticed that the kind of people who use this atrocious word
are often the same people who refer to your letter of, say, the 12th
"*ult.*" or "*inst.*" or make an appointment for the 14th "*prox.*," although
the odds are that they haven't the faintest idea what the Latin words
ultimo, instantem, and *proximo* mean. Sometimes, however, they use
the mysterious expression "Your communication of even date" and
then I confess that *I* don't know what *they* mean. Even with what? Do
they use it as the opposite of "odd"—the 12th as opposed to the 13th?
Or do they mean "yesterday's date" or "today's date"—in either case
why "even"? I simply cannot guess. There are a whole lot of peculiari-
ties connected with the correspondence of small businessmen. If their
Christian name happens to be John, they often abbreviate it to Jno.
I have been thinking about this curiosity for a long time; but for the
life of me I can think of no plausible explanation of it, nor any advantage which John may suppose he gets, by so ridiculously describing
himself.

THE SERVICES' principal contribution towards Latinity is "personnel."
Although we took it from the French, it came originally from Latin
persona, meaning a mask worn in the theatre, therefore the character
wearing it, therefore a personage, and so a person. The excuse for "personnel" is that it is a short and comprehensive term for "men and
women," indispensable now that the Services recruit both; though in
fact we find that the word was used in Brassey's *Naval Annual* in 1886,
long before the Wrens were thought of. *The Times* in a leader described the creatures who are nowadays denominated by this word as
follows:

> Though in theory they are human beings, they have only to be
> called personnel to lose their full status as human beings. They do
> not go, they proceed. They do not have, they are (or more often are

[1] *Hamlet.*
[2] *Richard II.*

not) in possession of. They do not ask, they make application for. Their minds, in so far as they may be deemed to have minds, are stocked not with the glories of knowledge but with irrelevant and unmemorable statistics, such as their father's nationality at birth and the date on which they were last inoculated against yellow fever. Once they either kept things or gave them up; now they must retain or surrender them. Want (it is true) they do not know, nor need; but deficiencies and requirements are just as inconvenient. They cannot eat, they can only consume; they perform ablutions; instead of homes they have place(s) of residence in which, instead of living, they are domiciled. They are not cattle, they are not ciphers, they certainly are not human beings; they are personnel.

The leader-writer compared the individual who let loose "personnel" into the English language with the kindly nature-lover who first liberated a pair of grey squirrels—and so incidentally added to the problems of what Rodent Operators call Pest Elimination. If we excuse a Mr. Osborn on the grounds that he put the word in italics and so (in 1857) could plead that he was only quoting from the French, then the culprit seems to have been none other than the novelist Thackeray. He used the phrase "personnel of the Universities" in 1861.[1]

It happens that the most remarkable specimen of deformed and disgusting prose in the whole of my collection contains this word "personnel," seen in association with three other pests, "overall," "bracket" and "yardstick," as one might see a slug, a snail, an earwig, and a nauseous caterpillar feeding upon the same lettuce-leaf:

Personnel requirements are furnished on experience tables which normally consider approximately one per cent of overall strength a day as a common yardstick. Casualties are well within this bracket.

If you read this three times you can just catch a faint glimpse of what the author meant to say—and so discover how far he fell short of saying it. He was not, however, a minor civil servant. The quotation is from a statement issued by General MacArthur's Headquarters at the most critical period of the Korean War. When I discovered it, in my daily paper, I had a moment of panic. I felt that if our side were really

[1] *Four Georges.*

capable of thinking like that, and writing like that, we were bound to lose.

For contrast, in 1943, I read another general's despatch and was persuaded, by the terms in which it was written, that we should inevitably triumph. It was addressed to the British Prime Minister. It ran:

Sir:
The orders you gave me on August 15th 1942 have been fulfilled. His Majesty's enemies, together with their impedimenta, have been completely eliminated from Egypt, Cyrenaica, Libya and Tripolitania. I now await your further instructions.

It made me want to cheer. But what about those Latinisms,—"impedimenta," "eliminated"? Do I contradict all I have been saying by approving of them here? Not at all. Such words are excellent and effective in the hands of a man *who knows how to use them*; and General Alexander, when he composed his telegram to Sir Winston Churchill, knew exactly what he was doing with that ponderous "impedimenta," that large and sweeping "eliminated." He was writing in the grand manner to one who conducted affairs in the grand manner always; and so doing, uplifted us all.

LAST but not least among the ill-users of Latin are the Communists. It always surprises me that the People's Voice should speak in a dead language: proletariat, dialectical materialism, coexistence, collectivization—such words might have fallen from the cracked lips of a dry-as-dust don half-mummified in his library, with cobwebs in his hair. No people, without a capital P, ever spoke so—nor gabbled such unbelievably *dreary* words as antideviationism, indoctrination, or unilateralism over their pints of beer. You would not think that anybody with a fire in his belly could bring himself even to pronounce them; nor that the kind of ideas which were once expressed by that great shout in the streets, *Aux armes, citoyens!* could possibly be contained within such a mealy-mouthed phrase as "The ultimate objective is the liquidation of the bourgeoisie." Nevertheless the Communists do use phrases such as these, and communicate ideas by such words as "antideviationism," and in some extraordinary fashion are even moved by them. I suppose the real reason is that international Communism feels acutely the lack of an international language, and so is glad to borrow from anywhere the

96 *You English Words*

kind of words which with slight alteration can be fitted into many
tongues. Esperanto, which I should have thought would have suited
the Party well, appears to have been unacceptable,—I do not know why;
so there was nothing for it but to go a-scavenging among the leavings
of the classical scholars, and we find the workers at one with the dons
in regretting that Latin ever ceased to be the common tongue of edu-
cated persons throughout the civilized world!

HOW LATE it continued to be a common tongue I learned with surprise
when I was reading about Dr. Johnson's visit to France in 1775. The
Doctor's French was not very fluent, and we are told that he mostly
spoke in Latin, for the excellent Johnsonian reason that "there is no
good in letting the French have a superiority over you every word you
speak."

He seems to have got on quite well. His spoken Latin was probably
not unlike some of his spoken English, for he always sought to compose
his sentences in a classical style and, when he failed, was not above making a second attempt, translating what he had said into something
nearer to Latin. Boswell shrewdly noticed this:

> Talking of the comedy of "The Rehearsal," [1] he said, "It has not wit
> enough to keep it sweet." This was easy;—he therefore caught him-
> self, and pronounced a more round sentence: "It has not vitality
> enough to preserve it from putrefaction." [2]

Even if the words in any given sentence were necessarily short he
usually contrived to introduce one big word which stood out like a giant
among pygmies; for example: "Sir, there is no settling the point of
precedency between a louse and a flea"—a sentence which from time to
time is happily quoted during Parliamentary elections by those of the
disillusioned who remember their Boswell.

Johnson took a real pleasure in the long words: even when he was
dying. Dr. Richard Warren, Physician to the King, paid him a visit
and in what Boswell describes as "his usual style" hoped that his famous patient was better. We are not told how his bedside manner

[1] By George Villiers, Duke of Buckingham.
[2] *Life of Johnson.*

reacted to the terrible answer which came rumbling back from the stricken giant beneath the tumbled blankets:

No, Sir, you cannot conceive with what acceleration I advance towards death.

That particular sentence was spoken in deadly earnest and in awesome dread; but on other occasions, I am sure, he would introduce the unusual word into his conversation for fun, and in order to startle and confound his attentive audience. Sir Winston Churchill, although his style stems more I think from Macaulay than from Johnson, betrays the same half-mischievous delight in surprising his listeners with a long word. Addressing the House of Commons in Secret Session on June 25th, 1941, he made a very grim speech concerning the Battle of the Atlantic, which was going against us; begging the M.P.s to say nothing which might give comfort to the enemy, he declared:

It would be a great mistake for us to ingeminate and emphasise our woes.

I wonder how many Members recognised the rare 17th century word "ingeminate," which comes from Latin *ingeminare*, to redouble, and hence means "to emphasise by reiteration."

Dr. Johnson seems to have conjured up new words out of his own learning. He was the first person, apparently, to speak of "inspissated gloom." The word is simply Latin for "thickened, made dense," and Johnson used it in connexion with Shakespeare's description of the ominous nightfall in *Macbeth*. "Conglobulation" is another of his extraordinary conjurations out of Latin. He used it to settle an argument about swallows. In his time the most learned men in England believed that these birds hibernated in the autumn and emerged from their winter-quarters in the spring. Migration to the south was inconceivable; for how could such "poor little birds," asked Gilbert White, bear up against what in good classical English he described as "the meteorous turbulences" which they would encounter upon such a journey? [1] Moreover, he had noticed that the swifts in autumn seemed "bleached, and, as it were, what country people call piss-burnt, like an old weatherbeaten wig." This, he reasoned, was due to the sun's heat, and if they

[1] *Natural History of Selborne.*

followed the sun into lower latitudes they would be still more bleached when they returned!

No; he was sure they had some "secret dormitories" if only he could find them. So he poked about with his walking-stick into the mud at the edge of ponds; he prodded the thatch of cottages, he investigated chimneys. But he never found any swallows, and the hypothesis remained unproved.

But Dr. Johnson, who was not a naturalist, was untroubled by scientific scruples. He had no doubts about the matter at all; he added a fine fancy to Parson White's theory, and asserted it as a fact; and he reinforced his dogmatism, lest any should dare contradict him, with this most rare word of thunderous Latinity.

"Swallows certainly sleep all the winter," said he. "A number of them conglobulate together, by flying round and round, and then all in a heap throw themselves under water." [1]

BOSWELL RECORDS that another time, during an argument about *The Beggar's Opera*, the Doctor collected himself "as it were to give a heavy stroke," and declared:

There is in it such a labefactation of all principles as may be injurious to morality.

It was difficult to know, at any given moment, whether or not the Doctor meant to be playful. "We sat," Boswell goes on, "in a comical sort of restraint, smothering a laugh, which we were afraid might burst out." The meaning of "labefactation" is "weakening, overthrowing" and it comes from the Latin *labefacere*, to make totter or fall. "Anfractuosity" was another of these conversational bludgeons which Dr. Johnson wielded with considerable effect. Once again it is almost pure Latin,—from an adjective meaning winding or roundabout. "Sir, among the anfractuosities of the human mind, I know not if it may be one, that there is a superstitious reluctance to sit for a picture." The great man might have said "involutions" or "intricacies"; but those words would have been comparatively commonplace. After all, he had not long since defined with wonderful precision some 41,000 words in his *Dictionary*. He would have been less than human if he had not now and then trotted out a rare one.

[1] Boswell.

Whether he was writing or speaking, his style was always a reflection of himself. It mirrored equally his grandeur and his bearlike ponderous play. "I'll come no more behind your scenes, David," he said to Garrick, "for the silk stockings and white bosoms of your actresses excite my amorous propensities." Another version of this sentence substitutes "bubbies" for "bosoms"; and I think I can hear Samuel Johnson saying it. I am sure I can hear him speaking, half in fun and half in earnest, that most characteristic observation about Sunday and how it should be kept:

> It should be different from another day. People may walk, but not throw stones at birds. There may be relaxation but there should be no levity.

As usual, the Latinate word comes in beautifully at the end, rounding off the sentence, laying down the law.

THE PASSAGE in Dr. Johnson's *Lives of the Poets,* in which he describes the lamentable end of Edmund Smith, is one of the best examples I know of the classical style in English. Mr. Smith had made up his mind to write a tragedy in verse on the subject of Lady Jane Grey.

> Having formed his plan and collected materials, he declared that a few months would complete his design; and that he might pursue his work with less frequent avocations, he was, in June 1710, invited by Mr. George Ducket to his house at Hartham in Wiltshire. Here he found such opportunities of indulgence as did not much forward his studies, and particularly some strong ale, too delicious to be resisted. He ate and drank till he found himself plethoric; and then, resolving to ease himself by evacuation, he wrote to an apothecary in the neighbourhood a prescription of a purge so forcible, that the apothecary thought it his duty to delay it till he had given notice of its danger. Smith, not pleased with the contradiction of a shopman, and boastful of his own knowledge, treated the notice with rude contempt, and swallowed his own medicine, which, in July 1710, brought him to the grave.

There has never been devised a better medium than this Latinate English of the 18th century, for telling such an anecdote with a straight face,—what we nowadays call "dead pan." See how Gibbon plays the same trick when he summarises with impeccable gravity the career and achievements of Emperor Gordian the Younger:

> His manners were less pure, but his character was equally amiable with that of his father. Twenty-two acknowledged concubines, and a library of sixty-two thousand volumes, attested the variety of his inclinations, and from the productions which he left behind him, it appears that the former as well as the latter were designed for use rather than ostentation.[1]

This is my favourite passage in Gibbon, even surpassing the famous sentence concerning the end of the schism:

> Of the three Popes, John the Twenty-third was the first victim: he fled and was brought back a prisoner: the most scandalous charges were suppressed; the Vicar of Christ was only accused of piracy, murder, rape, sodomy, and incest.[2]

Johnson, it has been said, "hewed a passage through the Alps, while Gibbon levelled walks through parks and gardens."[3] It is a fair comparison of their two styles, both classical, but the one magnificently ponderous, the other exquisitely urbane. Of all our great writers—except perhaps Sir Thomas Browne—Gibbon is surely the one who had read most Latin. He spent more than twenty years in study and scholarship, between the time when he "sat musing on the steps of the Capitol . . . and the idea of writing the decline and fall of the city first started in his mind," and the publication of the last three volumes in 1788. He must have been almost thinking in Latin by then; and if we bear in mind still the comparison with vintage port, then we shall hear in the following passage the measured periods of a man who takes his inspiration from the old wine, but whose cool head is not affected by it. This is an after-dinner prose-style, incomparable of its kind, but no more for everyday use than the Cockburn '27. The circus-girl, whom he writes of, later married Justinian, and became the Empress Theodora: a strange elevation, says Gibbon, which cannot be applauded as a triumph of female virtue.

[1] *Decline and Fall of the Roman Empire.* Gordian wrote several works of literature, and he had three or four children by each of the concubines.
[2] *Decline and Fall of the Roman Empire.*
[3] George Coleman: *Random Recollections.*

She neither danced, nor sung, nor played on the flute; her skill was confined to the pantomime arts; she excelled in buffoon characters; and as often as the comedian swelled her cheeks, and complained with a ridiculous tone and gesture of the blows that were inflicted, the whole theatre of Constantinople resounded with laughter and applause. The beauty of Theodora was the subject of more flattering praise, and the source of more exquisite delight. Her features were delicate and regular; her complexion, though somewhat pale, was tinged with a natural colour; every sensation was instantly expressed by the vivacity of her eyes; her easy motions displayed the graces of a small but elegant figure; and either love or adulation might proclaim that painting and poetry were incapable of delineating the matchless elegance of her form. But this form was degraded by the facility with which it was exposed to the public eye, and prostituted to licentious desire. Her venal charms were abandoned to a promiscuous crowd of citizens and strangers, of every rank and of every profession; the fortunate lover who had been promised a night of enjoyment was often driven from her bed by a stronger or more wealthy favourite; and when she passed through the streets, her presence was avoided by all who wished to escape either the scandal or the temptation. The satirical historian [Procopius] has not blushed to describe the naked scenes which Theodora was not ashamed to exhibit in the theatre. After exhausting the arts of sensual pleasure, she most ungratefully murmured against the parsimony of Nature; but her murmurs, her pleasures, and her arts, must be veiled in the obscurity of a learned language.

The five footnotes which, in the *Decline and Fall*, disfigure this impeccable piece of prose refer to the appropriate authorities in Latin and Greek, and provide the relevant quotations. If the curiosity provoked by them led schoolboys and undergraduates to improve their Greek and Latin, then this may be one of the very few examples in history of the end justifying the means.

THE LAPSES of great writers, as well as the highest endeavours of some little ones, have demonstrated to us how the classical style can be overdone: how the urbanity can decline into a sort of sterile formalism, and the reverberating Johnsonian utterance become as a mere post-prandial rumbling of wind. Dr. Johnson himself fell sadly from his great eminence now and then, and made, as you can imagine, a resounding flop when he did so. Possibly we should not blame him for spoiling one of the best epitaphs in the English language by beginning it "Poor Peyton expired this morning"; for such was the fashion of his time. But another epitaph, that upon David Garrick, jolted even Boswell into protest:

> I am disappointed by that stroke of death which has eclipsed the gaiety of nations, and impoverished the public stock of harmless pleasure.

If such a model had been widely followed, I dare not think what would have happened to the English language. Fortunately we have possessed for the better part of four centuries a most fortunate exemplar and corrective against overwriting, over-Latinising and *sesquipedalia verba* in general. The Bible, first in Tyndale's wonderful translation and then in the Authorized Version which owes so much to Tyndale, is set down in the plainest English imaginable; though in such Books as *Isaiah, Ecclesiastes* and *Job* this plain English has somehow taken fire from the Hebrew poetry, so that whole chapters seem to be written in words of flame. Essentially, however, throughout the whole Bible the phrasing is simple, the style straightforward, and the manner at times even colloquial—"For lo, the winter is past, the rain is over and gone." [1] I have often heard people use "over and gone" in that sense when they are talking about the weather in the village street or in the pub; and I have wondered whether the expression got into our speech by way of the Bible, or whether it was a familiar one among Englishmen in Tyndale's day. He was never a man for high-flown poetry, and it is clear that he loved the speech of the common people and wove its rhythms into his translation:

> Whither thou goest, I will go; and where thou lodgest I will lodge; thy people shall be my people, and thy God my God; where thou diest will I die, and there will I be buried. [2]

So much for "the Bible in the vulgar tongue"—vulgar but majestical! The Book of Common Prayer has had a powerful influence in

[1] *The Song of Songs.*
[2] *The Book of Ruth.*

the same direction. Indeed its effect upon the thoughts, the speech and the writing of Englishmen may have been even more profound than that of the Bible, because it has so often worked upon us unbeknownst at the critical moments in our lives:

> Man that is born of a woman hath but a short time to live, and is full of misery. He cometh up and is cut down like a flower; he fleeth as it were a shadow.[1]

The English language was proof against serious debasement while sentences like Ruth's, and that last one from the Burial Service, were landmarks in an Englishman's thinking, as his Parish Church was a landmark in his sight.

INDEED, we should have been a pretty contemptible people if we had ever permitted the pompous, the "overwritten," the slick and slovenly, above all the mean in spirit, to enjoy more than a brief fashion and a fleeting vogue in our writing and speaking; for, as if it were not riches enough for any one language to possess King James' Bible and the Book of Common Prayer, ours can boast a Shakespeare as well. Moreover, by the happiest coincidence in our history, his extraordinary genius and prodigious craft were matched to the critical hour, when the language had suddenly come into an enormous heritage, and when our poets were wondering what the devil to do with all this wealth from the Renaissance. Even Marlowe's head was turned by the vision of that cornucopia of wondrous words. Though he poured them prodigally into his poetry, he never quite learned how to weld them together with the old. But Shakespeare, striding into the turmoil and confusion, recognised at once that those new, melodious, overexciting "Romance" words and the tough, plain, uncompromising Anglo-Saxon ones were by no means incompatible; they might be joined together to make an instrument more powerful than any English poet—perhaps any poet anywhere—had possessed before.

The wonder is not that Shakespeare handled words better than any Englishman had done until he came upon the scene; it is that he did so more superbly than anybody since. Nor did it matter to him what *kind* of words they were,—as it did to the translators of the Bible, for example, who were committed to the grandeur of austerity. Shakespeare

[1] *Burial Service.*

seized upon the whole huge, various and newly-enriched vocabulary and found it barely sufficient for what he had to say. He did not need the great words all the time. When the theme and mood of a scene demanded it, he was capable of the utmost economy; but if the occasion called for extravagance then he called up all the most tremendous words at his command and squandered them recklessly—upon Lear defying the cataracts and hurricanoes, upon Juliet crying out to the fiery-footed steeds, upon Claudio foretasting the terror of being dead, upon Timon hurling curses at great Mother Nature herself

> *Whose womb immeasurable and infinite breast . . .*
> *Engenders the black toad and adder blue,*
> *The gilded newt and eyeless venom'd worm,*
> *With all the abhorred births below crisp heaven . . .*

For contrast, here are five lines of the sparest dialogue. King John has a word or two with Hubert concerning the young Prince Arthur:

KING: Death.
HUBERT: My lord?
KING: A grave.
HUBERT: He shall not live.
KING: Enough.

Those ten words tell us a terrible lot. Here are eight which say even more. Indeed I doubt if there are two sentences in English so pregnant with dreadful meaning:

MACBETH: Duncan comes here tonight.
LADY MACBETH: And when goes hence?

Shakespeare could do the most extraordinary things with monosyllables alone. "Unarm, Eros; *the long day's task is done And we must sleep.*" [1] Ten more of the simplest English words, and how much do they say to us! But it's in *Macbeth* that we are made most aware of the short sharp words knocking upon the mind with blows as urgent as those with which Macduff and Lennox, hammering on the gate, knocked up the drunken Porter.

---

[1] *Antony and Cleopatra.*

> *The times have been*
> *That, when the brains were out, the man would die*
> *And there an end; but now they rise again.*

NOW SEE what happens, when following a succession of such monosyllables Shakespeare introduces *unexpectedly* one or two of those tremendous new words which like lofty Spanish galleons had sailed into the language as lately as the Armada into the English Channel.—The familiar words first, to lull the mind and soothe the ear:

> *Will all great Neptune's ocean wash this blood*
> *Clean from my hand? No, this my hand will rather*
> *The multitudinous seas incarnadine.*

If you repeat the lines aloud you may even feel yourself catching something of the excitement and the sense of daring adventure which Shakespeare knew when he wrote them. "Multitudinous" had never been used in English before; and as an epithet for the sea it was audacious and beautiful, it suggested the vastness of ocean by conjuring up a picture of innumerable ripples and waves. As for "incarnadine," the adjective had been in use for a dozen years when Shakespeare by a stroke of his quill in the mighty line turned it into a verb.

THIS IS ONLY one aspect of his craft, this matching of the "words of learned length and thunderous sound" with the short staccato English ones. But it is something which never ceases to delight and astonish me, how by their very brusqueness the brief Anglo-Saxon words set off the melodious tetrasyllables, and how the long and the short together make a sort of thunderstorm poetry,—a bright flash illuminates all, and while we are still half-blinded by it, the rolling reverberations are in our ears: "mandragora" . . . "fantastical" . . . "majestical" . . . echoing in our consciousness like cannonades among the hills. Those "multitudinous seas" provide one good example. There is one still better, a valediction which may well have been Shakespeare's own farewell to the Dark Lady whose loved and hated and tormenting image had borne him company through all the years of passionate creation. It is spoken at the moment of Cleopatra's death; and you feel that perhaps Shakespeare is laying a ghost when, by an act of supreme exorcism, he conjures the little serpent into her bosom and causes her at the very end of her long journey to breathe: "Peace, peace! Dost thou not see my baby at my breast, That sucks the nurse asleep?" She falls back; and Charmian says those lines which contain perhaps the most extraordinary conjunction of words in English literature. Genius at fever-pitch must have dictated it; and by a miracle the two unlikely words fused together—the learned precise term of the Greek mathematicians, the roughly-affectionate countrified Middle English noun. Fusing, they generated a light as splendid as sunset; and no girl in history has ever gone out of the world in such a glory:

> *Now boast thee, death, in thy possession lies*
> A LASS UNPARALLEL'D.

CHAPTER 8

Pickings and Stealings

WHEN SHAKESPEARE DIED in 1616 English was already the richest language in the world, richest in synonyms and shades of meaning, in the words of poetry and the words of science, in words to serve philosophers and words to serve lovers, in everyday words for men who talk in taverns. Yet even these were not enough for all the uses which English ingenuity could put them to. We always wanted more: and during the next 300 years we ransacked the five continents for words. It might be said of us, as Moth said of Holofernes and Don Armado, "They have been at a great feast of languages, and stolen the scraps." [1] No other language, I am sure, has such a capacity as ours for gathering up and subsequently absorbing other people's scraps. The French, it is true, have lately discovered a taste for some English expressions, *"le boxing," "le club," "le bifteck,"* week-end, sweater, rugby and sandwich. With the exception perhaps of *"le coquetêle,"* so spelt, our words neither look nor sound very happy in French and are deplored by the academicians, who are stern and puritanical and at heart opposed to any word or phrase that was not used by Molière. So from time to time the surprisingly strait-laced French become troubled about these alien words, which they regard as seducers of pure speech and corrupters of language. Compare the behaviour of us British, who were assailed not long ago by a ferocious enemy sworn to overwhelm us by means of a lightning war, which he called a *blitzkrieg*. Having dealt with our assailant, we fell with delight upon the boastful word, gave it a new meaning ("bombardment from the air") chopped off its tail, and took it willy-nilly into our language, where it is so firmly established now that English history books of the future will certainly contain such chapter-headings as "England under the Blitz, 1940-1."

[1] *Love's Labour's Lost.*

It is an odd thing, and may be indicative of a long-standing discord and contrariety, that English in modern times has borrowed fewer words from German than from any other Continental language. The only ones I can think of are shale, wolfram, yodel, kindergarten, the unpleasing word mangelwurzel—and plunder. In case our ancient grudge prompts us to suggest that the latter word is characteristic of the nation whence we had it, let us remember that one of the words which English soldiers got to know during their service in India, and found so useful that they brought it home with them, was the Hindi word *lūt*—"loot"!

WE HAVE TAKEN a handy vocabulary from the Indian languages,— mostly words for which we had no equivalent before. For instance until recently our Army was, as it were, dressed by India—puttee (a bandage), dungaree (from *dungri*, a coarse cloth), khaki (dust-coloured), topi (a hat). The name of this rather absurd headdress is often misspelt *solar* topi, on the grounds that it must be something to do with the sun; in fact *sola* (spelt thus) is the name of the pithy shrub from which the hat is manufactured.

It was our soldiers, of course, who brought back the Hindi word *khushi*, meaning pleasure, and attached it during the First World War to any job habitually performed well out of range of shot and shell. (Our own word "cushion," though quite unrelated and derived from Old French, may possibly have influenced some people who picked up the alien word from the soldiers.) During World War II, when it became increasingly difficult to get out of range of H.E., this word "cushy" somewhat changed its meaning and is now used for any soft job. I get the impression that it may be gradually dying out.

Hindi words more secure in English are pundit, bungalow, pyjama, bangle, yoga, jungle, pukka of course, and the sahib who goes with it, nabob and shampoo,—from a word *champo* meaning massage. "Thug" is firmly established; it comes from the name of a fraternity of professional murderers who terrorised parts of India during the 1820's. "Mongoose," the charming Rikki-tikki-tavi animal, is a word from Marathi. "Curry" comes from Tamil. "Dinghy" is Bengalese. Lastly, "Juggernaut" comes from *Jagannath*, an idol of Krishna; our lesser leader writers delight in it, using it as a word for anything slow and inexorable, as the processes of bureaucracy.

IT IS FUN to look at a map of the world and see where the words come from. I daresay there is hardly a territory, however wild and far away, that has not at some time or another yielded its tribute to our tongue. When the small-town weekly somewhat short of news makes headlines about the cow that ran amok on her way to market, it is using a word (meaning "furious") which comes from Malaya, whence we have also sago, bamboo, and orang-utan, literally "wild man of the forest." When our M.F.H. says that shooting foxes is taboo, he is expressing his rather confused ideas by means of a Tongan word for "sacred" brought home by Captain Cook from one of his Pacific voyages. When the Gas Board installs what we still call a geyser in our bathroom, we are likening the water-heater to a particular warm spring in Iceland, which bears an Old Norse name meaning "to gush forth." when the triumphant chess-player says to his opponent "Check Mate" he probably does not know that he is speaking corrupted Arabic. The phrase is *Al-shah mat*, the King is Dead! It originally came from Persian. We speak another Persian syllable when we talk of the butcher's van. The fine word *caravanserai* implied a company of merchants or pilgrims travelling together,—

> *Away, for we are ready to a man!*
> *Our camels sniff the evening and are glad.*
> *Lead on, O Master of the Caravan:*
> *Lead on the Merchant-Princes of Bagdad.*[1]

The caravan-site with water laid on and sanitary arrangements provided is a far cry from the Golden Journey to Samarkand; and so is the vehicle laden with sirloins and steaks and legs of mutton and pork chops.

Every day of our lives in our speaking and writing we use, probably without knowing it, some fragments of a dozen or more languages. If we talk about "a bit of a schemozzle" we are speaking Yiddish. If we say we are in a blue funk about something we are using a Flemish word *fonck*, perturbation. The frightful wars we have fought over Flanders gave us ample opportunity and excuse for learning that word.

If we speak of zero hour we are using Arabic; of a wagon, Dutch; of the esplanade, Spanish; of broccoli, Italian; of a shawl, Persian.

[1] James Elroy Flecker: *Hassan*.

"Tulip" is Persian too,—it comes from a word meaning turban, and so might a bed of tulips make you think of the bright-turbaned guests at a Sultan's *divan*. To Gerard the herbalist they were "strange and forein flowers," newly introduced: "The bloud-red tulip with the yellow bottome" is his dramatic description of one kind.

The chimpanzee at the Zoo was given his euphonious name by some people called the Bu who inhabit the forests of Angola. From Peru comes the odd-looking Quechuan-Indian name of the odd-looking beast, the llama,

> *With an indolent expression and an undulating throat*
> *Like an unsuccessful literary man.*[1]

Indeed the dictionary is a Noah's Ark, in which all the strange creatures from the ends of the earth find their proper places, and liven our language with their outlandish syllables: the kangaroo, meaning "the jumper" in Aboriginal Australian, the giraffe named in Arabic, the zebra in Amharic, the panda in Tibetan, the porcupine meaning "spiny pig" in Latin, the dromedary meaning "the runner" in Greek, though in fact he only does about 10 miles an hour. Here is the squirrel, also named in Greek, through a corruption of *sciouros*, shadow-tail. Here is the opossum from the lands of the Algonquin,—bringing his own private verb with him, "to play possum," to lie low. And here we find the mournful-looking gnu, or *nqu*, thus named in a Hottentot dialect by the Cape Bushmen of South Africa. The Dutch settlers have another word for it, which to English ears suggests a creature more weird and formidable than this ox-like antelope: they call it the wildebeest.

THE POTATO'S NAME comes to us through Spain from Haiti; the tomato's, also via Spanish, from Mexico. It is interesting that the Spanish words are *patatA* and *tomatE*. The final "o" which both have in English is due apparently to our simple belief that a DagO always ends his words like that. "Dago," by the way, comes from the Spanish Christian name *Diego*,[2] and was first used in the United States as a rather contemptuous term for all Latins.

Sometimes these exotic words made long and complicated journeys before they got to England. "Cannibal" is a good example. The Caribs

[1] Hilaire Belloc.
[2] James.

were American-Indian tribes who lived in various islands off the coast
of Venezuela; the inhabitants of Cuba believed them to be eaters of
human flesh. I don't know whether this was true, but during a stay in
Trinidad I was taken to visit one of the last of them, her whom they
called the Queen of the Caribs, and she was such a gentle old lady,
fragile as a piece of old papyrus, that I find it difficult to believe her
ancestors could have eaten anybody. However, the people of Cuba held
a different opinion; and in their speech *cariba* became *caniba*, in which
form Christopher Columbus heard it. He brought it home from his
voyage of discovery in 1493, and soon it got into Spanish as *canibal*,
and thence into English.

The Caribbean language is extinct, or nearly so; but a few syllables
of it are preserved through our taking over this word and one other,
"canoe," which came from a branch of the language, long ago withered,
called Taino.

Another common word which we can think of as a ghostly whisper
from a dead civilization is "chocolate." The Spaniards took it home
from Mexico; for it is really an Aztec word, *chocolatl*, meaning " a
food made by mixing the seed of *cacaua-atl* with those of a tree called
pochotl." The "tl" at the end of a word is generally a mark of its Aztec
origin; [1] wherefore the Mexican names tickle the ear with their strangeness—that of the mountain Popocatepetl, for instance, and that of the
extraordinary salamander which never grows out of its tadpolehood
even when sexually mature, a ghastly Peter Pan animal from the lakes
of Mexico City, which they call the axolotl.

FROM THE North American Indians, we have taken their characteristic
words tomahawk and wigwam, totem and moccasin and squaw. I love
the exciting Redskin words and I wish we had more of them—whenever
I encounter in print such tribal names as Mohican and Passamaquoddy,
Cherokee, Chickahominy and Sioux, they leap out at me shouting their
war-cries and waving their tomahawks in the air! I see again the shining
vision that every boy sees, the sumachs and maples ablaze in the Fall,

[1] Unless of course the word is spoken by a citizen of Bristol. The port was
originally called Bristowe. But its natives appear to have a strange defect of speech,
which causes them to tack an "l" on to the ends of their words, though they themselves do not know that they do it. I expect they say chocolatl; and if you asked
them whether they meant chocolate, they would say "I said chocolatl, didl I?"

the swift tumbling river, the birch-bark canoe, the warpaint, the headdress with the scarlet-tipped feathers that match the maple-leaves. I
found a score of these exciting names all together in an old Encyclo-
pædia the other day. The tribes were classified rather priggishly according to their moral state, e.g. the Sacs and Foxes "showed considerable
improvement," the Dog-ribs were "wild and indolent"—but how could
they be both?—the Beavers were "rather stationary," an extraordinary
condition, but not so bad apparently as that of the Chinooks who were
"stationary or worse." The Aleuts were "decaying," the Kafbobs were
"destitute," the Klickatats "badly influenced by whites," as were the
Puyallop and the Winnebago, whereas of the Kickapoo the censorious
ethnologist commented laconically, as he might of so many of us,
"Progress hampered by liquor."

The quaintest word which we have acquired from the Red Indians,
—yes, even for all I know from the drunken Kickapoo themselves—is
the word "mugwump." It comes from Massachusetts *mugquomp*, and
means a Big Chief.

of course the commonest kind of loan-words—as foreign words are
called when we take them over unaltered—are those which are connected with some well-known idiosyncrasy, custom, manufacture or
characteristic of the people they are borrowed from. Obviously we have
no English word for the Eskimo's igloo; so when we want to refer to
it, we use his. As a nation comparatively unmusical we were glad to
borrow the Italian words solo, soprano, piano, fortissimo etc. as well as
some other specialties of that nation, the vendetta, the stiletto, the
prima donna, the inferno, the casino, the grotto, the replica, the dilet-
tante, and the gusto which characterises the Italian people. In the same
way from the Irish we have taken over the "blarney" [1] which is generally regarded as one of their specialties, with "shamrock," "brogue,"
and their delightful name for a girl, "colleen"; also their unique and
vociferous elemental spirit, the banshee, which comes from Gaelic
bean sidhe, fairy woman. "Hooligan" is taken from the name of a
particularly wild Irish family that became notorious in London during
the 1890s.

---

[1] Kissing the stone at Blarney near Cork is supposed to give you "a cajoling
tongue and the art of flattery or of telling lies with unblushing effrontery." Lewis:
Topographical Dictionary of Ireland.

Welsh gives us "bard" and "coracle,"—a kind of boat used on the Dee. Scottish Gaelic naturally provides the topographical words, loch, bog, cairn, glen, and the bird ptarmigan, as well as plaid and clan; and one is happy to notice that both the "whisky" and the "galore" in the title of Sir Compton Mackenzie's book are native to the west of Scotland. "Galore" is Gaelic *gu leior*, enough; "whisky" is an Anglicised version of *uisgebeatha*, water of life. This is parallel with the French phrase for brandy, *eau de vie*, the Latin *aqua vitae*, and the Scandinavian word for their own ardent spirit, *akvavit*. Temperance reformers disapprove of all these words.

"Whiskey," by the way, is the Irish spelling. Otherwise, the stuff seems to be called whisky in every language under the sun. The French translated Sir Compton's title, when the book was filmed, as *Whisky à Gogo*. The word Scotch, we are often told, should be used solely for the drink; the people are Scots, their adjective Scottish. Nevertheless Sir Walter Scott, R. L. Stevenson and Robert Burns described their fellow countrymen as Scotch, and so do many of the modern Scottish writers.

But everybody is agreed that only whisky distilled in Scotland shall be called Scotch. It is said that the British Ambassador once had to draw the attention of the Swedish Government to the fact that a straw-coloured liquid, manufactured in Stockholm, was being described as Scotch whisky. The Swedish Foreign Minister said he would look into the matter; and having done so expressed his profound regret, but felt compelled at the same time to draw the attention of His Britannic Majesty's Government to the regrettable custom of describing a coarse variety of the turnip as a Swede . . .

BY ACCEPTING a foreign word into our language we admit, as it were, the foreigner's exclusive right to choose an international name for that particular thing. It is fascinating to observe what sort of things, in the case of each country, we have considered to be their special perquisites. Australia's is surely the boomerang. Portugal's include port, caste, and palaver,—our sailors picked up the last one from the natives along the Guinea coast, where the Portuguese traders had left it. Sherry is named after Jeréz in Andalusia, and from Spain too come cargo, desperado, and also, I believe, the name of the suit of spades in a pack of cards—which has nothing to do with digging but is named after *espada,* a sword. One surprising importation from Spain is "cockroach," our adaptation of *cucaracha,* the Spanish name for the insect we generally call a black beetle, though it is neither a beetle nor black,—it belongs to the same family as the crickets and earwigs, and is reddish-brown, except when newly emerged; it is then cream-coloured, and such specimens are described as "white blackbeetles," making absurdity complete.

From the West Indies we have two words which must have originated in the forests of Africa, travelled across the Atlantic in the terrible slave-ships, and survived in the Plantations; they live on to haunt the minds of the great-grandchildren of the slaves,—"voodoo" and "zombie." The latter really means a dead person dug out of his grave and reanimated so that he can be used for labour; there is still a strong superstition in some of the islands that powerful magicians can use the dead so. Lately the word has crept into English slang, meaning a dopey or half awake person.

The Hungarian language, Magyar, is quite unrelated to ours. It belongs to a group which includes the languages spoken by the Finns, the Esthonians, and some Mongol ex-cannibals called Samoyeds. For us Indo-Europeans it is a terrifying language in print; but it has enriched our English hotchpotch with the words "goulash," "paprika," possibly "coach" (from the town of Kocs where such carriages were first made?), "vampire" the blood-sucker,—and also the female vamp who is derived from it—and best of all "hussar," a word which for me seems to epitomise the pre-war Balkans,—their innumerable Regiments, their beautiful uniforms, their little wars fought between harvest-home and the first snow, their courage in absurd causes, their cavalry charges, and oh! the glint of the sun upon the last, the very last perhaps in human history, of the bright but bloodstained swords!

THE SPECIAL BELONGINGS of Japan, concerning which we have conceded that its own names are better than any of ours could be, are the kimono, the practice of jujitsu (literally "pliant art"), the geisha girl (originally a "dancing person," though she sometimes interprets that function pretty liberally) and the ceremonial form of suicide, hara-kiri (a "belly-slitting," generally by its owner). From China, as well as giving its name to our porcelain, we have accepted the word kowtow and also pidgin, for the quaint jargon so called, it is said, because the

Chinese found difficulty in pronouncing "business." His shot at it was *bidginess*, shortened to *bidgin*, hence pidgin English,—"business English"—and hence possibly our phrase "That's not my pigeon"—not my concern. We have another phrase "Not for all the tea in China,"—so perhaps it is not surprising that the Chinese word for that commodity should be heard more often than the English one in our Naafi canteens. The word is "char," a corruption of *chai*, and I imagine our soldiers first had it from Hong Kong.

Russia has named for us its own dreary and treeless steppes, the little quadruped sable which produces a valuable fur, and two specialties of its own, the mammoth and the Bolshevik. The latter word means "a member of the majority" but in English slang we have perversely given it the opposite implication: a bolshie is one who is always "agin the rest." The long-extinct mammoth which the Russians found deep-frozen in the Siberian tundra was named by them *mamont*. The "n" was left out by a compositor when the word was first printed in English, and from this accident it has never recovered. "Th" in the 18th century was still an occasional spelling for the sound of "t," so *mamot* became mammoth in the first Russian grammar published in England. It is much too late now for any pedant to put things right; for the word is firmly fixed in advertisers' English as an adjective expressive of size. They even offer us a mammoth package of cereal, which is bigger than king-sized, apparently.

THAT THE RUSSIAN should name his mammoth and, more recently, his sputnik, the German his U-boat, the Norwegian his ski, saga, troll, and fiord, the Italian his spaghetti and his gondola, the Frenchman his revue and his soufflé on behalf of the whole world seems right and proper; but I cannot for the life of me see why we have allowed the Arabs the privilege of christening "alcohol," which their Prophet forbids them to drink. It would not matter if solely the laboratory spirit were so called, but we have permitted a combination of policemen and puritans to foist upon us the horrible term "alcoholic liquor," which apparently comprehends our Château-Lafite and our Taylor 1927, our Rüdesheimer and our Chevalier-Montrachet, our Napoleon brandy and our Château Yquem,—indeed everything fermented or distilled, from Red Biddy to Romanée-Conti.

In any case it was by a misunderstanding that "alcohol" got its

name. *Kohl* is the powder with which Arab girls paint their eyes; and
very effective it is when those dark eyes are the only features you are
allowed to see, and they are like the fishpools in Heshbon, by the gate
of Bath-Rabbim. Now in order that it should act upon the eyelids as
a stain, the powder has to be very fine; therefore antimony is heated
and vaporised so that black dust is produced by sublimation. In much
the same way wine when heated gives off a vapour which cools into an
essence; therefore, for no better reason than that it was made in somewhat the same way as the eye-powder, the spirit so obtained was called
al kohl by analogy. I must say this strikes me as a poor excuse for giving
the stuff such a revolting name. But the origins of Arabic words are
often very mysterious. Our "coffee," for example, comes from *qāhwah*
(*kahvé* in Turkish), which word "is said by Arab lexicographers,"
according to the *O.E.D.*, "to have originally meant 'wine' or some
kind of wine, and to be a derivative of the word-root *qahiya*, 'to have
no appetite.' "

The Arabs have also given us the little-loved word "algebra," and
many more beginning with "al,"—which is simply the Arabic article
"the": alkali, almanac, alembic, alcove, alfalfa. "Artichoke" was *alk-
harshūf*, and came to us by way of Italian during the 16th century,
when the herbalist Gerard thought little of its roots and wrote of them
gloomily: "They yield to the body a raw and melancholy juyce and con-
taine within them great store of winde." "Zenith," and "cipher" date
from the time when Arabian scholars in Alexandria led the world in
mathematics. Cotton, sofa, calibre, admiral, magazine, harem (literally
"forbidden"), syrup and gazelle are samples of the great assortment of
words we have taken from this old enduring language, which Islam in
the course of its conquests and conversions has carried across half the
world. To "garble" is another; and our soldiers as you may imagine have
garbled the sense of some of the words they have picked up during their
campaigns in North Africa. *Mufti* in Arabic means one who expounds
the law. When an Army Officer acted as a magistrate he wore civilian
clothes; hence through confusion the word was used for "civilian dress
when worn by a person entitled to wear uniform." [1] *Baksheesh* meant
simply a present, without any implication of "greasing the palm." A
houri is by no means a tart, as some of our simpler fighting men have

[1] Field-Marshal Lord Wavell, as quoted by Mr. Eric Partridge in *Origins*.

supposed; the word means, literally, "a gazelle-like woman of Paradise," and in particular she resembles a gazelle because of the liquid darkness of her eyes,—painted no doubt with *al kohl!* The infidel soldier obviously can have little hope of houris either in this world or the next, and had better content himself with a "bint." In Arabic this means no more than "girl," though a *saida bint*—"good-day girl"—is a prostitute. Returning warriors have introduced the word into English slang, where it is used as a rule rather affectionately.

FOR ONE SWEET WORD I can forgive the Arabs even their algebra. The jasmine which our cottage-gardeners call jessamine was first named in Persia. In Arabic *yasmin* became the name of a scent, and hence presumably a name given to girls. Hassan, drunk with love and words, and especially with the two doting syllables of this particular word, sang a song consisting of beautiful sounds mixed with very little sense, beneath a balcony in the Street of Felicity by the Fountain of the Two Pigeons:

> *How splendid in the morning glows the lily;*
> *   with what grace he throws*
> *His supplication to the rose: do roses nod the*
> *   head, Yasmin?*
> *But when the silver dove descends I find the little*
> *   flower of friends*
> *Whose very name that sweetly ends, I say when I*
> *   have said, Yasmin.*
> *The morning light is clear and cold; I dare not*
> *   in that light behold*
> *A whiter light, a deeper gold, a glory too far shed,*
> *   Yasmin.*
> *But when the deep red eye of day is level with the*
> *   lone highway,*
> *And some to Meccah turn to pray, and I toward thy*
> *   bed, Yasmin,*
> *Or when the wind beneath the moon is drifting like*
> *   a soul aswoon,*
> *And harping planets talk love's tune with milky*
> *   wings outspread, Yasmin,*

> *Shower down thy love, O burning bright! for one*
> *night or the other night*
> *Will come the Gardener in white, and gathered*
> *flowers are dead, Yasmin!* [1]

AN ARABIC ADJECTIVE meaning "of, on, for or by a journey" itself jour-
neyed far south and wriggled its way into Swahili, whence our White
Hunters during the 1890's picked it up as "safari" and gave it the meaning of an expedition after big game. And so we come to the sunburnt
lion-coloured "veld" (it means "field" in Dutch) and to the hunters'
words, "trek" and "spoor," which seemed all the more exciting for being
so laconic when we first met with them in some boys' adventure story.
Both came from Afrikaans, which also gave us "commandeer," from
"commando," which originally meant a punitive expedition or raiding-
party of Boer settlers. We spoke of Commandos during the Boer War,
but thereafter the word fell out of use until 1940, when our Army,
driven ignominiously from the Continent, was bound for honour's sake
to consider ways and means of going back there. The small companies
of volunteers which it trained for the first raids across the Channel were
called Storm Troops—a bad name at that time if only because it was
copied from the German. Then they were called Leopards, for they
would be stealthy, silent and swift, and as Sir Winston Churchill put
it would "spring at the throats" of the enemy. At last somebody had the
brilliant idea of reviving that old Boer word "commando," and Sir
Winston with his instinct for the right word seized upon it joyfully.
The deeds of the commandos ensure that it will stay in English forever.

There is a word of darker significance which comes from South
Africa. I do not know if the Boers invented the cruel whip of rhino-
hide; they certainly didn't invent the name for it, which is said to derive from Malay and ultimately from Urdu; but the fact remains that
sjambok has become an "international" word which many languages
have taken over from Afrikaans and put into their dictionaries, where
it stands as a sort of silent indictment against the Afrikaaners. Indeed
it is even used figuratively to express a tyranny of whips and violence:
"sjambok-rule." Words, because they are often the mirrors of behaviour, do indeed rise up and sit in judgment upon a whole nation

[1] James Elroy Flecker: *Hassan*.

now and then. Italian dictionaries contain a verb, *abbacinare,* concerning which the Reverend Dr. Trench exclaimed in horror: "What whole
processes of cruelty are sometimes wrapped up in a single word!" For
abbacinare means "to deprive of sight by holding a red-hot metal basin
close to the eyes." In German dictionaries—and as far as I know in
those of no other modern language—you will find a word which means
"malicious joy at another's misfortune, gratification of pent-up envy,
pleasure in the downfall of those one has formerly cringed to and en-
vied." The word is *schadenfreude.* It is often to be found in English
writing, but is printed in italics; we haven't yet taken it into the language, though we have no equivalent word of our own.

"Slave" is a good example of a word whose very existence is an indictment of a nation at the bar of history; for it is none other than a
version of Slav, the name of the Eastern European people. The German tribes so often overran and conquered these races that they were
reduced to a condition of servility. To be a Slav was to be a slave; and
in such a "transferred sense" the word was first used in the 9th century, though the conquests and the enslavements continued long after
that. "Slave" came into English in time to be used by Chaucer; it
found its way into many other languages too; though not one person
in ten thousand, I daresay, realised its significance when in 1942 the
Germans made another of their great expansions to the eastward, and
the Slavs became slaves once again.

In much the same way does the word sjambok indict the Boers—
Boer, by the way, is Dutch for "farmer" but also has the sense of back-
woodsman, an outlander, a country lout, wherefore we have our word
"boorish." Perhaps in the first instance it was the language rather than
the people themselves that was responsible for this grumpy association.
Even the Dutch of the homeland appears ugly and tongue-twisting to
Englishmen—hence our phrase Double Dutch; the Boer version of it
called Afrikaans simply appals us. It may be, as I have been told, a very
good language for dirty-story-telling round a camp fire; but on the few
occasions I have heard it spoken I have been horrified by the ape-like
utterances which it involves.

"BOSS" AND "SPOOK" are Dutch words which we had by way of American English; but we took over a whole vocabulary directly from Dutch
through our commerce with Holland and our mutual seafaring to and

fro,—in fact many English words connected with ships and sailors were Dutch originally: hoist, deck, yacht, buoy, marline, splice, dock, swabber, furlough, bulwark and of course skipper. From Holland too we got our snuff and the word for it, our brandy (*brandywijn*), and our dope (*doop*). The "hop," for flavouring beer, was introduced into England from the Low Countries during the reign of Henry VIII; and the dictionary, which reflects almost all our doings, records this minor incident of commerce faithfully, for we took over the Dutch name with the plant. About the same time, very fittingly, we accepted into our slang their word *bouse*, which we now spell booze.

The diminutive suffix -kin comes from the Dutch, e.g. as in manikin,[1] lambkin, firkin, kilderkin, and pipkin, which sounds like a petname for a child but turns out to mean a small earthenware jar or pot. Herrick wrote a quaint *Ternery of Littles, Upon a Pipkin of Jelly sent to a Lady:*

> *A little meat best fits a little belly,*
> *O sweetly, Lady, give me leave to tell ye*
> *This little pipkin fits this little jelly.*

The oddest of such words is certainly "sooterkin," which as well as being an obsolete term for a sweetheart is defined in the *O.E.D.* as "an imaginary kind of afterbirth formerly attributed to Dutch women." The illustrative quotation which follows serves only to deepen the mystery, so far as I am concerned:

> There goes a Report of the Holland Women, that together with their children, they are delivered of a sooterkin, not unlike to a Rat, which some imagine to be the off-spring of the Stoves.

CONCERNING ANOTHER RATHER curious word which we had from the Dutch, a pitiful story is told. It is said that refugees from religious persecutions in the Low Countries who came to work in England in the seventeenth century were unable to make any reply save *niet weet,* "I do not know," to the questions which the English asked them. The English, of course, expect every nationality to understand their language if only it is shouted loud enough; so doubtless they fairly hollered

---

[1] Dutch *mannekin*.

at the Dutchmen, who like the canaries they had brought over with them pathetically chirped "*Niet weet! Niet weet!*," wherefore we decided in our rough island fashion that they were "nitwits," and so christened them. Later nitwit got into our dictionaries as a word for all poor fools.

IN ONE RESPECT I think we have repaid the Hollanders ill for their contribution to our language. Nations when at odds are apt to play mischievous games with words at each other's expense. We have often quarreled with our neighbours the Dutch, because of naval rivalries and commercial competition; and for these and other reasons we have sought to score off them by inventing such derisive phrases as a Dutch bargain (one-sided), a Dutch auction (mock), Dutch comfort ("Thank God it's no worse"), a Dutch concert (everybody playing a different tune), Dutch nightingale (a frog), a Dutch feast (when the host gets drunk before his guests have had a chance to), a Dutch headache (a hangover), a Dutch treat (when everybody pays his share), a Dutch husband (bolster laid alongside one in a bed), a Dutch widow (prostitute), Dutch courage (induced by drink) and so on. To cap it all we have even attributed to them the invention of a kind of contraceptive. This of course is a familiar trick of nations who are anxious to be as nasty as possible to a neighbour. We exchange contraceptives, as it were, with the French; and also the most unpleasant diseases. We spoke of syphilis as the "French" or the "Spanish pox"; across the Channel it was called "the English disease."

I HAVE LEFT our nearest neighbour until last, in this discussion of our pickings and stealings and beggings and borrowings. Our debt to French is enormous; after all, our language has only followed the human example in borrowing from the people next door. We saw how the baggage-train of William the Conqueror included enough Norman French and adapted Latin words to transform the English language within a couple of centuries. Since then through our trade and our wars, our travels and our diplomacy, we have added in each century a hundred or two French words to our store. A few examples of them will serve as amusing footnotes to the history of Anglo-French relations. We borrowed "moustache" as early as the 16th century; also "fricassée," "portmanteau" and "piquant," and that excellent word

You English Words

which in French is more versatile than in English,—*machin*, machine. During the next hundred years, when our French contacts were closer, we seized joyfully upon the theatrical words ballet, burlesque, tableau, and décor, also parterre, coquette, some military words—dragoon, stockade, parole—and chagrin, champagne and soup! During the 18th century the words connected with *la guerre* go like a column on the march, corps, manœuvre, sortie, tricolor, espionage, dépôt, fusillade. High society introduced salon, bureau and etiquette. In various ways we acquired émigré, régime, canteen, coterie and cul-de-sac. The word "picnic" came into English about this time. "Rissoles" appeared on the menu. Fashionable women spoke of "rouge." We welcome "brunette" and re-learned "blonde," which oddly enough had been used in 1481 by Caxton ("The rayes of the sonne make the heer of a man abourne or blounde") [1] and thereafter forgotten.

FORTUNATELY THE VICTORIANS, though so strict in some ways, had no qualms whatever about this kind of miscegenation. We had no stuffy old Academy to watch over our language like a chaperon (from French, 1720) and worry about what company it was keeping. During the 19th century English learned a lot of new French manners. Fashion brought over such words as crêpe, béret, suède, cretonne, rosette; French chefs taught us sauté, mousse, fondant, gratin; soldiers laid down barrages, issued communiqués, carried marshal's batons in their haversacks; society mingled only with the élite, was chic, went to the matinée, attended premières, dined in restaurants, made its daughters débutantes and found them suitable fiancés, maintained its prestige, deplored enfants terribles and kept its amour propre. The century ended with Aubrey Beardsley and *The Yellow Book* in a rather macabre and fin-de-siècle mood.

ENGLISH IS the richer for those French words, I think; we should not use them too often, but now and then they can give a sharper edge to a meaning, as it were, than the nearest of our home-bred words can do. There is no *exact* equivalent of, let us say, chic, naïf, enfant terrible, débâcle, or raison d'être. Almost every auctioneer's catalogue of household furniture bears witness to the indispensability of chiffonier and

[1] *The Mirror of the World* (trans.).

jardinière. All the same it surprises me that so many French expressions should have stayed in English so long without showing any sign of changing either their spelling, pronunciation or meaning, or becoming adapted to a wider use. In the old days things were very different. *"Pensée"* arrived in 1500 and was changed to pansy within thirty years. (It was the French, of course, who first had the charming idea of naming that contemplative-looking flower after "a thought.") *Quelques choses* quickly became "kickshaws" for the first Elizabethans; "Any pretty little tiny kickshaws, tell William Cook," said Justice Shallow, thinking perhaps that the pigeons, the two hens, and the joint of mutton he had already ordered might fail to satisfy the great appetite of Falstaff. Earlier than Shakespeare, it took us a mere sixty years or so to anglicise *dent-de-lion* into "dandelion." And coming down to Dickens' day, Mr. Smauker was swift to take the refined society word *soirée* and reduce it to the terms of a lower-middle-class England. "A friendly swarry," said he, "consisting of a boiled leg of mutton with the usual trimmings." The later introductions, on the other hand, remained confined to "polite speech," elegant letter-writing, and literary usage; and I daresay the reason is that they have always been the property of a fairly small social group, which has used them for limited and peculiar purposes, e.g. as substitutes for words which might seem "risqué" or too outspoken in English; for their sheer snob-value; for making private communications in front of servants (a practice which nowadays strikes us as horribly rude); and in order to observe the conventions of a society where certain expressions were, shall we say, *de rigueur,* such as that of adding *Répondez s'il vous plaît* to an invitation, because the request sounded less peremptory in French.

My mother, who died three years ago at the age of 85, was certain to use some French word or phrase quite naturally in the course of almost any conversation; and in doing so she was simply reflecting the fashion of a Victorian country-house girlhood. Although she had had a French governess for a time, as the custom was, she had hardly learned the elements of French grammar; and she couldn't read the language at all, nor write it, nor talk it save in the form of these sayings, which she spoke with an excellent accent: distingué, savoir faire, comme il faut, ça va sans dire, outré, nous verrons, gauche, touché, roué, ennui, hors-de-combat, sangfroid, négligé, en passant, par excellence, double entendre, rendezvous, recherché, résumé, passé, métier, penchant, contretemps, joie de vivre. She used these expressions so often that whenever I meet with them now I can almost hear her voice. I used to think the habit was rather absurd; but as I have been writing them down I have asked myself in each case whether there was a good brief English equivalent. Except in the case of distingué, gauche and en passant, I couldn't find one. Take the noun "rendezvous," for example. "A place appointed for a meeting" is the best we can do—and that is five words instead of one. And is there not, often, some implication of *time* as well as of place? "I have a rendezvous with Death At some disputed barricade," wrote Alan Seeger early in the Great War,

> *I have a rendezvous with Death*
> *At midnight in some flaming town,*
> *When Spring trips north again this year,*
> *And I to my pledged word am true,*
> *I shall not fail that rendezvous.*

He kept it. As for the French word itself, unadapted, unaltered in any way, it is completely at home in English poetry; so it should be, for we've been using it, believe it or not, since 1591.

CHAPTER 9

From Greece and Rome

O F COURSE IT is only a smattering of words that we have taken over lock, stock and barrel from a foreign language. For the most part our words came deviously, making their way by winding paths through the minds of generations of men, even burrowing like moles through the dark subconsciousness. Fancied likenesses, far-fetched associations, ancient prejudices have acted upon them. Superstitions, misapprehensions, old fables, mythologies, taboos, the jests of simpletons and the vaulting imagination of poets have all played a part in shaping them. During their labyrinthine journeys in time and space they have often changed their form, spelling, pronunciation and, especially, their sense. A very good example is the word "treacle," of which the origin is to be sought in the Greek *therion*, meaning a wild beast. The association is so unexpected that it would probably have stuck in my mind without the fortuitous mnemonic of the Lyle's Golden Syrup tin, familiar at the school tea-table, which carried a picture of a lion's carcass with bees flying out of it, and a caption from the *Book of Judges*: "Out of the strong came forth sweetness." This of course has nothing whatever to do with the derivation of "treacle"; but it ensured that I should never forget the curious connexion with wild beasts.

Now *therion*, by an extension of its meaning, came to signify "any dangerous or savage thing"; and since poisonous serpents were within this category a word was coined, *theriake*, for "an antidote against snake-bite." This became *triacula* in Low Latin and *triacle* in Old French; and in due course the word arrived in English as "treacle" but with the meaning: "A medicinal compound used against bites and poisons." Such a salve, which the apothecaries in their grand way called an alexipharmic, generally consisted of aromatic and soothing herbs like rue, garlic, germander and valerian, all of which incidentally are still known as Poor Man's Treacle or Countryman's Treacle in parts of the English countryside.

To make a good salve, it was necessary to bind together, with some harmless sticky stuff, the bruised or fine-chopped leaves. What better stuff for the purpose than thick black molasses? And so you see by what devious processes the Greek wild beast becomes at last the treacle which was mixed with dollops of brimstone for Smike and his companions at Dotheboys Hall.

TURNING OVER THE pages of an etymological dictionary, you begin to realise how much our language, whether homely or high-faluting, owes to Greece and Rome. The plumber is so called because in his trade he uses *plumbum*, lead; the carpenter was originally *artifex carpentarius*, a maker of wagons; and we have dentist from *dens*, vet from *veterinarius* ("pertaining to cattle"), artist from *ars* and his easel from *asellus*, a little ass, which seems extraordinary until you compare it with our English expression "clothes horse." If we say we don't care a jot we are using as a metaphor the Greek "i," *iota*, which is the smallest Greek letter. "Asparagus" is simply the Greek word for a sprout or shoot. "Asbestos" is Greek for inextinguishable. *Hupokritēs* meant an actor on the stage; and so a hypocrite is a person who pretends to beliefs and feelings which are not his own. *Aegis* was the dreaded shield of Zeus, made for him by Hephaestus. We treat the Cloud-Gatherer with little respect when we speak of a fête being held under the aegis of the Women's Institute. *Agonia* meant a contest, primarily in athletics. You have only to look at a photograph of anybody winning the 100 yards to understand how it came in its English version to have the sense of "agony."

Hundreds of our useful words,[1] and some of our most splendid ones, are taken direct from Greek. Labyrinthine, pandemonium and phantasmagoria are three beauties. "Labyrinth" may in fact belong to a still older language, out of Asia Minor or perhaps ancient Egypt; it is an appropriately mysterious word. "Pandemonium" (first used by Milton) has the awesome literal meaning of "the abode of all the demons." "Phantasmagoria" seems to have been invented by an enterprising showman in 1802 in order to advertise an exhibition of optical illusions produced by the magic lantern. Nowadays, however, it generally means

[1] For example: orchestra, dogma, cinema, phenomenon, enigma (something "spoken darkly" or in riddles), museum, clinic, pylon, acrobat, phase and philander.

"a series of drifting phantoms" such as you might see in a dream or a fever.

We have great Greek words for most of our physical diseases and for all our psychological troubles, not forgetting cremnophobia, "fear of falling from cliffs," and hagiophobia, "excessive dread of holy persons or things." If you are a fancier of rare and extraordinary words, here is a prolific hunting-ground. Another lies in the direction of ancient magic, where high-sounding Greek combinations were used to inspire awe and create an atmosphere of mystery. "Alectoromancy," for instance, meant "divination by a cock picking up grains." There are scores of these "mancy" words, interesting by reason of the glimpse they give us of the extravagances of the seers. Divination was even performed by dropping melted wax into water (ceromancy), by mirrors (catoptromancy), by salt (halomancy) and by mice (myomancy). I have no idea what experiments or observations were involved in myomancy, and I should like to know more about this long-forgotten chapter in the relationship of mice and men.

ALL THE -ologies are named in Greek, e.g. palaeontology, the study of ancient things, and so are most of the ancient things themselves, such as the dinosaur, "the terrible lizard," and the pterodactyl, "the feather-fingered creature." Greek also provides us with a useful if peculiar vocabulary denoting the rarer kinks, vagaries and idiosyncrasies of the human race, such as a craze for setting things on fire, pyromania; the printing or painting of filthy pictures, rhyparography; fish-worship, ichthyolatry; love of corpses, necrophilism; the belief that one has turned oneself into a wolf, lycanthropy; and the contemplation of the navel for the purpose of attaining philosophic calm, omphaloskepsis! There is even a word expressive of the healthy male appreciation of a good-looking feminine bottom: callipygian; which Sir Thomas Browne explains as referring to "women largely composed behind." [1] Fashions change; and nowadays we should be more likely to describe such women as steatopygous,[2] fat-rumped. As somebody punned in Latin, *Ars est celare arsem!*

Because Greek is such a handy language for new-word-making, the

---

[1] *Pseudodoxia Epidemica.*
[2] Anthropologists apply this word technically to describe an abnormality found in the women of Hottentot Bushmen, especially a tribe called the Bongos.

professors have naturally played their little games with it. For instance, H. L. Mencken being asked by a striptease-girl to suggest a
more dignified term for her profession put forward "ecdysiast," from
Greek *ecdysis*, a shedding or throwing-off, as a snake sheds its outer
skin. I am told that this word is now current among the more high-
minded stripteasers in the United States, indeed according to Mr. Ivor
Brown a Society of Ecdysiasts, Parade and Specialty Dancers has been
formed to protect them against persecution and to defend their rights.[1]

I do not know whether "ioblepharous" can be said to exist in English; I heard it used by a don, by no means "remote and ineffectual,"
but observant of women's make-up, to describe a "violet-lidded" girl.
The Greeks used to paint the eyelids of their female statues blue;
and the adjective was *ioblepharos*.

"Triskaidekaphobia" must have been another scholar's fanciful
formation; it is alleged to mean "fear of Friday the thirteenth," and
would seem to be genuinely useful, for there is no way of describing that
superstition more briefly. Seven syllables, however, have proved too
many for the layman's tongue; and the word remains a donnish jest, as
does "floccipaucinihilipilification," the longest word in the O.E.D.[2]
which is made up of several Latin words meaning "at little" or "at
nothing." The whole conglomeration therefore signifies "the action or
habit of estimating as worthless." No doubt there are many more such
ingenious inventions, which learned men in lighter moments juggle
with as gravely as sealions balancing sticks upon their noses. Long may
they continue to do so, those Dons of Might such as Belloc wrote of,

> *Who shout and bang and roar and bawl*
> *The Absolute across the hall,*
> *Or sail in amply billowing gown*
> *Enormous through the Sacred Town,*
> *Bearing from College to their homes*
> *Deep cargoes of gigantic tomes:*

[1] *Say the Word.*
[2] Thomas Love Peacock used a longer one in *Headlong Hall*—osseocarnisan-
guineoviscericartilaginonervomedullary, thus describing in 51 letters the structure of
the human body. A Dr. Strother beat him by one letter with a word indicating the
composition of the spa waters at Bristol: aequeosalinocalcalinosetaceoalumino-
socupreovitriolic. Perhaps the longest word used in ordinary speech was Mr.
Gladstone's antidisestablishmentarianism.

Dons admirable! Dons of Might!
Uprising on my inward sight
Compact of ancient tales, and port
And sleep—and learning of a sort . . .[1]

APART FROM SUCH jokes as triskaidekaphobia, the joining-together of Greek elements has provided scores of words which we could hardly do without—chrysanthemum (gold + flower), cosmopolitan (world + citizen), phosphorous (light + bearer), panorama (all + view), heliotrope (sun + turning), chlorophyll (light green + leaf), pachyderm (thick + skin), xenophilism (foreigner + liking), logorrhoea (word + flow), photography (light + writing), telephone (far-off voice), helicopter (spiral + wing). Even your thermometer is named in Greek (heat-measurer); and the mercury inside it is so-called after the swift God who bore Zeus' messages and wore the wings upon his heels. And when you ask for the cereal at breakfast you are paying your respects to Ceres, the goddess of corn.

WE HAVE TAKEN a lot of words from mythology, naturally enough; and we have made some strange uses of them. During the late war, when suddenly at dusk the air became filled with a sad discordant mooing, it occurred to me that we could hardly have chosen a more inept name for the instruments which were making the noise.

"The name of those fabulous animals (pagan, I regret to say) who used to sing in the water has quite escaped me." Mr. George Chuzzlewit suggested "Swans." "No," said Mr. Pecksniff. "Not swans. Very like swans, too. Thank you." The nephew . . . propounded "Oysters." "No," said Mr. Pecksniff . . . "nor oysters. But by no means unlike oysters; a very excellent idea; thank you, my dear sir, very much. Wait! Sirens! Dear me! Sirens, of course." [2]

Odysseus made his men put wax in their ears, and bind him tightly to the mast, when they rowed past the Sirens' isle; so he alone of men was able to listen to the singing and yet survive; for the voice of a Siren (a creature part woman, part bird) was so sweet that sailors, unable to resist it, were lured ashore to their doom. But our wartime sirens

[1] *Lines to a Don.*
[2] Dickens: *Martin Chuzzlewit.*

played a tune such as the old cow died of; they had a blood-chilling
effect upon some people, whose hearts, as they put it, "missed a beat"
whenever they heard them. Before long London learned to shrug its
shoulders at them in its own fatalistic way; and in the midst of their
cacophony, on New Year's Eve, 1940, I heard a Cockney singing to a
well-known hymn-tune:

> *Sireens, sireens, sireens,*
> *Always bloody well sireens . . .*

The long "e" was no innovation. Kipling wrote during the First World
War of

> *Five maned trawlers with their sireens blowing*
> *Heading the whole review.*
> *"Sweep completed in the fairway.*
> *No more mines remain.*
> *'Sent back Unity, Claribel, Assyrian, Stormcock*
> *and Golden Gain."* [1]

MR. PECKSNIFF no doubt would have called a sylph a fabulous animal.
Mr. Crummles saw the likeness of one in the unrivalled Miss Petowker
of the Theatre Royal, Drury Lane. "She's the only sylph *I* ever saw,
who could stand upon one leg, and play the tambourine on her other
knee, *like* a sylph." [2] Today the word is most often used in the sense of
"a successful product of slimming." Indeed nowadays we treat these airy
spirits of the woodland and the waters with scant respect. Fishermen
deceive trout with tiny hanks of draggled feathers which they call
nymphs; and outside the company of anglers the word is more likely to
be heard in the form of "nymphet," meaning an adolescent wanton,
such as Lolita. Mr. Nabokov did not, however, invent "nymphet."
Drummond of Hawthornden used it for a little nymph, and so did
Michael Drayton in *Poly-Olbion:*

> *Of the nymphets sporting there*
> *In Wyrrall, and in Delamere.*

"Nymphomania" was invented about 1800 for "morbid and uncon-

[1] *Mine Sweepers.*
[2] *Nicholas Nickleby.*

trollable sexual desire" on the part of a woman. Once a purely medical term, it is now become a catty-cocktail-party word, used by envious women to describe others more ardent or acquiescent than themselves. Nympholepsy is a very different kind of frenzy, which only poets can really understand. The word comes from the idea that a man who beholds a nymph falls into a kind of hopeless rapture; hence it implies the desire of the unattainable, and the despair that goes therewith.

"VOLCANO" FROM VULCAN whose fiery forge lay in the heart of the mountains; "martial" and the month of March from Mars the God of War; "erotic" from Eros,—and also that booksellers' word for dirty books,—I read an advertisement the other day, "WANTED, Any high-class Erotica"; "fauna" from the woodland God Faunus and "flora" from his sister; "jovial" from Jove whom we also swear by: through these and many other words the Gods of Greece and Rome speak to us still. "Hermaphrodite" comes from the name of that unfortunate son of Hermes and Aphrodite who went for a swim in a fountain and found himself merging into the nymph Salmacis who lived there, so that the two bodies became one. Sailors use the word figuratively—"hermaphrodite brig" [1]—and Kipling called his Royal Marine "a kind of giddy Harumfrodite." As for Aphrodite herself:

> *Clothed round with the world's desire as with*
> *raiment, and fair as the foam,*
> *And fleeter than kindled fire, and a goddess,*
> *and mother of Rome—*

she who

> *Came flushed from the full-flushed wave, and*
> *imperial, her foot on the sea.*
> *And the wonderful waters knew her, the winds*
> *and the viewless ways,*
> *And the roses grew rosier, and bluer the sea-blue*
> *stream of the bays—*[2]

I must say it seems to me that we do dishonour to the language, and demonstrate a streak of shabbiness in ourselves, when we take the

---

[1] Square-rigged forward, schooner-rigged aft.
[2] Swinburne: *Hymn to Proserpine.*

Goddess' name in vain for the contemptible pills and potions and
powdered beetles which grubby backstreet chemists sell: and describe
these fraudulent philtres as—the Goddess forgive us—aphrodisiacs!

WE MAKE PARTIAL AMENDS for this affront if it is true that the word
April is named after Aphro (a pet-form of Aphrodite) because it is the
love-month, at any rate in Mediterranean lands. Even here, where the
wind blows so chilly in the spring, we have a saying that when the little leaves on the elms are the size of a mouse's ears, then is the time for
love; and the opening elm-leaves are just so big when the cuckoo comes.
April is a lovely word, and it dances in our poetry—Aprille with his
shoures sote, proud-pied April, and best of all:

> He came all so still
> Where His mother was,
> As dew in April
> That falleth on the grass.[1]

OF ALL THE words the Gods have given us, the strangest is surely "panic."
I think it is a terrifying word. It comes from *to panikon deima*, "fear
caused by Pan" and an important part of the meaning is that the fear
is *groundless*. Unexplained noises heard by night in the mountains; or
deep in the woodlands, a tiny sigh on the windless air, a scuffle among
dead leaves where neither bird nor beast was to be seen,—these were
the sounds attributed to Pan, and the irrational terror caused by them
is named after him. We use the word loosely nowadays; one even hears
of panic on the Stock Exchange. But true panic is a very different
thing, it is fear of something universal and protean, which inhabits the
darkness, the air, the trees, the sky, the earth herself. We use some long
Greek names for it, such as claustrophobia if it happens in an enclosed
space, and agoraphobia if it happens in the open, and for the sake of
completeness phobophobia which is simply fear of being afraid; but
whatever we call it, this is the same ancient "panic" the Greeks knew.
I have experienced it twice in my life. The first time was at nightfall in
a wilderness. All about me there fell an unnatural silence; and suddenly
this very silence grew loud, and began to shriek at me. I knew then what
the author of Deuteronomy meant by a "howling wilderness"; I cow-

[1] *I Sing of a Maiden.*

ered in the face of its howling and I should have fled but there was nowhere to flee to, I should have hid but there was not a tree nor a hole in the ground to give me refuge.

The second time was during the war. I was told to do a weather flight, which involved going very high, and as I was at that time normally a pilot of old submarine-hunting Swordfish I had never had occasion to fly really high before. I went up, up, up alone into the deepening blue, until the Spitfire seemed to hang upon her propeller in a remote vast emptiness, and suddenly an awful fear of the loneliness seized me, and with it a painful longing for the earth and homely things. I thought I should go mad if I stayed up there any longer; I eased the stick forward a shade and then Pan took charge altogether. I pressed it hard till the aeroplane plunged like a bronco, the engine revved and roared, the wings began to scream, and the blessed, blessed earth rushed up at me brown and green and dirty-looking but oh! so beautiful in contrast with that cold blue uninhabited sky.

A WORD I find sinister in a different fashion is the naturalists' term for a caterpillar: "larva," which comes from Latin, in which language it has an uncomfortable, spine-chilling, prickling-at-the-back-of-the-neck connotation. It means the walking spirit of a dead person, but carries the implication that the unresting dead one is in pursuit of the living. Because such a spirit is faceless, the word in Latin acquired the additional meaning of "a mask."

By a most daring fancy, our old naturalists adopted it as the scientific name for a caterpillar; because such a creature wears a disguise, the future insect is not recognisable in the present grub, its form is a "mask" which will one day be cast off. The name dates, of course, from the days before science and the humanities set themselves at odds; a good natural historian was generally a fair classical scholar, and he used the classics to make his communications concerning science more vivid, imaginative, logical and accurate. So science and poetry coexisted,—the use of "larva" for a caterpillar, and of "pupa" for the next metamorphosis, is a truly poetic employment of words. The great naturalist Linnaeus was the first to use "pupa" in this sense, in 1758. It is simply the Latin word for girl-child, hence for a doll; and Linnaeus' adoption of it was a stroke of genius, as you will realise if you look at the underside of a moth's pupa and see the shape of its face, eyes and embryonic wings like little arms sedately crossed in front of its body, all wrapped as if in swaddling-clothes which emphasise its likeness to a doll. Other words from the Latin *pupa* or French *poupée* are puppy (as it were a toy dog, a dog-doll) and pupil, in both senses,— that of the eye is so called because of the tiny image reflected there. From *poupette*, a baby doll, we get puppet and also poppet, the term of endearment.

BECAUSE THEY ARE the creatures of our fallible minds, words owe their existence as often to errors, superstitions, confusions and sheer ignorance as they do to our imagination, sharp eyes, keen ears, affections, prejudices, sense of fun, irony or any other of the attributes of this thinking reed, as Pascal described man.

"Hysteria" for example arises out of a medical misconception. Because women were more liable to acute and dramatic emotional disturbances than men, the doctors came to the conclusion that these vapours must be due to the faulty functioning of some organ which men hadn't got. They decided this could be none other than the uterus; and so "hysteria" gets its name from Greek *hustera*, the womb.

From a medical superstition of the Middle Ages comes the name of a greenish stone which was said to give relief to the pains of colic, especially those which occurred just under the short ribs, or near the groin. For this reason the Spanish doctors called this stone *piedra de ijada*, the stone of the side. Thence by ellipsis and mispronunciation we get our word "jade."

Another superstitious derivation is that of "sinister." The Latin word means "on the left" and the augurs who sought to predict events believed that omens, etc. observed on the left-hand side were unfavourable, wherefore the word gets its uncomfortable meaning.

Careless pronunciation, the running together of syllables, and our typically English habit of mumbling, combined with ignorance of a word's true meaning and contempt for anything we do not understand, have occasionally enriched the language by accident. "Termagant," for instance, is a corruption of Tervagant or Trivigant, a noisy knockabout character who appeared in the old morality plays, where he was described as "a Mohammedan deity." A similar corruption gave us "mammet," an image or puppet (now obsolete but familiar in Shakespeare). It derives from the belief that Mahomet was worshipped by his followers. So did we demonstrate our remarkable ignorance concerning the faith which affirms unequivocally: "There is no God but God."

"Ragman rolls" were certain deeds, documents, schedules, catalogues, etc. written upon rolls of parchment, and in particular they were the instruments of homage done by the Spanish nobles to King Edward the First. Slovenly speech turned this into "rigmarole," an excellent word by which we still express our disapproval of legal documents.

Often enough our dislike of foreign pronunciations goes hand in hand with our ignorance; and then perhaps there is born such a word as "nincompoop," possibly from *non compos mentis,* or "dandelion," the happiest of accidents, for whereas *dent-de-lion* described but one not very noticeable characteristic of the plant, its notched leaves, "dandelion" contrives to pack into its nine letters a complete and vivid description of the dandy flower, the show-off, the shaggy-one, golden-maned, bold as a lion and so on.

Another flower-name, "rosemary," provides an even better example of our English way with words. Being partly maritime, the herb was given the Latin name *ros marinus,* "sea-dew." Pleasant enough,—but that *ros* offered a temptation which the English can rarely resist, to make "rose" out of any syllable that sounds remotely like it, while *marinus* naturally suggested "Mary," another name we love. So we dedicated the herb to the Virgin, as it were, and in doing so twisted the Latin out of all semblance of its meaning. Who cares? We made a name for the homely herb that aptly matches it, that has endearing associations, and that is most perfectly suited to our tongue:

> *For you there's rosemary and rue; these keep*
> *Seeming and savour all the winter long.*[1]

The learned would perhaps describe the process which gave us "dandelion" as folk-etymology, that is to say "the popular perversion of a form of words in order to render it apparently significant." [2] I am always a bit suspicious about any expression or concept involving the word "folk," partly because I find it so often associated with the ponderous, patronising and intellectual approach to country people ("folk-speech," "folk-customs," even, ye Gods, "folk-psychology," which, you

[1] *The Winter's Tale.*
[2] O.E.D.

have probably guessed, is a word invented by the *Herrenvolk* themselves, *völkerpsychologie*) and partly of course because of its nauseous
application to fairies: the Little Folk. I have even read a solemn assertion that "foxglove" was originally "folks' glove," fairies' glove,
which is precisely the sort of piffle folk-lorists are apt to fall for.

FROM TIME TO TIME in this book we shall have occasion to take note
of words which, quite clearly, have been made by poets. The poets may
have been individuals, learned or simple but possessed of the seeing
eye; or possibly a whole series of imaginations have worked upon a
word, polishing it bright as a pebble that has been in the stream for a
couple of hundred years. However it happened, nobody can deny the
poetry of "dandelion"; nor of "comet," which perhaps occurs to me
because it too possesses a flaming mane! *Komē* is Greek for hair; *aster
komētes* was a long-haired star; hence via Latin, Old French *comète*
for the heavenly body with its hair streaming in the firmament which
appears on the Bayeux tapestry. Here is a good example of the pleasure
you can get from this hobby of investigating words. "Comet" becomes
a word of great splendour when you know its derivation; and whenever
you meet with it, especially in poetry, it will "mean more" to you because the image which it calls up in your mind will be more vivid and
complete,—

> *Incens'd with indignation Satan stood*
> *Unterrifi'd, and like a comet burn'd*
> *That fires the length of Ophiucus huge*
> *In th' arctic sky, and from his horrid hair*
> *Shakes pestilence and war.*[1]

Milton's superb Satan is awesome and terrible and possessed of majesty, because the poet knows that if you allow yourself to think of
God's adversary otherwise, you detract from the glory of God. Notice
"incens'd," meaning "set on fire" in the literal sense; not just annoyed!
And notice "horrid," bearing its older meaning of rough, bristling,
shaggy. In fact, Satan's mane of fire streamed out behind him like
that of Halley's Comet in 1066!

[1] Milton: *Paradise Lost.*

CHAPTER 10

From the Heart of England

I T WAS SURELY a poet coining words in sport who hit on "skin-flint" some time during the 17th century.

He first of all told someone else's wife,
For a farthing she'd skin a flint and spoil a knife
Worth sixpence skinning it.

So Edward Thomas imagined his *Lob,* the Puckish incarnate spirit of England, word-making as he wandered to and fro through the country-side. He it was, according to Thomas, who christened the wren Jenny Pooter, and the wild clematis Traveller's Joy; and he who said of that same niggard housewife that "She had a face as long as a wet week." "Skinflint" uses metaphor brilliantly to achieve its ironic end; as in-deed does "cheeseparing" also, [1] for it even conjures a mental picture of the hunk of nearly-petrified mousetrap which most readily lends itself to being pared. I like all such words which seem to have sprung from the rich and comic imagination of Englishmen; and I was lucky enough to grow up within hearing of plenty, having been born in a part of the English countryside where the people used lively and traditional idiom without any feeling that it was old. Throughout my boyhood I was somewhat bilingual. From my parents I had the conventional English of their kind, but from a Gloucestershire nanny, some farm-boys, some poaching ragamuffins, and the back-alley kids of my native country town I picked up the older speech and the words that do not come by book-learning. The earliest I can remember is "tosty-ball" and it brings back the smell of the cowslips and the shine of the sun as I sat on a green bank and learned to make a cowslip-ball, when I was three or four. It is one of those words which inhabit that strange twilight of understanding in which the very old and the very young can meet and

---

[1] Likewise "chawbacon," a word almost Hogarthian in the strength of its caricature.

communicate with one another,—where both describe a tea-kettle as "shooky," guelder-roses as "whissun-bosses," a piece of sore, ragged skin at the quick of a nail as a "backfriend," and where "sleepydust" is something which they have in common. "Chobblings" is another such word. My old nanny meant by it "pulped fragments, as of apples chewed and ejected by rats." It was from her that I learned the apt children's name for the seed-capsules of the mallow, or the larger ones of the hollyhock. "Cheeses," we would call them, and indeed they were just the shape of a Double Gloster. "Chusha-wagga," by the way, was our term for the pale cheese made from skim-milk, and we sang a rhyme about it which ran:

> *Two pints of milk and three of slobber.*
> *Fire wunt fret it,*
> *Water wunt wet it,*
> *Knife wunt cut it,*
> *Dog barks behind the door*
> *Cos a' cawnt yut it.*

Cheese came into many of our sayings. For some reason which I shall never understand we spoke of the first crisp little leaves on the hawthorn as "bread and cheese." And the yellowhammer sang to us in springtime

A little bit o' bread an' *no* cheese

—as he does to me still.

Our quaintest phrase of all described the effect when reflected sunlight or moonlight was thrown on to the ceiling from the surface of, say, water in a bowl, or a looking-glass. We called it "Jack-a-making-pancakes," with the happy and novel imagery which springs from the clear sight only of children or of poets.

BY THE TIME I was ten the little boys of the Tewkesbury alleys had become my birdsnesting companions and mentors; and my ready tongue had learned from them scores of words and phrases which I instinctively preferred to their politer equivalents; moreover I pronounced them in the proper way, e.g. "assudbackuds" for hind-before, "werret" for worried, "goodsarted" for good quality, "furderafild" for farther off. To the utter dismay of my parents, the whole shape and

pattern of my speech became for a while that of rural Gloucestershire.
If I did not actually conjugate the negative present tense of "to be"

> I byunt
> Thee bissunt
> 'E yunt

at any rate my possessive pronouns were "hisn," "ourn," "yourn,"
"hern." I'd say "on" for "of," a time-honoured usage which perhaps
our emigrants took with them to America,—" 'Do you know who made
you?' 'Nobody as I knows on,' said the child . . . 'I 'spect I grow'd.' " [1]
Then I used "shut on" for rid of and "smart" for good—"I be
feeling smartish." For "every other day" I would say "every otheren
day" and for "next to" I would say "anenst" (but so did Ben Jonson in
The Alchemist). I used the old past participle "boughten"—of, say, a
cake. A fire was a "blizzy," to put it out was to "dowt" it, "to becall"
meant to berate, a "misword" was an unkind one, and a clout on the
head would make me "swimey," with a long "i." For all I know I may
even have learned to employ the equivocal word "middling" with a
precise regard for its nuances of meaning, when "very middling" means
extremely ill but "pretty middling" is fairly well considering.

I LOST my Gloucestershire accent, and the manners of speech which
went with it, when I was sent away to school; but no sooner had I left
school than I began to acquire yet another set of words, those of field
and farmyard, through being articled to a country auctioneer. All this
was great good luck for me, and though I can no longer quite naturally
slip back into the rough speech of the West Midlands, I have cherished
its rhythms, its sayings and its dialect as part of my heritage. Even to
write the words down is to bring back boyhood. The "miskin," for instance, sometimes called "mixen," was the dung-heap, tepid within,
where I grubbed with bare hands for the little red worms which are best
for roach-fishing. "Beestings" meant the first milk to come from a cow
after her calf had been born. A "shuppick" was a pitchfork,—you need
a practised eye to see that the word is simply "sheaf-pike." A "stank"
was a temporary dam in the brook, which made the cows a drinking-
place in dry weather.

[1] Harriet Beecher Stowe: *Uncle Tom's Cabin*

"Squitch" was couch-grass, and a "squitch-fire" was a bonfire of it. The word is a corruption of "quick," which we also use for the haw-thorn. It refers, not to rapid growth, but to tenacity of life; in fact we use it just as the Apostles' Creed uses it, in that phrase which had a certain strangeness when as children we had to learn the Creed by heart: "From thence he shall come to judge the quick and the dead." We had to be told that it meant "living"; but later we met with the same usage in *quick*silver and *quick*sand. The *quick*thorn is so-called because it is deathless and ineradicable. Cut it, plough it, dig it, let the beasts graze it down to the very "quick," yet it will spring again as soon as the husbandman's back is turned. It once composed the forest floor of England, and if some plague were to wipe out all Englishmen it would do so again, marching out from the hedges to fill the fields be-tween them, splitting open the tarmac roads, butting its way through the floors of the empty houses, toppling over the decaying furniture within them . . .

"Quick" comes from Old English *cwic*, which is akin to Latin *vivus* and Greek *bios*. "Wick" is another version of it, current in some parts of England. A little to the north of where I live they use the expression "wick as a cricket," meaning lively.

"DAGS" WERE the elf-locks in a sheep's wool, matted with mud and ex-crement; "dagging" was the job of cutting them off,—in Australia now-adays they have dagging-machines. The straw in the barn was tied into "boltings." Four of them made up a "thrave." "Sockage," which I now recognise as "soakage," was liquid manure; but save when we referred to artificial fertilizers we never used the word manure, which originally meant "to work with the hands,"—hence to cultivate, and hence to enrich the soil. We preferred the old Scandinavian "muck" which went so well in the saying "Where there's muck there's money." Incidentally Francis Bacon, whom one would not expect to use such a word, was the originator of the proverb "Money is like muck, not good unless it be spread." [1]

BEFORE I WAS seventeen I was making out the sale catalogues of what we described as Live and Dead Farming Stock,—an odd expression, but

---

[1] *Essays* 15 *"Of Seditions and Troubles."*

the O.E.D. allows that "dead" can be applied to things naturally without life as well as to things that have been alive; and of course we all speak of a Dead End.—In my village some time ago there was a notice-board which said: "DEAD END—to River, Inn and Church"; but the parson protested, and it was taken down.—The dead Farming Stock which I used to catalogue would include such items as a seven-tine scuffle, a set of ducksfoot drags, a swath turner, a rick borer, a corn kibbler, a two-shear skim, a heel rake and a bouting plough; but the list of live-stock would perhaps have puzzled a townsman even more, for example:

Lot   9. Heifer in milk and in calf, served 22nd March
Lot 10. Her lug teat
Lot 11. Half-legged gelding "Prince"
Lot 12. Two Gloster Spot hilts
Lot 13. Six hoggets . . .

"Lug teat" is an expressive term for the demanding calf that feeds fat from its mother. "Prince" is called "half-legged" because his build is betwixt and between the hack or hunter with its fine legs and the cart-horse with its shaggy ones. The hilts (in some parts called gilts) are young sows, and the hoggets, though our townsman might suppose them to be little pigs, are yearling sheep. Other words for a sheep, according to its age and sex, are teg, theave, wether, and chilver . . . Here, indeed, is a whole vocabulary of farm-words which, if they haven't "been in England as long as dove and daw," [1] have at least been here as long as the parish church with its Norman Tower. For instance, when the farmer kills a pig and his wife prepares to cook the appetising odds-and-ends (for it's said there's nothing you can't eat, save the squeal), then she is likely to use some terms which go back to the 12th or 13th centuries; e.g. "haslet" and "chitterlings." The latter is first recorded in 1280: a manuscript tells of women quarrelling as they wash the "inwards" or "chitterlings" in a stream. The word has such an agreeable sound that if it were not associated with a pig's tripes it might well be used as a term of endearment. "Haslet," or as we call it "aslet" with a long "a," is a collective term for the pig's "fry"—the liver, heart, etc. which is also spoken of as the "nightcap" or "Tom-hodge." [2] The

[1] Edward Thomas: *Lob.*
[2] The equivalent in the case of a sheep is the "pluck"; of a calf, the "gathering."

thin membrane or diaphragm in which the farmer's wife wraps up her faggots is known as the "apron." The fatty lining of the stomach, which is rendered down into lard, is the "leaf"; and when all the lard has been melted off it the residue is called "scratchums" or "scratchings." Frugal cottage-wives used to make a special kind of cake to use up the scratchums; and indeed you can read a history of hard-living and rural poverty in some of these terms concerning the parts of the pig; for even the fat which comes off the now despised chitterlings has no less than two West Midland words to describe it: we call it "mudgin," or sometimes "tippit," as we choose. We even have a name for the ears, nose and tail, pickled together. They are called "souse."

SURELY THERE IS a distinctive homespun character about these country words. They are down-to-earth, inelegant, yet wonderfully expressive: "moithered," for instance, which still gives me a better idea of sheer bewilderment than "muddled"; "scrawny," [1] a word we use a lot for lean, starveling, desiccated; "shrammed" (starved with cold) and "clammed" (starved with hunger)—note that we use "starved" in both senses; "sorney," for someone who is a little "daffy" or soft. These, and dozens more, I probably heard before I had any words of my own; that old Nurse would have said that I was "nesh" in the sense of delicate, difficult to rear (Chaucer used it so), and she might have added that I was "tissucking" martal bad. You can make your own guess about the derivation of "tissuck"—from Latin *tussis*, a cough? or an illiterate corruption of "phthisical"? or simply echoic of the sound of coughing as, "cagmag," to argue, echoes the harsh voices of neighbours disputing over their garden-fence?

Of course I don't claim all these words for the West Midlands. Many are common to a dozen dialects; and a few of the rough, tough expressions which salted the speech of our people when I was a boy stand now on the fringe of conventional English, if they do not indeed belong to it,—for instance those three lazy words which signify different ways of walking and each of which contains as it were a whole paragraph of criticism and shrewd comment within the space of a few letters: "slummocking," "traipsing," "mooching." The last one always

[1] It is apparently of Scandinavian origin, and is related to that odd word which we meet with in *Lycidas*: "Their lean and flashy songs Grate on their *scrannel* pipes of wretched straw."

has an extra implication of up-to-no-goodness added to its sense of
"skulking": a hint of the "miching," from which word it probably derives—"Marry, this is miching mallecho, it means mischief." [1] Some
other good words of country character, but which I expect are common
currency in most parts of England, are watty- or kecky- for left-handed,
scrabble, gawky, dollop, lashings (perhaps a corruption of lavishing?),
scrambling (makeshift), unked (dismal or lonely), lungeous (rough
in play, especially of young colts or footballers) and brevit, meaning
to pry or prowl or to do both at once, like Michael Drayton's owl,

> *Breviting by night*
> *Under pretence that she was ill of sight.* [2]

Then there's "plim," to swell or fill out, as bacon does in cooking, or the
ears of corn do in a wet July, or a newly-hatched butterfly's wings do
when it begins to spread them. It is related, of course, to "plump" and
"plum," and Hardy uses it in *Tess of the D'Urbervilles*: "Don't that
make your bosom plim?"

"Gallus" is another of these widespread words, splendidly and ag-
gressively Non-U, but as rightfully and naturally a part of the English
language as fish and chips is part of the English diet. It is said to be
a form of "gallows" and it has come into use as an adverb of forcible
emphasis in much the same way as "bloody" has—"gallus bad weather
we be getting."

WE IN Worcestershire, Warwickshire and Gloucestershire have a
score or so of words frequent in our speech, which we believe to be
our own and by which we suppose (perhaps wrongly) we should recognise a man from the heart of England if in London or Timbuctoo we
heard him using them. "Cazulty" (casualty) is a typical one; we use it
as an adjective in its old sense of chancy, precarious or uncertain,—
"There's no tellin' what to be at in such cazulty weather." "Tabber" is
another: "He came a-tabberin' upon my winder"; but here we have
the authority of a prophet, although minor,—Nahum anticipating the
doom of Nineveh writes of maids "tabering upon their breasts."

"Notomise" is a queer one; it means a skeleton, and presumably has
the idea of "anatomize" confusedly mixed up in it. It is rare nowadays;

[1] *Hamlet.*
[2] *Owl.*

but I can remember hearing an old person speaking of someone who looked very thin and ill: "He's nobbut a notomise." Another lively expression with the same meaning, which is still common with us, goes gruesomely: "He's nobbut a waarm'd-up carpse!"

"Caddle" is a word which I haven't met with outside West Midland country speech. It has the affectionate meaning of "to nestle, or want to be petted." I imagine cuddle and caddle are closely related, and that kittle makes up the trio,—Kipling's MacAndrew confessed with shame that he had spied upon

The couples kittlin' in the dark between the funnel stays.[1]

WE HAVE—or had, for only the old men use them now—some peculiar swearwords. "Baggernation-take-it" is perhaps a polite version of "buggeration"; but what can you make of "Gon-sharn-it" and "Gon-shume-it" which I often heard the farm-labourers say when I was a boy? They might have meant "Consign it (to blazes)" or "Consume it (in everlasting fire)" but they seemed to be weightier oaths than that, they were never uttered at random but were provoked by a long series of misfortunes piling up one upon another.

To "buffle" is to stutter; and to "biver" is one of our strangest local words,—it is best defined as "to quiver, as lips do" and it brings to my mind a pale-faced little boy, with red-rimmed eyes and a sloppy mouth, who was cruelly bullied by the bigger boys at the first school I went to. He became so terrified that whenever one of his tormentors approached him his lower lip began to tremble uncontrollably, and continued to do so until he burst into tears. This was "bivering." Now I find the word "bive" in the O.E.D., from Old English *bifian*, to shake or tremble; and this is clearly the same as our "biver," yet the six examples of its use given in the dictionary (beginning with one by King Alfred in 888) are all earlier than 1250. Is it possible that "bive" or "biver" have not reappeared in English writing since then, and that the speech of Worcestershire yokels has kept the word alive for seven centuries?

UP ON THE Cotswolds recently I heard a very rare adjective (though the noun is common enough), "pommel" meaning "rounded and fat"; and

[1] *MacAndrew's Hymn.*

I remembered finding it long ago in *Reynard the Fox* by John Masefield, who for all I know may have picked it up on Cotswold too:

> *A pommle cob came trotting up*
> *Round-bellied as a drinking cup,*
> *Bearing on back a pommle man,*
> *Round-bellied as a drinking can.*

It was the red-faced clergyman from Condicote, and

> *His white hair bobbed above his head*
> *As halos do round clergy dead.*

The jolly word "pommel" comes from Latin *pomellus*, a little apple.
I don't know why Masefield chose to spell it so oddly. The poet Montgomerie used it as a noun for a woman's breasts:

> *With ivory neck and pommells round*
> *And comely interval.*[1]

"FLIM" IS A WORD which we use for limp or pliable; I have no clue to its
derivation. "Scrat" as a verb is obvious, but only in the Midlands have
I heard it used as a noun: "If she 'adn't bin such a scrat they ud all a
bin in the wukkus afore now." "Swink" for to toil or overwork is more
than a thousand years old; it alliterates well with "sweat," and Chaucer
uses it often. But in Gloucestershire it has a quaint past-participle
which I shall always associate with a very fat man whom I met one
hot day as he came out of a hayfield. He was a minor Falstaff, "larding
the lean earth"; down his round red face poured runnels as on a steep
hillside after rain. Like Chaucer's canon, it was "joye for to see him
sweate." His small piggy eyes twinkled though his shoulders sagged, as
he leaned on the gate and said to me:
"I be fair forswunk, I be."

"TEART" (tart, sharp, as of cider or the east wind) is a word which we
also use of pain, and it has so strong an association for me that I can
almost feel the smart if I repeat it. "Peart" on the other hand means
lively, almost perky, though when we say someone is market-peart we
mean that the perkiness is carried to excess. He has been to market and

[1] Alexander Montgomerie: *Bankis of Helicon* (1586).

spent a lot of time in the pub. He is not exactly drunk, but the drink has induced a liveliness which may manifest itself in acrimony, argufying or even in fighting. When we know a man is market-peart we humour him, or give him a wide berth.

"Chat" is fairly well known as a noun meaning a small branch or twig, but we make a verb of it,—we say we are "goin' chattin' " in the same way as "goin' 'oodin',"—chatting means collecting material for kindling, 'ooding of course suggests that bigger branches and logs will be carried home.

To "moot" has two meanings with us: a subject is raised for discussion, an idea is "mooted"; but the pigs, if they haven't got rings in their noses, will go "mooting" with tiresome consequences. I came across this notice not long ago in the *Dean Forest Mercury:*

WARNING TO PIG OWNERS

Notice is hereby given that any pig found running in the Forest and mooting turf will be considered to be insufficiently ringed and may be impounded without further warning.

Deputy Surveyor

The word "mooting" accords well with the wonderfully archaic phraseology which comes pat off the tongues of all who are concerned with common rights. For instance the owners of those mooting pigs were taking advantage of what is called the "common of mast." This is the Foresters' right to turn loose their "hogs and pigs, ringed, levant and couchant," in "time of pannage," which is the time when the acorns fall from the Queen's oak-trees. All the Forest rights are controlled by "Agisters," who in the New Forest still wear uniforms of leaf-green. As well as the right of pasturing stock, there is "the allowance of turbary"—an entitlement to cutting turf for burning—and the "allowance of fuel," a right to go upon "the open wastes and gorsey and furzey grounds of our Lady the Queen" and collect the fallen boughs, dead wood and kindling.

TO THAT VERB "kindle," used in a very different sense, I owe a marvellous revelation which I received at the age of eleven, that Shakespeare was not after all a schoolroom bore, on a par with Julius Cæsar and

Ovid, but had been a boy like me, walking the paths I walked, speaking the same tongue. It happened like this. A touring company gave an open-air performance of *As You Like It* in the grounds of my school. I had never seen Shakespeare played before, and I should much rather have been practising at the nets. Before long, however, a pretty, tomboyish Rosalind had won my heart; and it was she who spoke the words which had such a profound effect on me. "Are you native of this place?" asked Orlando; and with a little curtsy she gaily answered:

As the coney, that you see dwell where she is kindled.

My whole spirit leaped at that! It was as if I were suddenly translated into a secret communion and companionship with this adorable tomboy, with whom I knew I should never have the chance to exchange a word. She called rabbits coneys; and so did I. When they had their little ones, she called it kindling; and so did I. On the strength of having (as it seemed) so much in common with her, I fell in love.

During the ten days or so while this affair possessed me (it was my very first, and I was as melancholy as Jacques) I read the whole of *As You Like It* several times. I walked hand in hand with my Rosalind through the Forest of Arden (which soon became, of course, a sort of Forest of Tewkesbury, the place where *I* was kindled). I imagined myself showing her the badger's sett, the otter's padmarks by the stream, the pair of sparrow-hawks, the coneys.

In time this Rosalind faded from my mind's eye; but Shakespeare remained. I had strayed from *As You Like It* to *A Midsummer Night's Dream* and thence to *Romeo and Juliet* and *Henry the Fifth*, where I was delighted by the line about "hateful docks, rough thistles, *kecksies*, burrs." When we were schoolboys we always used "kecks" or kecksies as a collective noun for all the umbelled flowers at the hedgesides in the spring, as well as for their dry hollow stems which we whistled through in winter. The word has a dry withered sound, which somehow matches them. Not long ago I found it in a poem called *The Idle Flowers* by Robert Bridges, where it clearly means the dry stems, not the umbels:

> *Bugloss and Burdock rank*
> *And prickly Teasel high,*
> *With umbels yellow and white*
> *That come to kexes dry.*

AND SO, as my reading of Shakespeare widened, I was reminded again
and again by some special use of a word or by the familiar rhythm of a
sentence that the man who spoke to me across three and a half centuries had spent a boyhood not twenty-five miles (as the crow flew)
from my own home; had looked with a sharper eye than mine at the
same sort of wild creatures, fished the same streams, delighted in the
same spring flowers, heard the same birdsong, and learned from the lips
of old people the same proverbs and tales.

Whenever I read the plays, I am reminded of it still. Shylock talks
of the ewes "eaning" in the very terms of a Cotswold shepherd. When
Cleopatra "hoists sail and flies" in the sea-battle it is as if she had "the
breese upon her, like a cow in June." The "breese" is the gadfly that
sets the cattle galloping off with tails in the air. Beatrice in *Much Ado*
is bade to "steal into the pleach'd bower,"—to "pleach," of course, is
our hedge-layer's word for interwine.

In *Coriolanus* and in *Pericles* we find "malkin" (or mawkin) used
in much the same sense as in the West Midlands today—a slattern or
untidy slut, one who looks a "fright," hence a scarecrow. And "doxy"
still means a sweetheart,—"With heigh! the doxy, over the dale." [1] I
have heard an old Warwickshire fellow lamenting his lost youth, and
the doxies at Stratford mop-fairs long ago. At one time the word meant
the good-for-nothing mistress of a rogue and a vagabond: a beggar's bag-
age, in fact. The O.E.D. does not commit itself to a derivation, but
Mr. Partridge in his *Dictionary of Slang* suggests that it may come
from Dutch *docke*, a doll. So for "beggars and doxies," now read "guys
and dolls." *Plus ça change* . . . in these matters. Mr. Justice Shallow
sighed in wistful recollection of the *bona-robas* he had known in his hot
youth at Clement's Inn. Florio's *Italian-English Dictionary* (1578) defined *Buonaroba*: "As we say, good stuffe, that is a good, wholesome,
plum-cheeked wench." And as we say today, or did only yesterday, "A
bit of stuff."

Nowadays, I think, the nearest West Midland equivalent to doxy
is "liebeside," or, as they put it in neighbouring Somerset "lie-by."
"Why, her wad'n never no better'n Squire's lie-by, and now her's
anybody's."

1 *The Winter's Tale.*

"PARLOUS" TURNS UP in Shakespeare several times,—"Thou art in a parlous state, shepherd," [1] just as we might say on Cotswold still. Feste in *Twelfth Night* saying "I shall be shent for speaking to you" uses the very accents of my childhood, when to be "shent" meant to be kept in at school. "Nayword" (by-word), "bemoil" and "crowkeeper" (an odd expression for one who keeps *off* the crows) are Shakespearian words which are still spoken in the countryside round about Stratford. I have heard a cattle-dealer say to his friends after the pub has shut "Shall we shog off?" even as Corporal Nym did; and that proverb of half-humorous resignation, "There's small choice in rotten apples," comes as readily to Warwickshire tongues as it did to Hortensio's. Children call an apple a napple; and also an uncle a nuncle as the Fool did in *Lear*. And a Cotswold man meeting another nowadays might well ask "How a score of ewes now?" (i.e. how much are they selling for?) even as old Shallow asked his Cousin Silence.[2] Our Cotswold farmer would pronounce the word "yows"; but so, I daresay, did Shallow.

Above all, there's the Nurse, whose choice of words and rhythms of speech seem to me exactly the same as my old Nanny's, of whom I have told you. "Tetchy" was one of her favourite words; so was "parlous." She, like Juliet's nurse, would use the word "stint" in its old sense of "break off, stop," even as Chaucer used it when he wrote of the nightingale "that stinteth first when it beginneth sing"—and as I still hear old people use it, in the counties that rub shoulders, not far from Stratford, at the place called the Four Shires Stone.

"BURRU" IS ANOTHER of the old words which survive in our country speech; we use it for a hollow out of the wind, a sheltered place,[3] whence of course comes borough. "Limmel," torn in pieces, is more difficult to derive unless one thinks of piece-meal and then of "limb-from-limb." "Croodle," to cower or crouch down, is to be found in the O.E.D.; so is "dunch," to jog with the elbow; but "craichy," weak, infirm, and shaky, is not recorded there; nor are "dummill," a useless article, and "morum," a clever trick or ingenious device. I cannot offer any suggestion at all concerning the origin of those odd but useful words.

[1] *As You Like It.*
[2] *King Henry IV, Part 2.*
[3] Also as an adjective, sheltered.

THERE IS an adjective which is common within a score of miles round about my native town, but which I have never heard spoken elsewhere. The word is "fritch," and it may be a corruption of "fresh," though it carries a much wider meaning. For it means vain, conceited, though not in a very bad sense,—a girl will tease another one: "You 'a' no call to be so fritch, even if you 'a' got a new frock on!" Fritch means, in fact, a mixture of "pleased with yourself," "looking good and knowing it" and "out for a bit of fun with the boys." It calls to my mind a picture of bright dresses in Whitsun sunshine, and the girls walking on a Sunday afternoon down the Lower Lode lane where for no known reason it was traditional to parade on high days and holidays, an Old Spanish Custom which was nevertheless observed at Tewkesbury in the days of my youth and probably still is, at the season

> *When showers betumble the chestnut spikes*
> *And nestlings fly:*
> *And the little brown nightingale trills his best,*
> *And they sit outside at "The Traveller's Rest,"*
> *And maids come forth sprig-muslin drest . . .* [1]

—or whatever the fashionable material may be.

I can still remember the agreeable surprise which those fritch girls used to occasion us, they were as butterflies come out of hibernation, because during the long winter we had somehow forgotten that so many of them existed, or at any rate that they were so pretty and gay. And they walked with a swing, and threw back their shoulders to show off their breasts, and turned round to laugh at us as they went by. All that meaning is packed into the little word fritch, though I have never heard it furderafild than the Malvern Hills on the one side and the Cotswolds on the other.

"HOYTING WITH the boys" would have been the old folks' phrase, spoken in disapprobation to describe the subsequent actions of the fritch wenches. The verb "hoyt" (or hoit) means, apparently, "to romp inelegantly." Romp, rumple and rampage are first cousins, as it were. "Rampage" is wonderfully expressive, I think: "On the Rampage, Pip, and off the Rampage, Pip; such is Life." [2]

[1] Thomas Hardy: *Weathers.*
[2] Dickens: *Great Expectations.*

Hoyden, "a boisterous noisy girl, a romp" is surely related to "hoit," though the word may also have some kinship with "heathen," originally perhaps a heath-dweller, hence a wild person from wild parts, and a non-Christian by implication.

ANOTHER WORD THAT the older women are apt to apply to the girls who are gay in the spring-time is "giddling." It is nothing to do with "giggling"; it means "flighty, feckless," with a hint of "flirtatious" too. It is always said in disapproval. "You 'a' no call to go along with they giddlin' girls," is what a mother says to her teenage sons, who never take any notice; they go down to the bottom of the Lower Lode lane in the weather the cuckoo likes, and when dusk falls they pair off with the fritch and giddling girls, so that there's a couple kissing and huggling at every stile along the meadows that go by the river towards Deerhurst.

"HUGGLING": a condition which Milton poetically, though as it happened also quite literally, described in the line

Imparadised in one another's arms.

To huggle is a much better word than to hug, better too than "cuddle," despite the O.E.D.'s most endearing definition of that act:

To press or draw close within the arms so as to make warm and cosy.

"Huggle" means rather more than that, especially after dark. I have told elsewhere [1] of the pleasure it gave me to discover this affectionate word in Stubbes' *Anatomie of Abuses* (1583), though his use of it implied puritanic disapprobation. He was complaining of the Rogues and Vagabonds that had become a pest in the countryside; the "Sturdy Beggar" he considered to be the greatest nuisance of them all, and noted that he did not always travel alone. "So long as he hath his pretty pussie to huggle withal, that is the only thing he desireth."

We still use huggle in our common speech; and like Mr. Stubbes, I am afraid, the old people use it especially when they are shocked.— "A-huggling they were bold-as-brass agyunst my gyarden-gyut!" But it is rare in literature, and I have only encountered it twice,—in Stubbes' diatribe, and in *The Ballad of Little Musgrave and Lord Barnard*,

[1] *Come Rain, Come Shine.*

that ingenuous and most sorrowful piece which nobody could resist quoting given half a chance. Lady Barnard, in her Lord's absence, "cast an eye on little Musgrave As bright as the summer sun" and shamelessly confided to him:

> "I have a bower at Bucklesfordbery,
>   Full daintily is it dight.
> If thou wilt wend thither, thou little Musgrave,
>   Thou's lig in my arms all night."

A "little tiny page," however, overheard and betrayed them; galloping hoofbeats startled the lovers out of their bliss. But little Musgrave was the frightened one:

> "Methinks I hear the thresel-cock,
>   Methinks I hear the jay;
> Methinks I hear my Lord Barnard—
>   And I would I were away."

> "Lie still, lie still, thou little Musgrave,
>   And huggell me from the cold;
> 'Tis nothing but a shepherd's boy
>   A-driving his sheep to the fold."

In burst Lord Barnard, whose fury expressed itself in disconcerting fashion:

> He lifted up the coverlet,
>   He lifted up the sheet:
> "How now, how now, thou little Musgrave,
>   Doest thou find my lady sweet?"

> "I find her sweet," quoth little Musgrave,
>   "The more 'tis to my pain.
> I would gladly give three hundred pounds
>   That I were on yonder plain . . ."

As well he might; for Lord Barnard quickly slew him, turned his attention to the lady, "cut her paps from off her breast, Great pity it was to see," and then proceeded straightaway to make arrangements for the obsequies, with a nice regard for social distinction and degree:

"A grave, a grave," Lord Barnard cried,
*   "To put these lovers in;*
But lay my lady on the upper hand
*   For she comes of the better kin."*

A CURIOSITY of English dialect is that of ascribing genders to inanimate things. Which gender seems to be a matter of choice. One would expect a machine to be feminine, and I have heard a labourer say "Her's busted proper" when his binder has broken down. On the other hand I am assured that in some parts of Worcester and Warwick almost every object is regarded as masculine—a spade, a pitchfork, a wheelbarrow, a hat—and the only feminine exceptions are boats, cars, church-bells, fire-engines, railway-trains and cricket-balls! Incidentally, the rules of cricket originally recognised that the ball was feminine and so described her:

> When yᵉ ball is hit up either of yᵉ Strikers may hinder yᵉ catch in his running ground or if she is hit directly across yᵉ wickets yᵉ Other Player may place his body anywhere within yᵉ swing of his Batt so as to hinder yᵉ Bowler from catching her . . .

But as I said, these genders are determined by local taste and opinion; there is no general agreement about them. In parts of Devon, I believe, the use of the feminine gender is so extremely rare that everything living or inanimate is spoken of as "he"—with the sole perverse exception of a Tom-cat.

I HAVE TRIED to give you an idea of the generosity in vocabulary, the richness in metaphor, of the speech which I used to hear at market or in the village pub, some thirty years ago. Max Müller, writing during the 1880s, credited the English farm-labourer with a total of some 300 words—a moron's portion; yet it was this very farm-labourer who handed down to us the words which I have quoted in this chapter. Moreover, he went to church every Sunday, and even if he listened with only half an ear he must have grown familiar with the Collects and the Lessons; through this a kind of glow was shed upon his speech, a reflection of the noblest English other than Shakespeare's that pen ever set down on paper or parchment.

Today that glow is fading or has gone out. However I believe that our country-people still have more words than comparable townfolk have. One evening last summer when I was fishing in our tench-pond three youths from Birmingham, who were camping nearby, came down to try their luck and sat themselves quite close to me. On the other side of me were two young men from the village,—one worked in a garage, the other was a cowman. The evening was still, and the pond is one of the quietest places I know; so I could listen to the talk of the country on my right and of the town on my left. The contrast was astonishing. The Birmingham boys were so poor in language that they had real difficulty both in communicating the simplest idea and in composing any but the simplest sentences. Now and then they would trot out a phrase not of their own composing which seemed to be an echo of the idiotic baby-talk of some pop-song. Otherwise they were utterly lacking in metaphor which might have coloured or given variety to their few score of monosyllables, their dozen or so of disyllables, which in any case were so truncated that they sounded like the grunts and groans and snarls of a primitive tribe. Three four-letter swear-words, pallid as clay, bespattered all their speech. Yet these young men, in their late teens, had spent several years at school, where books of all sorts had been provided for them free and without stint.

The cowman and the village mechanic on the other side of me talked about motor-bikes, cricket, fishing, weather and girls; they not only had an amplitude of conventional words for their ordinary needs, but also a subsidiary vocabulary expressly designed for communicating certain uncommon ideas or unusual experiences,—for example when the midges became tiresome they pulled some branches off a willow and lushed, that is to say they beat about them with green boughs; they would have used the same word for their defensive action during the taking of a wasps' nest. Their minds were well-stocked with old sayings, which they used aptly, and obviously enjoyed: of a mutual friend who was "always late for everything" and who had promised to come fishing but had failed to turn up, one said: "I dessay he's still racin' the snails round his gyardin'." Then they used the word "niflepin" for their fruitless fishing; it means "a pretended occupation, serving as an excuse for idleness." During a spell of silence some small creature scurried about among the reeds, and they described the sound as "fidthering" which means "making a little rustling noise such as that of a mouse or rat moving among straw." They seemed to have a sim-

ple precise word for almost every experience; for when they were dis-
cussing the state of a crop of pears in an orchard they used no less than
four words to describe the condition of ripeness and over-ripeness of
the pears on the different sorts of trees. "Frum" was ripe and in perfect
condition; "mawsey" meant soft and woolly; "sapy" suggested the pears
had gone sodden-like; "roxy" meant they were altogether decayed.
("Daddocky," by the way, also means decayed but is applied only to
rotten wood, e.g. a gatepost; whereas "rasty," although it means "gone
bad," is used specifically for bacon that has been hung too long, so
that the fat is "turning.")

WHERE DO SUCH words come from? Most, I suppose, represent survivals
of ancient words, corrupted perhaps, and kept alive because their syllables seem to have a pleasing aptness to the ideas they are intended
to convey. "Mawsey" *sounds* mushy-rotten, and "frum" has plummy
and plump associations. "Fidthering" of course imitates the rustling
sound as well as echoing the syllables of "feathering," suggestive of the
quietest possible movement,—"quiet," as Dylan Thomas put it, "as a
mouse with gloves." [1] A whole lot of ideas and associations may be
wrapped up in a single word, and we may be aware of some of them
only subconsciously. Now and then a word survives for no obvious reason, its original why and wherefore being long forgotten and its special
associations lost. In an old dictionary of Worcestershire words,[2]
printed in 1893, I came across the word "bull-squitter," defined as follows:

Much talk or fuss about a little matter.

This ante-dates the word which the Army shortened to "bull" [3] during
the later war by a good fifty years; and that word (bullshit) is described in Mr. Eric Partridge's *Dictionary of Slang* as "mostly Australian, 20th century. ?Ex-U.S." Is it possible that the word originated
with us in the form "bull-squitter," was carried out to America or
Australia, lay dormant like a seed in cold ground, and at last when the

[1] *Under Milk Wood.*
[2] Salisbury: *A Glossary of Words and Phrases used in S.E. Worcestershire.* I
have referred to it frequently while writing this chapter.
[3] In this version it has become so respectable as to be used in a House of Commons' debate.

climate was just right for it germinated, blossomed forth, and proliferated wherever there were disgruntled soldiers speaking the English
tongue?

But even if so, the mystery remains why bull-squitter was coined in
the first place as a word meaning "much talk about a little matter."
Why not, for example, cowpat or any one of a dozen expressions one
can think of containing the same unpleasing idea? I can no more suggest a probable reason than I can tell you why "neddy-grinnel" once
seemed to somebody an apt name for a dog-rose briar, and apparently
still seems so to country-people, for I heard a boy using it only the
other day. What it originally meant, what its associations were, what
was the basic idea behind it, nobody knows; yet, at any rate for a little
longer, it endures.

So do we cling to a good many words and phrases which, though
they seem to us perfectly expressive, we should not care to define or
explain to a stranger in the cold light of day. "What bist thee a-loffin
at? I should think thee'dst found a tiddy-'obin's nest and was a-loffin at
the young uns." "Tiddy-'obin" is probably baby-talk for little robin;
and its nest has become legendary in our language, an inexplicable
joke, secret, secure and deep-hidden in the hedgerows of fantasy.

Another bird of our wilder fancy appears in the phrase "A snoffle
for a duck." A busy man, occupied with some mechanical task, will
sometimes answer as follows if you ask him what he is doing and he
thinks you are being unduly inquisitive. "I am making," he will say,
"a snoffle for a duck"—and if this conjures up in your mind a picture
of a little bridle and bit fitted to a quacking duck's beak you will
probably realize that you have been politely snubbed.

Then there is the "skimmington." In this case the word itself is quite
easy to define. It is a rough play got up for the annoyance of an unpopu-
lar person,—or to show disapproval of some disgraceful act. We are too
good mannered to perform skimmingtons nowadays. Samuel Butler,
who was born in the shadow of Bredon Hill, describes one in *Hudibras*;
and the village next to mine, on the slopes of Bredon, had one only
about sixty years ago. There was a procession, an effigy of the unpopu-
lar person was carried, kettles and saucepans were beaten very loudly;
frying-pans were scraped rhythmically with knives; the effigy was burnt.
"Under *particular circumstances*," says one account mysteriously, "*certain articles* of wearing apparel are carried on sticks, after the manner

of flags." What circumstances? What articles? Above all, why skimmington? Only the echoes of our questions come back to us out of the
silent past.

"YOU NICKNAME GOD'S creatures," was one of Hamlet's inexplicable
reproofs to poor Ophelia; and so indeed do we nickname them, "mum-
ruffin" for the long-tailed tit, "vuzpeg" for the hedgehog, "pollywiggle"
for the frog's tadpole, "Jenny Pooter" for the wren, "writing lark" (or
scribbling schoolmaster) for the yellowhammer, "blue Izaak" for the
hedge sparrow. Molehills are "oontitoomps"; owl's pellets—those re-
gurgitated lumps of fur, feathers and bones—are "owluds' quids," the
likeness being to a "quid" of tobacco which a man chews and ultimately spits out. "Pillygrub" is a word which becomes interesting if
you compare it with caterpillar, which comes from Old Norman French
catepelose, a hairy cat. In my part of England old gardeners classify
caterpillars in three degrees. The brown hairy ones are palmer-worms;
all other hairy ones are pillygrubs; all smooth ones are canker-worms.
Joel the son of Pothuel made a similar kind of distinction between
pests when he wrote of a defoliated vineyard. He was not, perhaps, the
most miserable of the Minor Prophets, but the first chapter of his
Book is a very good example of what Dr. Johnson called inspissated
gloom:

> That which the palmer-worm hath left hath the locust eaten; and
> that which the locust hath left hath the cranker-worm eaten; and
> that which the canker-worm hath left hath the caterpillar eaten.
> Awake, ye drunkards, and weep; and howl, all ye drinkers of wine.

AMONG SCORES of delightful flower-names, which our people still prefer
to the ones in the botany books, are Creeping Jenny (Moneywort, also
called Herb Tuppence), Granny's Bonnets (Columbine), True-love-
knot (Herb Paris), Ladies' White Petticoats (Greater Stitchwort),
and Tittle-my-fancy, the little Wild Heartsease. Some of our current
names are older than the oldest Herbals. Gerard writes of the Goat's
Beard:

> It shutteth itselfe at 12 of the clock, and showeth not his face open
> until the next daies Sunne doth make it floure anew, whereupon it
> was called Go to bed at noone.

And indeed the countrymen who were boys when I was a boy demonstrate a blessed continuity by calling it Jack-go-to-bed-at-noon still.

We have a charming term, "gandygoslings," for the Early Purple Orchids, which are supposed to be Shakespeare's "Long purples That liberal shepherds give a grosser name." This grosser name relates to the shape of the roots, which in some orchids resemble testicles; hence the name orchis from Greek *orchis*, which means just that. Ruskin, when this fact dawned upon him, was profoundly shocked, and proposed that we should expunge the word from the dictionaries, and use "Wreathewort" instead. But not even the prim Victorians took much notice of such bashful artiness, and the word "Wreathewort" died a natural death. Goodness knows what Ruskin would have thought of our local name for the wild arum lily, which some call lords-and-ladies and others parson-in-the-pulpit. We call it "priests' pintle," in rude irreverence. Liberal shepherds had a lot to do with naming flowers and herbs in the old days; even lady-smock is not so innocent a term as it sounds. "Smock" used to mean, not only the garment, but the girl inside it; as we might vulgarly say, "a skirt." In the 18th century it was used as a verb—"To Smock and Knock It under the Greenwood Tree" [1] and in Dean Swift's *Polite Conversations:* "You don't smoke, I warrant you, but you smock."

"DWALE" IS A word which you may hear now and then in the speech of old country-people, from whose lips it drops ominously: it is a name for the Deadly Nightshade, or as Gerard called it in his *Herball* the Sleepy Nightshade which "causeth sleep, troubleth the mind, bringeth madness if a few of the berries be taken, but if more be taken they also kill and bring present death." Nightshade is a singularly beautiful, ominous and mysterious word. Were "night" and "shade" really conjoined so aptly in order to suggest the gathering darkness, the Valley of the Shadow? Or is there some prosaic explanation—that the belladonna was so called because it is a shade-loving plant?

"Dwale" is an older name and comes from the Scandinavian, where words resembling it have the meaning of "dead sleep," torpor and trance. It is a sombre syllable, a cross between dole and wail, heavy with doom; but nightshade is a dark word too, fitting for a plant so "furious

[1] D'Urfey: *Pills*, 1719.

and deadly," as Gerard describes it. Sweet music would both words make in the ears of Mr. Pugh, in *Under Milk Wood*. He is sitting opposite Mrs. Pugh, you may remember, and hatred possesses him as he swallows her cold grey cottage-pie. He is reading from the *Lives of the Great Poisoners*, on which he has put a brown paper cover so that she may be persuaded it is a theological work called *Lives of the Great Saints*. Sometimes he fetches out a pencil and underlines a sentence; sometimes he smiles in secret:

> Alone in the hissing laboratory of his wishes, Mr. Pugh minces among bad vats and jeroboams, tiptoes through spinneys of murdering herbs, agony dancing in his crucibles, and mixes especially for Mrs. Pugh a venomous porridge unknown to toxicologists which will scald and viper through her until her ears fall off like figs, her toes grow big and black as balloons, and steam comes screaming out of her navel.

Even John Gerard knew nothing as powerful as that.

I DO NOT pretend to know how our flowers got their old names, but obviously there wasn't a committee at work; an *individual* must have first performed each mystical act of christening. Now and then he was a learned herbalist or natural historian; but more often I think he was an ordinary countryman (perhaps illiterate, perhaps able to twist a scrap of second-hand dog-Latin to his purpose) who happened to possess a "seeing eye" and a quick imagination. When he spoke the name to others, its essential *rightness* caught their fancy; or perhaps, if it was not quite right, they themselves improved on it, sometimes deliberately, sometimes through misunderstanding or mishearing. Hence goldilocks and periwinkle, Solomon's-seal and lady's slipper, mouse-ear chickweed, Jackanapes on horseback (the oxlip), lamb's lettuce and weasel-snout. Hence old man or lad's love (how odd that the herb should be likened to both), spotted cat's ear, viper's bugloss, old man's beard, candytuft. Quaintness, especially if it seems to suggest tenderness or affection, is surely a factor in the survival of some of these old words. Poetic metaphor is another. Unknown, unhonoured poets were responsible for many of our words and more of our familiar sayings,— such words as "dimmit" for twilight, such sayings as "shut of day." Of the weather, especially, we speak as poets do, and wayfaring we call to each other out of the first snowstorm "So the old 'oman be plucking her geese," we cry "The wind be gwun down 'ill" when it backs or veers towards the south, we observe that " 'Tis dabbly weather" amid April showers, or if the day cannot make up its mind we grumble that " 'Tis neither Jim Crow nor Mary-Anne, nor one thing nor t'other." Who were Jim and Mary-Anne? No one knows or cares now; yet we cherish the phrase, as we cherish the old foolish weather-rhymes and such odd expressions as "the sun be a-draarin' up water" when the pale beams strike through a black cloud. We have a turn of phrase for every turn of the weather,—a word, incidentally, which is self-sufficient, so why do we nowadays read in the paper and hear on the wireless the silly expression "weather conditions"? This is a phrase which stinks of bureaucracy, and sounds as if it had been spawned among the lesser clerks in what we monstrously call the Meteorological Office,—how such a title as that ever survived the Premiership of Sir Winston Churchill I cannot imagine! I should have thought he would have insisted upon calling it the Weather Office. "Meteorological" (apart from any possible use it may have as a substitute for the breathalyser) is an ill-chosen word anyhow; it derives ultimately from Greek *meteoron*, something high in the air, and quite wrongly seems to suggest a science concerned with the study of meteorites instead of the rain, the clouds, the temperature, the winds. An associated Greek word, with the sense of "raising high," was used by Hippocrates as a name for the condition of flatulence [1]—a very different kind of wind!

NOW HERE ARE some typical sentences which we (speaking not of meteorology but of weather) are apt to say as we cock an eye at the sky: "Shouldn't 'oonder ef us didden get some wet-slobber ar sommat." "Wet-slobber" is half-snow, half-rain. "With et so muggy-waarm like, shouldn't 'oonder ef we ent a gwun to 'a' tempus." We hardly ever speak of thunder, except with reference to the actual sound; instead of "thunderstorm" we say tempest,—as folks did as long ago as 1530, according to the *O.E.D.*

On a sharp morning we say "It be a bit thin"—perhaps because our clothes feel thin in the cold? A quaint humour inspires many such sayings. "A duck's frost" isn't a frost at all; it means a night of mizzling

[1] Eric Partridge: *Origins.*

rain, such as a duck would enjoy. "It's black over Bill's mother's" is
what a North Worcestershire man says if he anticipates rain, but isn't
quite sure whether we're going to get it. Bill's mother's may be anywhere in the landscape; it's black over there, but the storm may miss
us. How did the saying originate? Was it a favourite saying of one local
character? Was "Bill's mother's" a cottage to the west of him, whence
most of our weather comes? Once again, no one knows.

CHAPTER **11**

A Host of Furious Fancies

There is a class of words called "echoic" in which country-men, children, simpletons and poets especially take delight, those which are formed by imitating natural sounds. Two uncommon examples, which I discussed in the last chapter, are "cagmag" and "fidthering"; but we can find hundreds in ordinary speech,—hullaba-loo, bumblebee, twitter, gargle, splash, squawk, hiccup. "Bubble" is one of the best. "Double, double, toil and trouble, Fire, burn; and, cauldron, bubble," chanted the Witches with obvious glee. They are words which one enjoys saying. "The surge and thunder of the Odys-sey" [1]—"Whistle, and I'll come to you, my Lad." [2]—"Sonorous metal blowing martial sounds." [3] All these are a bit more expressive than ordinary words, because of the echo which underlines their meaning. "I'll give you a walloping!" But "wallop" didn't always mean to beat. "So Sir Ector . . . walloped towards Sir Launcelot," says the *Morte d'Arthur*, in one of its boring accounts of those unutterably boring jousts. The word there means that he galloped, in so far as his great shire horse was able. "Gallop" is the most perfectly echoic of words:

> I sprang to the stirrup, and Joris, and he;
> I galloped, Dirck galloped, we galloped all three.[4]

You can hear every hoof-beat, and what does it matter whether or not you have the faintest idea—I haven't—what was "the good news" which they brought from Ghent to Aix?

I suppose it is likely that most of mankind's first attempts at word-making were of the echoic kind. Primitive tribesmen would surely name a bird or beast from its cry, as a baby does when it calls a dog a

[1] Andrew Lang, *As One that for a Weary Space has Lain.*
[2] Robert Burns.
[3] Milton: *Paradise Lost.*
[4] Robert Browning.

bow-wow, as the aboriginal Australians do when they speak of the kookaburra bird, and as English countrymen do when they call a green woodpecker a yaffle. The cuckoo, of course, *names himself* to a score of different nations as he wings his way from mid-Africa to Northern Europe every spring-time. Long before there was any human speech, he was calling cuckoo; who knows but that one day someone copied him, and there at last was a word!

The owl, I shouldn't mind betting, bears much the same name in the diverse languages of all the regions where he utters his cry by night. In Sanskrit he was called *ulukas*, whence by devious ways our "ululate," to howl.

FOR OBVIOUS REASONS, these "echoic" words go well in poetry:

> *His horse in the silence champed the grasses*
> *Of the forest's ferny floor.*[1]

Nothing could suggest the frightening quality of the silence better than the implication that the cropping of short grass sounded loud in it; and how perfectly the verb "champ" expresses that cropping!

Here is the wind in *The Trees they are so High*, that touching old ballad. Notice that when the wind blows very hard through the trees it is not a continuous, but a broken sound:

> *At the huffle of the gale*
> *Here I toss and cannot sleep:*
> *Whilst my pretty lad is young*
> *And is growing.*

Here is the sound the mill-wheel used to make, when almost every little stream had its corn-mill:

> *See you our little mill that clacks,*
> *So busy by the brook?*
> *She has ground her corn and paid her tax*
> *Ever since Domesday Book.*[2]

And here is Walt Whitman taking a deep breath of the air that came off the prairie and with lungs like bellows blowing it out again:

[1] Walter de la Mare: *The Listeners.*
[2] Kipling: *Puck's Song.*

I sound my barbaric yawp over the roofs of the world.[1]

Of course poets love to play tricks and little games with these echoic words. Edgar Allan Poe was particularly fond of them:

> *Keeping time, time, time,*
> * In a sort of Runic rhyme*
> *To the tintinnabulation that so musically wells*
> *From the bells, bells, bells, bells.*[2]

Tennyson invented his own chime:

> *The mellow lin-lan-lone of evening bells* [3]

and Browning set a couple of instruments playing an air together:

> *Bang—whang—whang, goes the drum, tootle-te-tootle the fife.*[4]

But Chesterton's *Lepanto* is the poem in which we really hear the drums, and the brave trumpets blowing, and the cannon in the distance:

> *Strong gongs groaning as the guns boom far,*
> *Don John of Austria is going to the war,*
> *Stiff flags straining in the night-blasts cold*
> *In the gloom black-purple, in the glint old-gold,*
> *Torchlight crimson on the copper kettle-drums,*
> *Then the tuckets, then the trumpets, then the*
> *   cannon, and he comes . . .*

It is a poem which invites a man to shout it; and indeed Field-Marshal Lord Wavell told [5] of a family he knew who were apt on high days and holidays to recite it in chorus. For my part I shall never as long as I live forget Mr. Robert Speaight reading it at the Cheltenham Literary Festival, and meeting its challenge to use the whole range and power of a splendid voice in the crescendo which ends each of the verses:

[1] *Song of Myself.*
[2] *The Bells.*
[3] *Far-far-away.*
[4] *Up at a Villa—Down in the City.*
[5] *Other Men's Flowers.*

Don John calling through the blast and the eclipse,
Crying with the trumpet, with the trumpet of his lips,
Trumpet that sayeth ha!
    Domino gloria!
Don John of Austria
Is shouting to the ships.

BUT TENNYSON of all the English poets is surely the one who uses onomatopoeia [1] best. He can make you hear (as Virgil could) the voices of small streams,—"Myriads of rivulets hurrying through the lawn." [2] He can strike steel against stone and startle you with its clangour—Sir Bedivere in armour is going between the rocks:

Dry clashed his harness in the icy caves
And barren chasms, and all to left and right
The bare black cliff clanged round him.[3]

He can break a great wave against your ear-drums, and bid you hark to the soft sizzle as in whiteness it dies away,—the army in *Boadicea*

Roar'd as when the roaring breakers boom and blanch on the precipices.

The alliteration helped him there. He confessed that it came to him naturally, he couldn't help it. Nor could Swinburne, obviously, for he sometimes alliterated himself into a sort of poetic somnambulism, in which, while the mind slept, the verses continued to flow forth, sibilant and senseless. On the other hand, no English poet could deny that alliteration was a necessary tool of his trade; and you can judge to what an extent people who read poetry associate it subconsciously with alliteration if you ask a fair sample of your friends to quote you the last line of *Lycidas*. Four out of five are likely to say

Tomorrow to fresh fields, and pastures new.

ALLITERATION, METRE, RHYME: what tricks we play with words!—to say

---

[1] "The use of naturally suggestive words, sentences or forms for rhetorical effect." (*O.E.D.*)
[2] *The Princess.*
[3] *Idylls of the King.*

nothing of anagrams, acrostics, crossword puzzles, puns, palindromes—
in which a sentence reads the same backwards as forwards: "Lewd did
I live, evil I did dwel." What strait-jackets do we squeeze words into,
for fun or for art's sake!—ode, sonnet, rondeau, triolet; stanza, couplet,
quatrain; hexameter, pentameter, iambic! Metre, I have read, may have
had prehistoric origins in the matching of words to the rhythm of the
tribal dance; if so, it is a far cry indeed from these wild orgiastic beginnings to, let us say, the trochaic tetrameter catalectic in which metre,
the most learned tell us, Tennyson wrote his *Locksley Hall*:

> *Better fifty years of Europe than a cycle of Cathay.*

There have been many good poets who have not even known the
names of the metres they wrote in; but Tennyson as it happened was
fascinated by prosody, and he amused himself by fitting the English
words into the old classical forms, for instance *Hendecasyllabics*:

> *O you chorus of indolent reviewers*

which is done to a metre of Catullus.

Of course English poetry, which depends on stressed syllables, cannot easily be matched to a pattern of "longs" and "shorts" such as
formed the basis of Greek and Latin verse. But a good many poets
have tried to do the trick, with varying degrees of success. Coleridge
was the most agile, I think, with his:

> *Trochee trips from long to short ...*
> *Iambics march from short to long:*
> *With a leap and a bound the swift Anapaests throng!*

and again, in imitation of Ovid:

> *In the hexameter rises the fountain's silvery column,*
> *In the pentameter aye falling in melody back.*

Those pentameters!—"Raspberry strawberry jam," we would whisper to
ourselves hungrily, doing prep in the cold classroom, still an hour to
go before the frugal supper! But as for hexameters—"the brave un-
tender hexameters," Humbert Wolfe called them—by the time you had
learned enough Latin verse by heart they became so accustomed that
you could almost shape your common speech into a lame and jogtrot
echo of them, as some people can speak blank verse and as Longfellow

must surely have been able to speak trochaic dimeters by the time he
had written 5600 lines of *Hiawatha*. He cannot, however, be considered one of the world's metrical experts. He loved to torment the
English words by corseting them in alien forms; and lacking the loving
craft of a Tennyson or a Coleridge he inflicted some notable cruelties,
of which one example will suffice:

> *Archly the maiden smiled, and, with eyes overrunning*
> > *with laughter*
> *Said, in a tremulous voice, "Why don't you speak for*
> > *yourself, John?"* [1]

WHAT TRICKS WE PLAY with words indeed! You might think that the
conventions of poetry were strict enough, and the writing of it was
made difficult enough, when the problem was simply to fit the aptest
and the best chosen words into a predetermined pattern of sounds;
without superadding the additional obligation of rhyme. Milton
thought so. In his preface to *Paradise Lost* he spoke of "the troublesome and modern bondage of Rhyming," which he described as "the
invention of a barbarous age, to set off wretched matter and lame
metre." How he would have deplored the antics into which it has led or
tempted some later poets,—Keats rhyming "pants" (the respiratory
kind) with "elephants," Francis Thompson of all people matching
"tankard" to "drank hard," and Byron in *Don Juan* butchering words
to make a rhymester's holiday:

> *What men call gallantry, and gods adultery,*
> *Is much more common where the climate's sultry.*

He cheerfully rhymed "persuaded" with "they did," "prided" with "I
did," and "surpass her" with "Macassar" (the hair oil against which
antimacassars were devised). His best, or his worst, effort in this
direction ran:

> *But—Oh! ye lords of ladies intellectual,*
> *Inform us truly, have they not hen-peck'd you all?*

Byron, of course, had a lot of fun out of these extravagances; but
many a poet in serious mood has lapsed into bathos through striving as

---

[1] *The Courtship of Miles Standish.*

it were against nature to achieve an impossible rhyme. Precise rhyming, whether on the level of Pope or of Cole Porter, is an exercise of much art. Words will not be pushed around, bullied or treated roughly towards this end; and their obstinacy is reinforced by the fact that the property of rhyming, "the consonance of terminal sounds," is one which words have got by accident. That a word x may happen to rhyme with words y and z does not mean there is necessarily an association of ideas,—though certainly on the "love dove skies above" level an association is found quite often. But how about, say, the charming word "verbena"? With hyena, subpoena and semolina it can have little in common! A few words have no rhyme-fellows at all; and a great many possess only one each, to the chagrin of limerick-makers, such as he who with confidence, ingenuity and verve started off as follows:

> *There was a young fellow of Samothrace*
> *Who put half a crown on a mammoth-race . . .*

OF COURSE MILTON's complaint was reasonable enough, since he was thinking in terms of long epic poems. *Paradise Lost* put into rhyme (which incidentally would have involved about 5500 couplets!) would have been as unseemly as a rhymed *Hamlet* would have been ludicrous, —though Shakespeare in the middle of an agonized passage certainly paid his tribute to the power of rhyme when he slipped a sudden unexpected internal one into the blank verse:

> *I should have fatted all the region kites*
> *With this slave's offal: bloody, bawdy villain!*
> *Remorseless, treacherous, lecherous, kindless villain!*

Treacherous, lecherous: how those two words startle and shock us and grip our attention. The power of rhyme is something of a mystery, I think. Memory is jogged by it, of course. Genghis Khan is said to have rhymed the battle-orders which he sent by illiterate despatch-riders to his subordinate commanders, who could not read; the easily remembered rhymes ensured that they were correctly delivered. But there must be much more in this than a matter of mnemonics, to account for the fascination and enchantment which rhyme exercises upon us all our lives. It is a kind of abracadabra—which word itself is a potent rhyme! In our earliest childhood "the cat sat on the mat"; it was never a dog!

We were told our first tales in rhyme: "Bye, baby bunting,[1] Daddy's gone a-hunting." We cherished superstitions about rhymes,—"You're a poet and don't know it!" we cried, when one turned up in speech by accident. Then for luck we had to say the name of a poet. Almost everybody said "Longfellow."

"Rhyming locutions," as they are called, are quite common in the language: we like to say "highways and byways," "fairly and squarely," "snug as a bug in a rug." Simple country people are apt to put warnings in rhyme, which impresses them as ominous and emphatic. ("Marry in May and you'll rue it for aye.") But we seem to think that such jingles are fitting also for Valentines and for fortune-telling, for the messages inside crackers, and for Christmas cards; and for expressing the joy of overflowing hearts,—"Tirra-lirra by the river, sang Sir Lancelot," [2] taking his cue perhaps from the birds which according to Autolycus in *The Winter's Tale* said much the same thing:

> *The lark, that tirra-lirra chants,*
> *With heigh! with heigh! the thrush and the jay,*
> *Are summer songs for me and my aunts,*
> *When we lie tumbling in the hay.*

Weather lore is put into rhyme: "Oak before ash, we shall get a splash; ash before oak, we shall get a soak"; and so of course are witches' spells. I heard plenty of both in my childhood, for that old Nanny I told you of believed every old saw and saying so long as it was in rhyme:

> *Leap Year*
> *Never brings a good sheep year,*

she would declare gravely every fourth spring. Such was the first "poetry" I knew. And old Nanny had a friend who was in a small way of witchcraft, that is to say she would charm away warts or cure a nosebleed or alleviate the pains of sciatica, which she called boneshave; if we asked her nicely she would recite to us some of her spells:

> *Flibberty, gibberty, flasky, flum,*
> *Calafac, tarara, lara, wagra wum.*

[1] It is thought to mean "fat," incidentally.
[2] Tennyson: *The Lady of Shalott*.

It was the rhyme that gave the mumbo-jumbo its authority,—and see how once again, to explain one rhyme I have used another!

THAT "MUMBO-JUMBO" is one of a large number of foolish and fascinating words, such as "hocus-pocus" and "higgledy-piggledy," which give pleasure to the child in us. The etymologists call them "reduplicated words." I cannot see why: "duplicated" is surely what they mean? "Hanky-panky," "hotch-potch," and "hurdy-gurdy" are good examples. "Hurry-scurry" is another, suggestive of wild haste, though perhaps "helter-skelter" is even wilder: "Helter skelter, hang sorrow, care'll kill a cat, up tails all, and a louse for the hangman." [1] Then there is "zig-zag," which sets two vowels in opposition to express the idea of rapid changes of direction. I cannot think of another word which so plainly carries its sense in its sound, without being echoic.

Now and then, this special kind of word-formation seems to bear the implication of contempt, for instance "gewgaw," a gaudy but worthless thing, "tittle-tattle," "chitter-chatter," and "namby-pamby." In other reduplications I think a kind of joke is involved, but it is such a small and simple joke (e.g. tit for tat) that our ponderous friends who associate simple-mindedness with the common people would doubtless describe it as a folk-joke: which itself sounds like a "reduplication." Such jokes are difficult to explain, so it's not surprising that the origins of most of these curiosities are recorded as "obscure." "Kittle-cattle"— which I cannot find in the *O.E.D.*—clearly comes from kittle, to tickle, therefore to puzzle; and so kittle-cattle are creatures difficult to handle, tricky, unsafe to meddle with. "Namby-pamby" is said to come from the name of Nam (pet-form of Ambrose) Phillips, who wrote pastoral poems of a sloppy and ultra-simple kind, upon which Pope wasted much cruel irony, though Dr. Johnson thought them pleasant enough.

The Doctor, by the way, employed an excellent reduplication, probably invented by himself, when speaking of Poll Carmichael, who at one time had a place in his household. "Poll is a stupid slut; I had some hopes of her at first; but when I talked to her tightly and closely, I could make nothing of her; she was *wiggle-waggle*, and I could never persuade her to be categorical." John Aubrey also uses a quaint one, in

[1] Ben Jonson: *Every Man in His Humour.*

his *Brief Lives;* at a time when everything was going ill with him he wrote: "This year all my business and affairs ran kim-kam."

Shakespeare seems to have enjoyed these oddities among words. We find "hurlyburly" in *Macbeth* and "hugger-mugger" in *Hamlet* (it means disorder or confusion); Hotspur described Glendower's old tales of Merlin and Welsh dragons as "skimble-skamble stuff," and Feste pretending to be Sir Topas the curate intoned to poor confined Malvolio, "Leave thy vain bibble-babble." Fluellen in *Henry V* says, "You shall find . . . that there is no tiddle-taddle nor pibble-pabble in Pompey's camp," meaning that there all was done with ceremony and sobriety; no nonsense, no goings-on. Shakespeare obviously thought the Welsh were particularly addicted to this kind of word—perhaps they were—for Parson Evans in *The Merry Wives,* of whom Falstaff complained that he made fritters of English, had his own back when he described the old knight as

> Given to fornications, and to taverns, and sack, and wine, and metheglins,[1] and to drinkings, and swearings, and starings, pribbles and prabbles.

My own favourite is "harum-scarum." It is no more than a rhyming combination based upon hare (by tradition, mad) and scare; but it conjures up a picture, by no means unattractive: "a mighty rattling harem-scarem gentleman." [2] And who can resist that wonderful limerick:

> *There was a young curate of Salisbury*
> *Whose manners were halisbury-scalisbury.*
> *He went about Hampshire*
> *Without any pampshire*
> *Till his Vicar compelled him to walisbury.*[3]

---

[1] A spiced mead, at one time popular in Wales.
[2] Madame D'Arblay: *Diary.*
[3] Anon.

CHAPTER 12

Many Inventions

Y ou see how temptingly the byways beckon in the course of
this quest for words? I was thinking of Dr. Johnson in bearlike play inventing "wiggle-waggle" to describe Poll Carmichael's vacil-
lations,[1] when it occurred to me how very few of our current words
had been invented by known individuals. Shakespeare undoubtedly
coined a good many, but some of them were pretty odd ones (discandy,
incorpse) which survive only in his works. It's likely that he was responsible for "auspicious" [2]—and of course "inauspicious" also, which
on the occasion of its first appearance upon the stage helped to make
an incomparable piece of poetry. Romeo cries out, in the vault beside
Juliet:

> *Here, here, will I remain . . .*
> *And shake the yoke of inauspicious stars*
> *From this world-wearied flesh.*

Surely no other word ever had such a première.

What "invented" words have got into the language and stayed
there, other than the Shakespearian ones? Ever the collector, I began to
gather a few together, beginning with "serendipity" which came about
through Horace Walpole's reading a fairy-tale called *The Three Princes
of Serendip* (an old name for Ceylon) in which the heroes "were always making discoveries, by accidents and sagacity, of things they were
not in quest of." It struck him that there was no noun in English
which described this fortunate faculty; and although it has only a
limited and literary use, his happy invention neatly fills the gap.

T. H. Huxley's invention, "agnostic," is likely to be more enduring.

---

[1] Nobody, as far as I know, has used it since!

[2] From Latin *auspex*, a corruption of *avispex*, a bird-watcher who deduced
omens from their flight. Such soothsayers must have had a high old time at the
migratory seasons, e.g. the Ides of March.

Huxley, who spent most of his later years in fierce controversy with bishops about Darwin and evolution, with Gladstone about the Gadarene swine, and with any Fundamentalists who dared to take him on concerning the literal truth of the Book of Genesis,—Huxley nevertheless grew sick and tired of being described by his opponents as an atheist, which he wasn't. So in 1869 he invented his word "agnostic" (from Greek *agnōstos*, unknowing) as a name for those who like himself could believe in God but were not prepared to deny the possibility of His existence. It offers a refuge for the humble honest doubter, halfway between the dogmatism of the churches and the arrogance of the materialists.

The first known user of a word was not necessarily, of course, the man who invented it; but I think we can assume that Tennyson coined "tip-tilted," which is nowadays a cliché of lovey-dovey novelists in the women's magazines, and has been so overworked that it is almost a vulgarity. But see it fresh as the dayspring in Tennyson's first delightful use of it, in the *Idylls of the King*. Lynette was the fair maiden, who had a mayblossom brow and a cheek of appleblossom, incidentally,

> *Lightly was her slender nose*
> *Tiptilted like the petal of a flower.*

We must give Tennyson credit for another invention, "airy-fairy," though later writers provided the hyphen and somewhat altered the sense. By "airy, fairy Lilian" he meant that she was light and delicate as a fairy; but the modern sense is nearer to "impractical," "highfaluting"—of projects and ideas.

A most ingenious invention, sometimes attributed to Sidney Smith, is "squarson," meaning a man who is both a parson and a squire. "You see, it's like a portmanteau—there are two meanings packed up into one word" (*Through the Looking-Glass*). Squarsons were a peculiar breed—such country clergy as on hunting mornings would hurry through "early service" with boots and spurs just visible beneath the skirt of the cassock! The extraordinary Victorian age, in addition to squarsons, produced squishops; but these were rare.

Lewis Carroll was a great inventor of nonsense-words, many of which ("frabjous" for example) now inhabit the lunatic fringe of the English language. One or two have settled down in our common speech, notably "chortle." It is so familiar and respectable a word that

we are apt to forget that it was one of Carroll's crazy hybridisations,—
"chuckle" crossed with "snort." In the very same verse we find "galum-
phing"—yet another invention. The O.E.D. defines the verb as "to
march on exultingly with irregular bounding movements," but you
must decide for yourself what kind of motion the sound suggests. Here
is the quotation from *Through the Looking-Glass*:

> *One, two! One, two! And through and through*
> *The vorpal blade went snicker-snack!*
> *He left it dead, and with its head*
> *He went galumphing back.*

> *"And hast thou slain the Jabberwock?*
> *Come to my arms, my beamish boy!*
> *O frabjous day! Callooh! Callay!"*
> *He chortled in his joy.*

I suppose we might claim that Swift's "Yahoo" has established itself in the language, in the sense of a degraded or bestial human being.
His even better invention, "Houyhnhnm," the name of the race of
noble horses who ruled the Yahoos, is also to be found in the dictionary, but few people dare to pronounce it and for my part I have never
been able to spell it without looking it up.

The odds against a new word surviving must be longer than those
against a great oak-tree growing from any given acorn. Indeed, for a
word to last even a year or two in the jungle of language the climate
and the season must be just right for it, and still the chances are that
before long some frost of neglect will wither it or some wind of change
blow it into limbo. Disraeli, trying to be clever, made up a verb out of
"guano," the rich manure formed of sea-bird droppings which comes
out of Peru (and which an old farmer of my acquaintance persists in
calling Pruve Iguana). Lady Constance in *Tancred* "guanoed her mind
by reading French novels." We may remember the word as a curiosity,
but it was never viable; and in a specimen-jar in the museum of language it finds its proper place.

For comparison see what has happened in recent years to "robot"
and "gamesmanship." Karel Capek's "robot" was not an invention exactly, for *robota* is a Slav word meaning servile labour; but he gave it
a new significance when he published his novel (later a play) called

R.U.R. in 1923. "Rossum's Universal Robots" were mechanical men, efficient for labour but lacking souls. A degenerate society came to be dependent upon their services; the Robots rose up and destroyed those who had created and exploited them. I should think that by now every civilized language has the word in its dictionaries.

Mr. Stephen Potter's "gamesmanship" recently got away to as good a start as "robot." Within twelve years of the publication of the book of which it forms part of the title,[1] the word is not only current wherever English is spoken but has fathered a whole family of "manship" words, at least one of which, the "brinkmanship" ascribed to the late John Foster Dulles, has been bandied to and fro as a missile in the cold war between Russia and the U.S.A. Long before "gamesmanship" was committed to paper I used to play snooker[2] against Mr. Potter and so had the advantage at a trifling cost of an exposition of what he meant by it. I am proud to have been as it were a flint (though one of many) from which the steel of Mr. Potter's wit struck this spark.

At any rate, it is a happy thought that one may have been in at the birth of a word. Such a claim was made by Lord Chesterfield, the enemy of Dr. Johnson. Everything I know about him suggests that he was a silly fellow, including this assertion of his, that he "assisted at the birth of that most significant word flirtation, which dropped from the most beautiful mouth in the world." Partridge derives it from Early French *fleureter*, to talk sweet nothings, related to *fleurette*, the diminutive of flower. His Lordship may be right, that he was the first man to hear it in English; but "flirt" itself goes back to the 16th century. I came across a delightful old French word, which apparently means the same thing. Cotgrave defines it as follows:

> *Gadrouillette* f. A minx, giggle, flirt, callet, gixie; (a feigned word, applicable to any such cattel).[3]

FROM THIS IDLE pursuit of words invented by individuals I was led on to another. It is a queer kind of immortality that a man gets when posterity takes his name and turns it into common speech. Who today remembers Captain Charles S. Boycott, agent in 1880 for the estates

---

[1] *The Theory and Practice of Gamesmanship or The Art of Winning Games Without Actually Cheating.*

[2] A mysterious word, for nobody knows where the name of this game came from.

[3] *A French and English Dictionary*, 1660.

of Lord Erne in County Mayo? Yet millions of people are using his name daily as I write this, in connexion with a campaign to bring pressure upon a Government whose policies they deplore. The gallant Captain himself would probably have been the last person to suppose that his name would last longer in our minds than those of many politicians, philosophers and poets. All he did was to carry out his master's orders and refuse to reduce the rents; wherefore the Irish simply *withdrew themselves from him*—their labour, their company, their smiles, their good mornings and good nights. Captain Boycott seems to have been a stout-hearted and obstinate man. He imported labourers to gather in his harvest; he had soldiers with muskets standing sentinel over the stooks. But in the end he was broken by the silence, the cold shoulder, the averted glance; and instead of collecting the rents, he fled the country.

Probably he does not deserve his place in the Rogues' Gallery of language, any more than does Dr. Joseph Ignace Guillotin, a humanitarian fellow, who thought it more kindly than hanging to decapitate wrong-doers by means of that typically French concept, a *machin*, called after him "guillotine." But we'll waste no sympathy on Vidkun Quisling of Norway, whose hanging in 1946 gave satisfaction even to the gentlest of patriots, and who lives on in ignominy through the noun "quisling"—one who betrays his country by collaborating with the occupying power. A lesser but long-enduring infamy is the lot of Mr. Elbridge Gerry, Governor of Massachusetts in 1812, who exercised great ingenuity in connexion with the electoral divisions of his State. He drew their boundaries in such a way that his party, although in a minority, was almost certain to win. Upon a map of Essex County these arrangements by a curious accident made a lizard-like pattern.

"A salamander," somebody said.

"A gerrymander," said somebody else.

And so another word was born.

MORE WORTHY AND beneficent characters are commemorated by the "greengage" which good Sir William Gage (*fl.* 1725) imported from France, may heaven reward him; by the watch-chain associated with aldermanic stomachs, called "albert" after the Prince Consort; by the load-line placed for safety upon the hulls of ships, through the efforts of Samuel Plimsoll, M.P.—I don't know whether he also gave his name to the canvas seaside shoes, nor if he did, why; by the type of cab which Mr. J. A. Hansom patented in 1834; by the gumboots nowadays called wellingtons, though they bear little resemblance to the riding boots which the Duke made fashionable; [1] and by the loose overcoat which gets its name from that gallant fellow Lord Raglan, who lost his sword arm at Waterloo and won his Field-Marshal's baton at Inkerman. The Earl of Cardigan, who served under him, fancied on the other hand a woollen jersey or "over-waistcoat," to which he gave his name; and which was perhaps a comfort to him during the bitter Crimean winter.

The "mesmerism" which Herr Doktor Mesmer demonstrated in Vienna about 1775 is nowadays called hypnosis, but we keep his memory alive through the verb "mesmerise,"—though we are apt to apply it loosely to the kind of terror that is induced in a rabbit by a stoat. He must take his place in this very mixed company, with M. Etienne de Silhouette, Mrs. Amelia Bloomer, Count Von Zeppelin, and General Henry Shrapnel (1761–1842) whose name has painful associations for many an old warrior who still carries about in his body some bits of fragmented shell.

Then we have that well-meaning old fool Dr. Bowdler, whose *Family Shakespeare* omitted all the words and phrases which might have brought a blush to a maiden's cheek; hence "to bowdlerise," to expurgate in a squeamish and puritanical way. "To grangerise" commemorates James Granger (*fl.* 1770) who invented the horrible hobby, as it seems to me, of interleaving books and sticking a miscellany of more or less relevant cuttings, portraits etc. upon the blank pages. Some people collect these "grangers"; for my part I love books too well to take pleasure in a good edition turned into a scrapbook by some bored young woman who had nothing better to do than fiddle with scissors and paste.

Although the word has such a limited use, I should like to admit "clerihew" into our collection of "words from persons." It commemorates Edmund Clerihew Bentley's aptitude for writing unscanned rhyming quatrains upon fanciful biographical themes, such as the famous one about Sir Christopher Wren, and my own favourite:

---

[1] Amid the enthusiasm which followed the victory of Waterloo, a hat, a kind of coat, a distinctive style in trousers, a cooking apple and the Sequoia tree (*Wellingtonia*) were also named after the hero.

Alfred de Musset
Used to call his cat Pusset.
His accent was affected.
That was to be expected.

And certainly we must not leave out "spoonerism," indeed we must give it an honoured place, as a light-hearted English equivalent of the Greek word *metathesis*, the transposition of letters and sounds. The Reverend Dr. W. A. Spooner (1844–1930) was Warden of New College, Oxford; and from time to time he delighted both undergraduates and dons with his quaint habit of *lapsus linguae*. He would complain, for example, of a blushing crow when what he meant was a crushing blow; and upon his lips the opening line of a well-known hymn became

Kinquering congs their titles take.

I do not know whether the schoolboys' horse-chestnuts do their titles take from the spoonerism; but we used to call them Kinkering Conks if they became champions at conkers.

"WORDS FROM PEOPLE," "words from places": you may hold such collecting-games to be as profitless as the acquisition of matchbox-tops, which is practised by human magpies who call themselves philluminists, in a horrible mixture of Latin and Greek. Nevertheless, if you would be a Prince of Serendip, "making discoveries by accidents and sagacity" of things you were not in quest of, let your imagination range to and fro for a while among the *places* which have contributed to our speech. Manufacturers and produce are responsible for many of the words—the best currants were grown at Corinth, gin came from Geneva, magnesia was found in the district of that name in Thessaly (whence also "magnet" because of the properties of the rock in which it was found). Damask originally came from Damascus, cambric from Cambrai, calico from Calicut on the Malabar coast of India, worsted from Worstead in Norfolk, and muslin from Mosul in Mesopotamia, while the duffel coat which the Navy made so popular gets its name from a coarse woollen cloth spun at Duffel near Antwerp. But consider by what stranger quirks of circumstance the names of places have given us our words for a victory celebration, a violent sort of abduction, a ball

bowled at cricket, a serpent, a manner of speaking, two sexual per-
versions, two colours and a style of beachwear; thus:

On the 17th of May, 1900, London heard of the relief of long-
besieged Mafeking. The city went mad with disproportionate joy over
what was not, in fact, a very great victory, and the verb "to maffick"
was coined at once. I looked it up in the *O.E.D.*, and serendipity at
once came into play; for I found a quotation from the *Westminster
Gazette* which revealed to me more about the night of Mafeking than
anything else I have read. Frenzied behaviour, wild drunkenness, every
sort of debauchery, may indeed have disgraced the streets; but here,
alas, is a more recognisable portrait of the Englishman in orgiastic
mood:

> The feathers . . . are sold for a penny each to enable "Mafficking"
> revellers to tickle other revellers' noses . . .

THE ABDUCTION IS called after Shanghai, a word which in this sense
carries the added implication that the victim is drugged or coshed,
dragged off to a ship, and forcibly enlisted as a sailor. I should have
thought this practice might just as well have been called "to Ports-
mouth," for our press gangs along the South coast were shanghai-ing
young men by the hundred during the Napoleonic Wars.

"TO YORK?" Surely it was a Yorkshire cricket team, during the 1880s,
that perfected the delivery of this unpleasant sort of ball? The *O.E.D.*
isn't certain; though it gives a selection of quotations concerning the
fate of Tunnicliffe and other famous batsmen. This must be very
puzzling to foreign students, who might reasonably suppose that the
word meant an adherent of the House of York during the Wars of the
Roses.

IT WAS AT Delphi, once known as Pūtho, that Apollo slew an enormous
snake; whence we get our name for the non-poisonous, constricting
monster which Kipling personalised as Kaa, beloved in our boyhood;
and of which, I am suddenly reminded, Hilaire Belloc wrote those two
lines of magnificent inconsequence:

> *I had an Aunt in Yucatan*
> *Who bought a python from a man.*[1]

So works serendipity.

The terse habit of speech comes from Greece also. The people who talked in that "laconic" way were the tough Spartans, who lived in Laconia. About the same time (700 B.C.) as they were acquiring their first fame in war, a passionate girl was writing superb poetry on an island in the Ægean. In one verse she invoked Aphrodite to help her gain the love of a woman, on the strength of which, plus some other tenuous shreds of evidence, it has been assumed that Sappho was homosexual, and so Lesbos, her beautiful island of poets and olives and good wine, gives its name to the wasteful perversion, as it seems to men, which is called "lesbian." Yet nobody knows whether Sappho was sixteen or sixty when she wrote those lines, nor whether it was merely the fashion for the girls of Lesbos to express themselves to each other in extravagant ways—as the Elizabethan young men did, to the confusion of some modern scholars.

Our name for the male perversion, of course, comes from the ancient wicked town in Palestine, Sodom. I have often wondered whether it was sheer ignorance or uncontrollable rage which caused the Marquis of Queensberry to mis-spell this word on the famous visiting-card which he handed to the hall porter of the Albemarle Club. "To Oscar Wilde posing as a somdomite," scrawled the demented Marquis; and with that extraordinary message the whole bleak tragedy began.

Our colours are from Italy, and are named after the brown earths of Siena and Umbria. How beautifully "umber" goes in English poetry,—in *Henry V*, when on the night before Agincourt each side catches sight of "the other's umber'd face" by the light of the campfires; or in these lines from *A Shropshire Lad*:

> *Wenlock Edge was umbered,*
> *And bright was Abdon Burf,*
> *And warm between them slumbered*
> *The smooth green miles of turf;*
> *Until from grass and clover*
> *The upshot beam would fade,*

[1] *The Bad Child's Book of Beasts.*

And England over
Advanced the lofty shade.[1]

BIKINI IS an atoll in the Marshall Islands; and here, soon after the war, the Americans let off some atomic bombs. I suppose the new fashion in exiguous bathing-wear appeared in the shops on Fifth Avenue about the same time as the island came into the news; and perhaps people forgot the black mushroom of smoke, and thought only of the palm-topped atoll, the blue Pacific, maidens basking on the sands. Yet this does not really explain it; the contrast is so remarkable that you might almost think there was a deliberate perversity in the association—of a pretty girl who has practically nothing on, with the elemental fury of nuclear fission, which in a fraction of a second could turn the bright flesh to grey ashes. "How with this rage shall Beauty hold a plea Whose action is no stronger than a flower?" [2] The reasons why a particular word "catches on" and stays in the language are often unknown, and in this case seem particularly mysterious. The mass-psychologists would probably diagnose from it some hidden nuclear neurosis, some secret sickness of our times.

CERTAINLY IT SEEMS as if an element of caprice enters into our word-making and word-choosing now and then. Though I am sometimes awestruck by the beautiful aptness of a word—comet, dandelion!—I am also from time to time bewildered by the currency of another, which may appear inept, ill-chosen and quite irrelevant to the idea it is meant to convey. "Bikini" is one example of this; "Whig" and "Tory" provide two more. How extraordinary that the opposed political parties which ruled or misruled England, turn and turn about, for more than 200 years should have been named respectively after a small band of Scottish insurgents, and after the wild embittered highway robbers of 17th century Ireland. The "Whiggamore" raid was a minor rebellion during which a rabble of Covenanters marched on Edinburgh in 1648. Why "Whiggamore"? Nobody knows. Some say that a "Whiggamaire" was one who "whigged"—beat, drove, urged on—a "mare," hence perhaps a horse-thief and cattle-rustler. This sounds highly improbable. Others say the word was taken from "whig" which

[1] A. E. Housman: *Fancy's Knell.*
[2] Shakespeare: *Sonnet 65.*

means "whey" in Lowland Scots, and was used as a taunt against the
sour-milk faces of the strict Covenanters. Yet others, while agreeing
that "whey" is at the root of it, assert that the association is with the
sour-milk and water which down-and-out tramps lived on during their
wanderings. This sounds improbable too. And in any case, why should
the horse-beaters or the whey-drinkers have given their name to the
rebels who attacked Edinburgh, and why should it then have been
abbreviated and attached to the Party which Dr. Johnson so hated that
he believed the Devil to have been the first Whig?

Likewise with Tory. *Toraidhe* in Irish means a pursuer,—no, a bit
more than a pursuer: "one who dogs your heels with evil intent." [1]
About 1640 the dispossessed Irish, being outlaws and having nothing
more to lose, did as you or I would have done,—took to the roads
and robbed the English settlers whenever they got the chance. They
were variously called bog-trotters, rapparees—a fine name!—and Tories.
About 1680 those people in Britain who wanted to exclude Catholics
from the Succession sought an offensive name for their Royalist, pro-
Papist, anti-Dissenting opponents, and chose the one which was applied to "the most despicable Savages among the wild Irish." [2] The
Tories with equal inconsequence named *their* opponents after the
horse-stealers or disreputable vagabonds of western Scotland. I can
understand that the two factions might wish to apply the most op-
probrious terms to each other; what puzzles me is why both sides so
readily accepted the validity of the nicknames, so that they were soon
declaring passionately from innumerable soap-boxes "I am proud to be
a Tory!" or "I was born a Whig as my father was before me, and I shall
die a Whig, praise be to God!" But who knows that the ordinary suffering individual Englishman did not have something to do with the
currency of these terms; who knows that we do not hear in them, faint
as a mocking echo far, far away, the secret laughter of *The Secret People* in Chesterton's poem?—

*It may be that we are meant to mark with our riot and our rest
God's scorn for all men governing. It may be beer is best.*

---

[1] Assertions that "Tory" derives from Irish *Tor a Ri*, "Come O King," are now
quite discredited.
[2] Roger North: *Examen.*

IT WAS a wise old schoolmaster, crusted as the port he loved, who first
pointed out to me the peculiarity of these nicknames for our political
parties. He was very interested in words, especially if there were problems and paradoxes attached to them. Knowing this, his form would
egg him on at least once a term,—"But *why* are they called Whigs and
Tories, Sir?"—and he would go jogtrotting off on his favourite hobby-
horse, while we congratulated ourselves upon avoiding the instruction
which is as naturally hateful to boys as if it were a tapioca-pudding of
the mind. Meanwhile the old fellow, who knew exactly what he was
doing, was planting unbeknownst to us some seeds of understanding
concerning the fundamentals of English political thought.

He taught me Greek and Latin as well as history, and here again
he showed his predilection for the odd or interesting word. There was
one in particular which we used as bait for him, and which he always
rose at like a trout to the mayfly. We had to choose our moment: just
after he had made one of his time-honoured, sardonic, pedagogic jokes.

"—Wouldn't you admit, Sir, that you were a bit of a cynic?"

"I would not. I enjoy my port too well for that. Diogenes and his
followers were so unwise as to make a virtue of living on bread and
water when they could have had—well, fried red mullet washed down
with an amphora of excellent Lemnian wine. They believed that hap-
piness was only to be achieved by satisfying one's minimum natural
needs in the cheapest and easiest way, and that nothing natural could
be improper or indecent; so they performed all their bodily functions
coram populo. This did not endear them to their neighbours; nor did
their privations lead to a cheerful disposition in themselves. So they
were called *kunikos.* Anybody tell us why?"

We all knew, of course; we had heard all this before; but it was
part of the game that we should pretend not to know until somebody
suggested diffidently:

"Er—would it be anything to do with a dog, Sir?"

"Precisely. From *kuōn;* because they were dog-like, snarlers, currish
ones. And so from *kunikos* we get our "cynic," one who is contemptuous of pleasure and disposed always to find fault,—or if you prefer
Oscar Wilde's definition: "A man who knows the price of everything
and the value of nothing."

I think he delighted to surprise and shock us. It was a way of holding our attention, part of his technique. But it was also an expression of

the anarch that lay hidden behind the façade of pedantry and port, Eton and Magdalen, Catullus (whom he'd translated) and County Cricket (which he'd played). Like a good many of the Classicists I have known since, he deeply mistrusted convention while devotedly serving tradition; and because the public-school conservatism of our young minds appalled him he took every opportunity of giving them a jolt.

"Melancholy," he would say, "that grave and beautiful word. How the poets love it. Keats wrote an Ode about it. Very well: derive it. *Melan*, black, *cholē*—You won't know that one. Gall. Bile. There you are. Melancholy, black bile,—charming."

Among his many and diverting prejudices was one against what he called the sloppy, sentimental and dismal hymns of the C. of E., of which he was a member. So I daresay it was he who told me that the word came originally from Greek *humen*, a membrane, which also meant a bridal song. My own dislike of *Hymns A. & M.* dated from my earliest church-going, when I somehow got it into my head that the book was called *Hymns A. to M.* and so there was another volume, *N. to Z.*, in the offing. My relief when I discovered this to be untrue was considerable. It pleased me at the age of sixteen or so, while singing words of little meaning to a devoutly dolorous tune in School Chapel, to let my imagination fill in the background of this word "hymn"—the white-robed bride in saffron veil and shoes, the singers and the flute-players, the girls and the garlands, the sacrifices to Zeus and to Hera, and the chanting of that strange marriage-song *Hymen O Hymenaee Hymen*, a mysterious phrase whose meaning not even the scholars can guess . . .

SO DID THE young imagination feed on these scraps of lore and learning which the old man with studied carelessness let drop. He had a number of pet words which he could always be relied on to talk about. "Cowslip" was one. He would point out to us, as part of his general theme that things were not always as charming and cosy as they seemed, the derivation of the flower's name, which has nothing to do with the velvety muzzles of cows but refers to their droppings: Old English *slyppe*, slobber or dung, whence also the "slops" which one empties! Having awakened our interest with this piece of "debunking" he would then, by way of counteractive, tell us why he thought the

cowslip was Shakespeare's favourite of all the 170-odd flowers which
he mentioned in his plays; he would read us the exquisite passage from
Cymbeline, where the "mole cinque-spotted" upon Imogen's breast is
likened to the freckles within the corolla of the flower; and we would
have, perhaps, a fleeting glimpse, a momentary understanding, of
Iachimo's sheer wonderment purging his concupiscence, and of Imogen's candlelit loveliness, made lovelier by our imagination of the sweet
defect in it.

So by devious ways he led us to Shakespeare. Each epidemic of
impetigo, which occurred in the rugger-season when we scratched each
other's faces with filthy nails, would prompt him to tell us that the
word "rascal" (Dr. Johnson's favourite synonym for a Whig) may
originally have meant "a scurvy knave," one with a rash (Old French
rasche) upon his skin. And he would quote Shakespeare to show us
the horror in which all skin-diseases used to be held—so that it was
natural to equate a person having a rash with a member of the rabble,
a fellow noted for his low and disreputable living, in fact a rascal.
"Scab" was used in the same way, long before it became part of the
unlovely vocabulary of Trade Unionism. Coriolanus, casting down his
imprecations upon the heads of the loathly and despised mob, asked
the murmurous citizens:

> *What's the matter, you dissentious rogues*
> *That, rubbing the poor itch of your opinion,*
> *Make yourselves scabs?*

He was, I daresay, to be regarded as a Fascist Beast; but nowadays the
workers bandy the nasty epithet among themselves, in the sense of one
who, whatever the rights or the wrongs of the matter, continues to
work while his fellows are on strike.

WHEN MY OLD schoolmaster had addressed a boy as an "oaf," which he
did very often, he would sometimes divert us with the explanation that
the word used to mean an elf's child, a changeling. In *The Merry
Wives of Windsor* it is spelt "ouph." From "changeling" the meaning
extended to include misbegotten, hence uncouth, doltish, a booby; and
so at last a lout such as roused the contempt of Kipling:

The flannelled fools at the wicket or the muddied oafs at the goals.[1]

[1] *The Islanders.*

A long way from elves' children but a pretty fair description, thought our classics master, of the boys at public schools!

"Cretin" was another of his favourite terms of abuse, especially when we were doing Latin Unseen; so it was only fair that in calmer moments he should explain to us how it came about that the French word for a Christian got the meaning of "congenital idiot." The people of Valois and Savoy, apparently, were the first to apply the word to a child who had come into the world without its wits; and in their patois *Chrétien* became *crétin*. A special sort of mental deficiency was endemic in their Alpine valleys; it was associated with goitre, and the idiot-children were particularly horrific, having immense heads and swollen necks, protruding tongues and furrowed foreheads; their intelligence was much lower than that of the brutes. Nevertheless, being human, they must possess immortal souls, which set them utterly apart from the brutes. So the good peasants reasoned. And in pity and tenderness they gave to the veriest monster the name which was an affirmation of immortality; for having been baptised the creature was at least *un chrétien*, and in due course would inherit the Kingdom of Heaven.

"—An assumption," my old schoolmaster would say, dropping for a moment his sardonic manner, "which I find most pitiful and brave."

CHAPTER 13

Some Monsters and Mysteries

T HERE MUST BE hundreds of words of which the known origins, at first sight, appear as wildly improbable as that of "cretin." The derivation of "fornication" is one that I *didn't* learn about at school. It comes from a Latin word meaning an architectural arch. The lowest (in both senses) of the brothels in Rome were built underground, being arched vaults, wherefore the word *fornix*, an arch, acquired the secondary meaning of "brothel." In Church-Latin this engendered a verb, *fornicari*, "to frequent brothels"; and thereafter as you may imagine it wasn't very long before ecclesiastics all over the place were sermonising against "fornication."

Although such derivations seem to suggest that mankind is more fanciful and less logical than one had supposed, it is fairly easy to see how the evolution came about, so long as the processes are shown to us step by step. But of course a great number of word-histories are imperfectly known. And concerning others, nothing is known at all. If I have given the impression that you have only to consult a good etymological or historical dictionary in order to discover the origin and derivation of any given word, I have greatly misled you. Neither the *O.E.D.* nor any of the other great dictionaries claims to be infallible or omniscient; and from time to time, by means of question-marks or equivalent symbols, they admit their doubts, or even their ignorance, about matters which a layman, in his greater ignorance, might well expect them to be informed.

About one of the best known lines in *Macbeth* they can tell us very little indeed:

> *Aroint thee, witch! the rump-fed ronyon cries.*

"Aroint" *apparently* means "Avaunt! Begone!"; we can deduce so much from the context; and since the phrase "Aroint thee, witch" occurs also in *King Lear,* in a crazy song which Edgar sings, it may possibly be a quotation from some old play or ballad that has since been lost.

As for the "rump-fed ronyon," the epithet suggests that she pampered herself, and fed on the best joints; but the noun, spelt runnion in most dictionaries, defeats them all. Dr. Johnson, using both spellings, suggested that one meant "a mangy creature" and the other "a fat bulky woman." The *O.E.D.* is too cautious to make a guess. It simply says: "An abusive term applied to a woman. Of obscure origin." This is all we know, save that the jealous Ford in *The Merry Wives* addressed Falstaff (who was dressed up as an old woman) as a runyon and a polecat, a witch, a rag and a baggage, all in the same breath.

So the only evidence we have for the existence of "aroint" and "ronyon" is that Shakespeare used both of them twice. No other writer has used them at all, save in deliberate imitation of Shakespeare. He may even have made them up.

OF COURSE THERE are scores of puzzling and extraordinary words in his plays, though sometimes the spelling makes them seem stranger than they are. "Deboshed," [1] for instance, is simply "debauched." But what are "bubukles," what is a "coystril," what is meant by "bisson tears"? The first word apparently means a kind of excrescence, some horrible hybrid between a bubo and a carbuncle: Bardolph's face was "all bubukles, and whelks, and knobs, and flames o' fire." [2] "He's a coward and a coystril," said Sir Toby, who like many a good man talked best when he was not quite sober, "that will not drink to my niece till his brains turn o' the toe like a parish top." [3] The top, by the way, was one kept for the use of the parishioners, a quaint but kindly provision of fun at the public expense in the days before the Welfare State was dreamed of. "Coystril" merely means a knave; Toby used it for the sake of the alliteration, which drunks always delight in. "Bisson" was a word meaning "purblind, short-sighted," and "bisson rheum" in *Hamlet* means "blinding tears." They were shed by the mobled queen; and that curious adjective means either that she muffled up her face or that she dressed untidily, which she certainly did: she was wearing

---

[1] *"Thou deboshed fish, thou,"* says Trinculo to poor Caliban.
[2] *King Henry V.*
[3] *Twelfth Night.*

> *A clout upon her head*
> *Where late the diadem stood; and, for a robe,*
> *About her lank and all o'er-teemed loins,*
> *A blanket, in the alarm of fear caught up.*

She had some excuse for this state of déshabillé, for she had just watched the hellish Pyrrhus "make malicious sport In mincing with his sword her husband's limbs."

The most splendiferous of all the rare words in Shakespeare is "orgulous." He only used it once; but to what effect!—

> *From isles of Greece*
> *The princes orgulous, their high blood chaf'd,*
> *Have to the port of Athens sent their ships.*[1]

It has nothing to do with "orgy," but comes from French *orgueil*, haughty, hence proud, swelling, magnificent. It went out of currency for more than two centuries, and was rediscovered by Southey and Scott. Nineteenth-century journalists seized upon it, and spoiled it by over use.

Other strange words used only once by Shakespeare (and never by anybody else, as far as I know) include "riggish," "ribaudred," and "wappened." The scholars can't tell us anything about them save that they are all pretty rude. "Amorously sportive" is a fair rendering, I should think, of the sense of riggish. Enobarbus said of Cleopatra:

> *Vilest things*
> *Become themselves in her, that the holy priests*
> *Bless her when she is riggish.*

Scarus, less charitably, described her as "Yon ribaudred nag of Egypt." You can make a guess what it means. As for "the wappen'd widow," it is a phrase of Timon's which appears in one of his comprehensive curses, and is pregnant no doubt with hideous implications, concerning which the well-mannered dictionaries do not speculate.

COMMON WORDS AS well as rare ones sometimes turn out to be etymological mysteries. You might think, perhaps, that so familiar a word as "butterfly" must have an obvious and well-known derivation. Far from it. There are three contradictory theories. The likeliest is that the

[1] *Troilus and Cressida.*

name refers to the colour of some of the commonest and earliest English species, especially the brimstone: "the butter-coloured fly." A rather far-fetched notion, on the other hand, attributes its name to the look and consistency of its excrement. But Dr. Johnson thought the name came from the time of the butterfly's first appearance in the spring, "the season of the year when butter is first made." That was before the introduction of swedes and turnips, annual rotations, and the winter feeding of cattle. Dr. Johnson's idea is ingenious, though it is probably wrong. He made, and admitted, a good many mistakes—as when the horsey woman indignantly asked him why he had defined "pastern" as the knee of a horse. The doctor replied cheerfully: "Ignorance, madam, pure ignorance."

SOMETIMES THE SCHOLARS may have a clue or notion concerning a word's origin, but the evidence which they seek in language or literature is lacking, and there is no definite proof. The pundits are in dispute, for example, concerning the derivation of the word "bastard." Some hold that it comes from primitive German *bansti*, a granary or barn, hence a "barn son" or "barn daughter"—one conceived or born there; others derive it from Old French *bast*, a packsaddle, hence presumably "begotten on a packsaddle," after the uncomfortable manner among muleteers!

These are bright ideas; but they lack proof. Nor is it certain that "to muse," for instance, derives ultimately from Latin *musum*, an animal's mouth, a muzzle, which some experts believe to be the ancestor of the Old French *muser*, to ponder or to reflect—*to pause with muzzle in the air*. It sounds far-fetched, and it is certainly not demonstrable; yet it may be an inspired guess that has hit the mark. After all, etymology is not to be compared with those sciences which can call calculations, measurements and physical tests to their aid. It is much more like a journey through the minds of men, in which the etymologist must fare alone, with only his learning, his experience and his intelligence to guide him. He may discover a clue now and then, or the track may be as faint as footprints on dry ground. It may disappear altogether. Thereafter he has no choice but to go by guesswork, as the baffled hunter does.

Now and then his guesses, even though brilliant, turn out to be wrong. Someone ingeniously derived "sincere" from *sine cera*, "without wax"; the idea being, I suppose, that if you despatch a letter or document *sine cera*, that is to say unsealed, anybody is liable to read it and the contents must be of a nature which you are not ashamed of— straightforward, open, sincere. I have come across this explanation many times, and I once heard a clergyman preach a whole sermon founded upon it; but alas, it turns out that there is no evidence for it at all. Latin *sincerus* means pure or clean; but beyond that nothing is known about the origin of the word.

"MARMALADE" IS A puzzling word which inspired a most enterprising guess, based upon a delightful though ridiculous anecdote. Mary Queen of Scots, the story goes, when out of sorts would refuse the tastiest delicacy, and could only be persuaded to eat if she were offered a conserve of oranges, which she was inordinately fond of. The preserve was therefore nicknamed *Marie malade*, hence marmalade. This is nonsense,[1] but full marks for ingenuity to the man who thought of it!

SOME OF THESE "phoney" derivations are plausible; some are wonderfully absurd. "Phoney" itself, by the way, has given rise to several. It has been said to come from "funny business"; to be associated with "telephone"; to originate in the name of a Mr. Forney, who sold imitation jewellery in America. In fact, as Mr. Eric Partridge demonstrated, its history, which is fascinating, goes back to an Irish word *fainne*, finger-ring, which Irish confidence-tricksters introduced into English underworld slang. A *fawny cove* was one who specialised in a trick involving a gilt ring which was passed off as gold. This was described in 1781. The word went out of English altogether and reappeared in America as "phoney man," a peddler of cheap imitation jewellery. It returned across the Atlantic in 1939, when American war-correspondents, who were widely quoted in England, began to speak of "the phoney war." It is now firmly established in the language as a respectable adjective meaning "false, sham or pretended." [2]

THE SCHOLARS THEMSELVES have been responsible for some of the strangest muddles, confusions and misapprehensions concerning the

[1] The generally accepted derivation is via French from a Portuguese word *marmelo*, quince, which in turn comes from Latin *melimelum*, a sweet apple.
[2] *Origins.*

meaning of words. Take, for instance, the very odd history of the word "shard," which most of us encountered for the first time in Kipling's *Recessional*:

> *God of our fathers, known of old,*
> *Lord of our far-flung battle-line,*
> *Beneath whose awful Hand we hold*
> *Dominion over palm and pine—*

So did we cheerfully and without very contrite hearts raise our voices at the school service on Remembrance Day. There was rather less assurance when we came to the

> *Heathen heart that puts her trust*
> *In reeking tube and iron shard.*

We didn't know what the last line meant. Guns and shells? I'm still not quite sure. "Shard" has a multitude of meanings. A cleft or a gap is an old one, still found in dialect. A fragment of broken earthenware is another. Satan smote Job with sore boils from the sole of his foot unto his crown "And he took him a potsherd to scrape himself withal." [1] This is a horrible thought, which I shy away from: Job sitting among the ashes and miserably scratching. But there's yet another meaning of "shard": a patch of cowdung, a cowpat. Now Shakespeare, myriad-minded as Coleridge said, filled the great storehouse of his memory with little things as well as big; and he had discovered during a country boyhood that some kinds of beetles bred in these cowpats, a trivial scrap of esoteric lore which however he did not forget. Writing a speech for Macbeth, he sought in his recollection for some small, ominous sound of the twilight which would emphasise the pregnant stillness of the hour; for Macbeth was waiting for the news that his murderers had slain Banquo. Shakespeare wrote:

> *Ere the bat hath flown*
> *His cloister'd flight; ere to black Hecate's summons,*
> *The shard-borne beetle, with his drowsy hums,*
> *Hath rung night's yawning peal, there shall be done*
> *A deed of dreadful note.*

[1] *The Book of Job.*

"Shard-borne"; born among the cowdung,—where in fact the adult beetle lays its eggs, which hatch into maggots, feed fat, turn into pupae, and hatch once more as perfect insects.

But Dr. Johnson, making his dictionary 150 years later, did not happen to know this particular fact of life. He assumed therefore that "shard-borne" meant "carried along on shards" and reasonably hazarded:

> Perhaps shard in Shakespeare may signify the sheaths of the wings of insects.

This was only a suggestion. Less scrupulous writers copied it, without the "perhaps." A Mr. Willus in 1811 fortified his confidence with a word from the Greek and declared authoritatively:

> *Shard* means the shell or hard outward covering of the tribe of insects denominated *Coleoptera*.

In this disguise the word got itself into learned treatises, even into poetry; and so at last we find this poor cowpat-word marvellously transmogrified in *Hiawatha*:

> *And the roof-poles of the wigwam*
> *Were as glittering rods of silver,*
> *And the roof of bark upon them*
> *As the shining shards of beetles.*

A FEW WORDS owe their very existence to "learned error" as it were. Momblishness, dog-ray, gofish, phantomnation, jimwhiskee, tantling, civantick, eposculation, journ-chopper are fair samples of these "words that never were," of which a list containing some 350 is printed at the end of the *O.E.D. Supplement*. We can look upon them as the sports, freaks, or minor prodigies of language. There is no such fish as a dog-ray; but the word "dory" (John Dory) was incorrectly printed "dorrey" in Holinshed's *Chronicle*, and the tired eyes or short sight of some later scholar turned this into "dog-ray" by accident. Dictionary-makers copied the misspelling, and making what seemed to them a pretty good guess defined the word as "a kind of dog-fish."

"Journ-chopper" represents an extraordinary corruption of "yarn-dealer"; in one dictionary it even became "journey-hopper." "Gofish" was a misprint for "goosish" (silly, stupid) in an early edition of Chaucer. It got itself fraudulently into three famous dictionaries. "Phantomnation" was defined in Webster's *American Dictionary of the English Language* (1864) as "an illusion (*obs.* and *rare*)." It was an illusion indeed. Pope in his translation of the *Odyssey* had written a line

> *The Phantom-nations of the dead.*

A philologist called Jodrell, who for some reason was prejudiced against hyphens, ran the two words together when he printed them in 1820, and defined the result as "a multitude of spectres." Various copycats kept this quaint error going, until even the great Webster printed the spurious word.

But "momblishness" is my favourite of all these bogus ones. It is defined in various dictionaries as "muttering talk." In fact it came about through misunderstanding of the Old French name for the flower forget-me-not, *"ne m'oubliez mye,"* which Chaucer corrupted to "ne momblysnesse." Nathan Bailey, compiling a dictionary in 1721, decided that it meant "muttering"; and an excellent word for "muttering" it would have been—if it had ever existed outside the imagination of the scholars!

THOSE OF US who are apt to make mistakes about words, to misspell or mispronounce them, confuse their meanings, or get them completely mixed up as Mrs. Malaprop did when she spoke of an allegory on the banks of the Nile,[1] may perhaps draw comfort from these lapses of the learned. And we all do make mistakes, of course. Many of them started as the misapprehensions of childhood and, growing up with us, became somehow inseparable from our habit of thought. I used to think that "darkling" was the present participle of a verb, so the phrase in Keats' *Ode to a Nightingale*, "Darkling I listen," naturally puzzled me very much. It was years before I discovered that "darkling" was an adverb, meaning "in the dark," and that there never was such a verb as "to darkle" until Byron, apparently by a slip of the pen, invented it in *Don Juan*:

> *The night . . . darkled o'er the faces pale.*

[1] Sheridan: *The Rivals.*

Now here's a queer thing. I believe it is possible—only just possible, chronologically—that Byron read Keats' *Ode* before he wrote that canto of *Don Juan*. If so, did Keats' "darkling" set off the same delusion in Byron's mind as it did in mine? At any rate, Thomas Moore, Thackeray and William Morris all subsequently made the same mistake; and so through a series of errors the verb "to darkle" found its way into the *O.E.D.* So long as it achieves a wide enough currency, a word that has come about through misunderstanding is nevertheless a word.

I was astonished and delighted recently, to discover that the verb "to mizzle" was really a word. The first time I came across "misled" in a book I pronounced it to myself "mizzled," for I had never heard it spoken. Even when, years later, I realized my mistake, it still seemed to me that mizzled was a most suitable word with which to express the plight of one "bewitched and bewildered." Imagine my triumph, therefore, when I was turning over the pages of the *O.E.D.* the other day and came across MIZZLE, v., "obs. except in dial., rare" meaning "to confuse, muddle and mystify." Apparently old Stubbes in his *Anatomie of Abuses* was using it in 1583. As usual he was disapproving of some people who were enjoying themselves. "Their heades," wrote he, "pretely [1] mizzeled with wine."

The verb has or had other meanings: to rain very finely, to disappear suddenly, and to make spotty "as when in winter the legs are put too near to a fire"!

A recent correspondence in *The Times* showed me that many other people had made the same childish mistake about "misled" as I did. A discovery which surprised me even more was that two of my friends, *unknown to each other or to me during boyhood*, shared my extraordinary belief that an "ashlar" was "a good stout stick cut out of a hedge." The reason seemed to be that all three of us, at some time during our youth, had happened to notice the title of a Kipling poem, which we had not bothered to read: *My New-cut Ashlar*. In fact the word comes from Latin *axilla*, an axle, also a board or plank, hence its English sense of "a square, hewn stone."

INDEED IT APPEARS that for almost every one of us there is some per-

[1] Prettily.

sonal *pons asinorum* of language which we can never cross without stumbling or shying. There are words which we dare not utter, because we used inexplicably to panic when we attempted to say them; there are others which we unknowingly misspell or mispronounce all our days, infuriating our friends even as their verbal lapses infuriate us. For our own disposition to error by no means reconciles us to the mistakes of others. A person who walks round my garden and admires my clemātis is only a little less abhorrent to me than a person who gives two syllables to "fiend." A distinguished broadcaster did this in a commentary on a recent Derby, in which a horse called *The Fiend* ran a good race; and he did so despite the fact that everybody else in the programme was pronouncing the word correctly. Indeed it often seems to us as if a person must be wilful or arrogant, to continue in his error, whereas the real cause is more likely to be a sort of blind spot in his understanding. He really *does not notice* when the word is pronounced rightly in his presence: he "hears" only what he expects to hear. Thousands of people who eagerly listened to news about "coupons" on the wireless during the last war, spoke of them as "kewpons" nevertheless. And I have an extremely intelligent and well-educated friend who persisted in pronouncing the Christian name of the late Mr. Bevan as if it rhymed with "manurin'," even though he must have heard it said correctly several times a week, both by his acquaintances and on the wireless.

Occasionally the mispronouncers win. Most dictionaries now admit that "sónorous" (which I should think would make my old classics master turn in his grave) is an acceptable alternative to "sonórous." And they allow the affectation of English Roman Catholics in calling Mass "Marse" (though the Latin is *Missa* and the French *Messe*), and the even stranger caprice of the musicians, who describe a composition as an "ōpus" yet concede that the "o" should be short every time they speak of the "opera." In these cases the lexicographers have presumably decided that the mispronunciations are acceptable on the grounds of wide-spread current usage; though I confess that "Marse" and "ōpus" set my pugging tooth on edge, as Autolycus would have put it.

OTHER PEOPLE'S PUGGING teeth, on the contrary, are more susceptible to grammatical mistakes, to split infinitives,[1] to sentences ended with a preposition,[2] or to mixed metaphors, in which I confess I take a perverse delight, for they sometimes call up images most wondrous and bizarre—"Not wild horses on their bended knees will persuade me"; "Leaving no worm unturned"; and that marvellous sentence of Mrs. Gamp's: "The words she spoke of Mrs. Harris, lambs could not forgive . . . nor worms forget." [3] There are characters, such as Mrs. Gamp and Mrs. Malaprop, who add splendour to language by their very misuse of it; and not all the careful pedantry in the world has given it as much glory as one bewildered sentence of poor word-intoxicated Pistol when he said of the dying Falstaff "His heart is fracted and corroborate." [4]

IT IS THE laying down of the law by people who have only partly learned the law; the sham scholarship; the phoney folk-lore; the affectation of know-alls that rouses *me* to anger in this matter of the use of words. For an example of sham scholarship, let me quote you that silly legend about the sirloin of beef. It was *not* knighted by James I, Charles II, or Henry VIII, though many respected writers have said so, and have given chapter and verse:

> Our King James First . . . being invited to Dinner by one of his Nobles, and seeing a large Loyn of Beef at his table, drew out his sword, and knighted it.
>
> (Swift, *Polite Conversations*, 1738)

[1] George Bernard Shaw, whose own prose was perhaps the most workmanlike written in the last two or three centuries, declared that "every good literary craftsman splits his infinitive when the sense demands it."

[2] Sir Winston Churchill dealt a heavy blow to this schoolmarm superstition against "ending with a preposition" by means of a Minute written in devastating mockery: "This is the sort of English up with which I will not put." Shakespeare ended with a preposition whenever he wanted to. An American poet, Mr. Morris Bishop, recently demonstrated that it was possible, if inelegant, to end a sentence with *seven*:

> I lately lost a preposition;
> It hid, I thought, beneath my chair
> And angrily I cried, "Perdition!
> Up from out of in under there."
> Correctness is my vade mecum,
> And straggling phrases I abhor,
> And yet I wondered, "What should he come
> Up from out of in under for?"

[3] Dickens: *Martin Chuzzlewit*.

[4] *King Henry V*.

King Charles the Second, dining upon a Loin of Beef . . . said for its merit it should be knighted, and henceforth called Sir-Loin.

(*Cook's Oracle*, 1822)

Dining with the Abbot of Reading, Henry VIII ate so heartily of a loin of beef that the abbot said he would give 1000 marks for such a stomach. "Done!" said the King, and kept the abbot a prisoner in the Tower, won his 1000 marks, and knighted the beef.

(Fuller, *Church History*, 1655)

The experts, needless to say, will have none of this rubbish. They insist that the correct derivation of sirloin is the obvious one, *sur*, above, + loin. The spelling, of course, may have been influenced by the various fables aforesaid.

SOME OF THESE "false etymologies," as they are called, have a much wider currency than any true ones. Rotary Club lecturers give talks about them; they turn up regularly in the correspondence columns of the newspapers; and never a year goes by but some deserving hack bundles a dozen or so into a chatty little article which he sells for a few guineas to a popular magazine. Good luck to him; he needs the cash! But I feel less charitable towards the pseudo-scholar who in order to show off his learning trots out at every opportunity some such statement as this: "Of course, 'bloody' is simply a contraction of 'By Our Lady'"—which is sheer piffle, and implausible at that. It is the "of course" that makes me want to wring his neck!

Then there is the *Rewards and Fairies* phantasy. Kipling took his title from a line by Richard Corbet (1582–1635), "Farewell rewards and fairies!"[1] There is nothing mysterious about it. But the silly argument goes that "rewards" here does not carry its usual and familiar meaning, but is an old name for elves, goblins, pixies or what not. The High Priests of the cult go so far as to pronounce it "roo-ards," in the hope, I suppose, that one of their listeners will rise to the bait and query the pronunciation.

"Roo-ards, old boy. Seventeenth century word for hobgoblins. Didn't you know?"

A pox on such pseudo-pedantry. The same kind of person will as-

[1] *The Fairy's Farewell.*

sure you that "O.K." comes from Choctaw (Red Indian) *hoke*, meaning "It is so," or that it represents a contraction of Scottish "Och aye." [1] He will assure you that "posh" came from "Port Out, Starboard Home" (the most comfortable, hence expensive cabins in liners to and from the Orient). There's not a jot of evidence for this. But initials in this connexion inspire the oddest flights of fancy: I have heard people solemnly assure their listeners that "S.O.S." stands for "Save Our Souls." Even the Attorney-General at the *Titanic* inquiry seemed to uphold this sanctimonious silliness: he "explained that the signal C.Q.D. meant 'Come Quick Danger' and this had been substituted for S.O.S., 'Save Our Souls.'" Why souls? The signal asks every mariner within reach to help to save *bodies!* In fact, the letters were chosen arbitrarily by the Radio Telegraph Conference in 1906, SOS (. . . — — — . . .) being those which were easiest to transmit and distinguish in Morse Code.

Mr. Know-all is apt to inform you that "beargarden" comes, "of course" from German *biergarten*, although we English baited bears in our parks, and roughs and toughs frequented the places set aside for the pastime, long before the Germans were drinking beer in theirs. He will derive the inn-name "Cat and Fiddle" from *Catherina fidelis*, who "was either Catherine of Aragon or Catherine the wife of Peter the Great"; and he will do this in order to appear clever, without knowing anything about the ladies concerned, without a coherent notion in his head *why* their faithfulness should be commemorated in the name of an English pub. Yet "Hey-diddle-diddle" [2] is one of the most familiar nonsense-rhymes in our language, and in itself offers a perfectly good reason for giving the jolly name Cat and Fiddle to such an establishment.

Another pub, the Goat and Compasses, is alleged to get its name from the phrase "God Encompasseth Us,"—though God knows why, unless the piety of their landlords was reflected in such inn-names during the Commonwealth. I am unwilling to believe it; indeed I

[1] Likelier guesses are that it stands for "Orl K'rekt" which some illiterate American packer abbreviated to O.K. when he checked the packages; that it derives from "Old Kinderhook," nickname of Van Buren, 8th President of the U.S.A.; or that it comes from the initials of a secret political society in the U.S.A. It got into English well before 1880.

[2] Believe it or not, an expert on nursery rhymes (J. O. Halliwell) even asserted that Hey-diddle-diddle was a corruption of a phrase in Greek!

should have thought that if any landlord ever called his hostelry the "God Encompasseth Us" he wanted his head looked at. Imagine a man trying to tell his wife where he'd been, after he had had a few beers there! [1]

In particular there is a bit of extra-special bogusness which we may find offensive rather than merely silly, because it relates to one of the most touching moments in English history, at the thought of which none of us need be ashamed to cry. Our "Roo-ards" friend may tell you that *"of course"* Nelson didn't ask Hardy to kiss him—he usually giggles at this point—but what he *really* said was "Kismet, Hardy," Kismet being Turkish for "destiny," "fate." Why Nelson as he lay dying in 1805 should have used this expression which did not arrive in English (via Arabic) until 1849 is not easy to explain. There is something Victorian-Nursery-Governessy about this story, I think: a feminine embarrassment at the thought of a man kissing a man ("which only foreigners do") and an utter lack of appreciation of the heroic atmosphere in which Nelson lived and died.

SO PEOPLE WHO talk about words should be very chary of saying "of course," especially in connexion with suppositions and speculations which the etymologists have put forward only in humility and with diffidence. As I have tried to show, this science is in the nature of an exploration through territory of which only a few areas have been properly mapped. There is a vast hinterland unknown. A good many of our commonest words came into the language mysteriously, none knows whence. The "lad" which Housman delighted to use, the "lass" which gave such pleasure to Shakespeare and Burns, have both been in English since the 13th century; but it is not known what they were derived from nor out of what language we took them. "Bad," "big,"— equally obscure—came in about the same time. In the 16th century "gloat" and "bet" arrived, apparently from nowhere. A little later "job," "crease" and "pun" first poked up their heads in print. Of their earlier history nothing whatever is known. The word "blight" slipped into the written language, probably by way of the speech of farmers or gardeners, about 1670. The learned did not know how to spell it,

---

[1] But I must not be too dogmatic; pub-names are mysterious things. There were, for instance, inns in England called "The Black Swan" *before* anyone had set eyes on the remarkable bird, which a Dutch navigator discovered in Australia in 1697!

so tried "blite" because they had heard of a plant of that name. Nobody knows anything about its derivation. "Slum" presents even more of a mystery, because its appearance "out of nowhere" in English literature happened in the 19th century, when the study of words was already far advanced. It was first spotted in 1812, as a "cant" word for a room. Dickens was using it in the current sense in 1851. So even in modern times a word can appear among us unnoticed, and without passport or credentials quietly establish itself in the language. One day somebody wakes up to its presence there, and begins to ask questions to which there are no certain answers. During the First World War our soldiers had a phrase "put the kibosh on the Kaiser." Nobody was very clear what it meant, save that it boded ill for the German Emperor, whose title being matched with kibosh came easily off the tongue. But what was this word "kibosh" doing, where did it come from? It turned out that Dickens had used it in 1836—"Hooroar," ejaculates a pot-boy . . . "put the kye-bosh on her, Mary." [1] Also it had appeared in *Punch*, 1885, in the sense of "something valueless." But how was it derived? What language did it belong to? Some thought it sounded Yiddish; many held that it had something to do with "bosh." But your guess is as good as mine, and probably as good as those of the experts, who in this case—as in many others connected with words—are by no means unanimous. I am reminded of the label upon a specimen exhibited in the Roman baths at Bath:

> Incised inscription. Read by Professor Sayce as a record of the cure of a Roman lady by the Bath water, attested by three witnesses; read by Professor Zangermeister as a curse on a man for stealing a tablecloth.

[1] *Sketches by Boz.*

CHAPTER 14

The Ever-changing Language

LANGUAGE, as we have seen, is ever-changing: no more settled than the sea or the sky. The only words of fixed form and meaning are dead ones, "Arch." and "Obs." The others, which continue to reflect our living thoughts, are subject to the inexorable laws of life, which forbid immutability. Changes affecting the language are going on all the time about us—in the newspapers we read, in the speech we hear, even in our own speech. Because the process is so gradual, we generally notice it as little as we do the leaf-change upon an evergreen tree. But occasionally for some reason or other it goes faster, and we catch a startling glimpse of a word in transition, as I did the other day when I waited my turn at the counter of a W. H. Smith bookshop. Most people were buying their morning papers; but the woman in front of me said: "I've called for Mrs. Robinson's books, please." The assistant went away and came back with a copy each of *Woman's Pictorial, The Exchange and Mart, Popular Gardening* and *The Anti-Vivisection News.* Mrs. Robinson's friend paid for them and went off with what she thought of as four "books" under her arm. For how long have the assistants in bookshops understood "books" to mean "magazines"? Not more than ten years, I imagine. But today even *Reveille, The Woman's Sunday Mirror* and I daresay *The Muck-Shifter and Public Works Digest* are all spoken of as "books" by many of their readers. The term is chiefly current among "estate dwellers" —which in my youth would have meant the Squire's tenants but now means those of the Council, though it seems to be widening its range. She was a representative of suburbia who recently was kind enough to tell me: "I've been reading your book in a book," by which I understood she had read it as a serial.

"Contemporary" is another word which in a dozen years or so has acquired a new meaning. The women's magazines (or books!) are mainly responsible for this. Sensibly enough, they lay great stress on present-day styles of house-decorating and furnishing, which they generally describe as "contemporary." Seeing this word so often used as a synonym for "modern," people are beginning to forget that it really means "belonging to the same time or period." It is not beyond the bounds of possibility that the process will continue and gain momentum, so that the older meaning of the word will become obsolete and the dictionary will have to make room for a new definition, something like this:

Contemporary, adj. modern, fashionable, up-to-date.

PEOPLE of a precise and pedantic turn of mind often feel very resentful concerning any change whatever in a word's usage. They are apt to ask, especially if they are schoolmasters, what is the point of their trying to employ words properly, if meanwhile the "*hoi polloi*" can play fast and loose with language and go unreproved,—so that the "vulgar error" of today is enshrined in tomorrow's dictionary as an "authority" for the wrong usage? One of these schoolmasters, for whom I confess I felt a sneaking regard, became very concerned during the darkest days of 1940 about our use of the word "evacuate." It was just after Dunkirk, an invasion seemed imminent, there was talk of moving all civilians who had not got essential jobs out of certain threatened areas. At this hour the indignant schoolmaster chose to write his Letter to the Editor. It pointed out, in precise terms and in a faintly querulous tone which seemed all the quainter against the background of bangs and sirens, that the misuse of the word "evacuate" was to be deplored. Dunkirk had been evacuated; but our soldiers had not. The seaside towns might have to be evacuated; but not their citizens, unless we proposed to empty each one by means of a stomach-pump. For good measure he added that he was dismayed by the appearance of that ugly neologism "evacuee." Meanwhile the bombs continued to fall.

The word "tremendous" was the subject of a similar pedagogic agitation not long ago. We were told that it should only be used in the sense of "that which makes us tremble"; [1] and no less a person than a D. Litt. described any other use of it as an "enormity." "Fabulous" is another great worry to such scholars, because they say it is in danger of losing its proper meaning of "belonging to a fable." It lost it long

[1] It comes from Latin *tremere*. Cf. *delirium tremens*, the trembling delirium.

ago! De Quincey in his *Confessions of an Opium-Eater* (1822) declared that he had taken "fabulous quantities" of the stuff. Miss Mitford (1852) wrote of someone's "fabulous passion for fish" and Lord Houghton (1859) of "houses let at fabulous rents." However I have some sympathy with the gentleman who wrote to *The Times* the other day complaining of an advertisement in which the publishers of a book had described it as "fabulously true."

It wouldn't be the first word to acquire an opposite meaning from its original one. A "casualty," at one time an accident, is now used almost exclusively to mean the victim of one. "Painful" once meant taking pains: "O the holiness of their living, and the painfulness of their preaching." [1] "Scan" is a word which is just now in the process of turning topsy-turvy. Properly, it means "to examine minutely, to look at searchingly" and by careful writers it is still used in this sense. But I suppose there is hardly a lawyer who has not received some such answer as this in reply to his question: "Did you read the document?"

"Well, I only just scanned it."

IN GENERAL, I cannot share the indignation of the schoolmasters concerning changes in the use of words. After all, change is a Fact of Life, and therefore of language. It is a quite untenable doctrine that a word should perpetually and in all circumstances carry exactly the same meaning; and if it were generally held it would put the poets out of business. For poetry depends upon metaphor; and metaphor is defined as "the transfer of a term to some object to which it is not properly applicable." Must we then say that there is one law for the poets and another for the people?—that it was all right for Julia Ward Howe to write in her *Battle Hymn of the Republic*:

He is trampling out the vintage where the grapes of wrath are stored

but that it is all wrong for us to speak of "vintage cars"?

The worst pedant in this respect I ever knew was an old gentleman who reproved his daughter for saying she looked "dilapidated" because she hadn't done her hair or made up her face after a game of tennis. I dared not argue with him because at the time I was courting the girl;

[1] Fuller: *The Holy State.*

so he launched himself into a lecture, saying that the word conjured up in his mind the image of the desolate ruin of some noble edifice such as the Parthenon, from which through slow decay during many centuries stone had fallen from stone . . . And so it may have done. But in the mind of an M.P. called Sir John Newport, debating in Parliament as long ago as 1817, it conjured up the image of his country's tottering finances; and in 1874 a writer as respectable as Ruskin was using it to describe *a pair of women's shoes*.

IF THE PUNDITS of language were to disallow these extensions of meaning, at what point would the prohibition stop? "Jargon" meant "birdsong" long before it meant unintelligible speech, or what Feste would have called vain bibble-babble,—

> *Sometimes a-dropping from the sky*
> *I heard the skylark sing;*
> *Sometimes all little birds that are,*
> *How they seem'd to fill the sea and air*
> *With their sweet jargoning!* [1]

In this sense Chaucer took the word from French *jargonner*, to warble (of birds); and it was so used until the last century. Since then the old meaning has disappeared, and we can now speak of "legal jargon" without causing the pedants to utter a single squeak of protest. And when we say a person is a snob, they do not ask us if we are suggesting that he is a shoemaker. But that was precisely what "snob" did mean until the middle 1800's. It then took on the sense of "ill-bred" or "not quite a gentleman." Thackeray through his *Book of Snobs* (1848) seems to have been responsible for its present meaning.

Tobacconist meant the smoker, not the seller of tobacco, when Burton wrote in *The Anatomy of Melancholy*: "Germany hath not so many drunkards, England tobacconists . . . as Italy hath jealous husbands." A curate used to be the rector or vicar, one having the "cure" of souls. The word "hosteller" (compare *hôtelier*), meaning one who kept an inn, descended in the social scale until it became "ostler," the servant who looked after the horses. A "typewriter" in 1885 had the

[1] Coleridge: *The Ancient Mariner*.

sense which "typist" has now: "The marriage of the type-writer and her employer is so frequent that it has passed into a joke." [1]

THE GREEK WORD *Nausia* means seasickness; when we are nauseated we are sickened. But in the 18th century people nauseated the offensive thing. "I nauseate walking; 'tis a country diversion; I loathe the country." (Congreve, *The Way of the World*.) Dr. Johnson was furious because a young woman of his acquaintance left the Church of England and became a Quakeress. "Madam, I pretend not to set bounds to the mercy of the Deity; but I hate the wench, and shall ever hate her. I hate all impudence; but the impudence of a chit's apostasy I *nauseate*."

What he really nauseated, of course, was that a woman should venture to have a mind of her own about theology, which was the proper concern of men only. "Sir, a woman's preaching is like a dog walking on his hinder legs. It is not done well; but you are surprised to find it done at all."

"NAUGHTY" USED TO mean poor (literally "possessing naught"). Langland used it in this sense: "Nedy men and naughty." "To admire" is literally "to wonder at"; shade by shade during many centuries it has acquired its present meaning of "to gaze on with pleasure." When old Capulet said of Romeo "He bears him like a portly gentleman" he did not mean that Romeo was fat, but that he bore himself with dignity. "Gestation" meant "carrying or being carried" long before it came to signify the process of carrying young. Doctors used to prescribe gestation (riding on horseback or in a carriage) plus "pure air and sea-bathing" during convalescence. As for "silly," it has had a score of meanings, ranging from pitiable to weak or frail, from rustic to simple or unlearned, although nowadays it is only used in the foolish sense. At times it has meant "scanty," at others "plain and homely" and in this sense was used by the poets so often in connexion with sheep that it became at one time a more or less conventional epithet for them.

IZAAK WALTON, sitting on a primrose bank and being moved by the spring beauty of the river-meadows, thought that they were "too pleas-

[1] Anon.: *How to Get Married.*

ant to be looked on, but only on holy-days." [1] And of course he meant "days set aside for religious observance" such as Good Friday—when incidentally *hali*but or "holy flatfish" was properly eaten! In fact holy-day became holiday, and took on its secular meaning, a very long time ago; and a modern Bank Holiday implies almost exactly the opposite of a holy-day, I suppose.

THEN THERE IS a certain type of drunk—effusive and over-friendly, soppy as a spaniel, much given to self-pity and liable to burst into tears —whom we describe as "maudlin." Here is a large extension of meaning indeed!—all the way from that Mary who anointed Jesus' feet to the sot who clings and sobs. I have a theory about this. I think probably puritanism and the painters are equally to blame. In the early simplicity of faith it seemed natural and only proper that a painter should choose the prettiest young girl in the town as a model for his Virgin. Then puritanism came like a frost in spring, blasting the bud of innocence. The prettiest girl was now regarded as too naughty, or at any rate insufficiently pious, to sit for the Virgin; but the artist was determined to paint her, so she became his model for Mary of Magdala instead. All went well until the next cold wind of puritanism began to blow about the world, chilling the very hearts of men, so that even a pretty Magdalene was disapproved of, since she might be said to glorify vice. The painters had to show her as snivelling into a handkerchief, red-eyed, even red-nosed, and thoroughly unattractive. The language, always quick to reflect our hypocrisies, took due note of this. Magdalene became maudlin, "mawkishly emotional, weakly sentimental"—greatly to the dismay of our old friend Dr. Richard Chenevix Trench. It could never have happened, he declared sternly, if "the tears of penitential weeping had been held in due honour by the world."

Now Dr. Trench was a professional moralist, flourishing in the favourable climate of the 1850's. He was also a good philologist by the standards of his day; and naturally enough, as a Victorian, he could not refrain from applying his moral judgments to the objects of his study. This had some rather peculiar effects upon his writing; we often find him reprehending the words themselves. For the more he studied the dictionaries, the more sorrowfully he came to regard them as reposi-

[1] *The Compleat Angler.*

tories of iniquity and record-books of man's fall from grace. "Indeed . . . it is a melancholy thing," he remarked in one of his lectures, "to observe how much richer is every vocabulary in words that set forth sins, than in those that set forth graces . . . How much cleverness, how much wit, yea, how much imagination must have stood in the service of sin, before it could possess a nomenclature so rich, so varied, and often so heaven-defying as it has."

It had never occurred to me, until I read that passage, that there were more wicked words than good words. On reflection, however, I think the Reverend Doctor was right. My edition of Roget's *Thesaurus* (1925) gives a choice of 61 different words meaning "drunk" against 4 meaning sober. They include mellow, cut, boozy, fou, fresh, merry, elevated, squiffy, groggy, beery, topheavy, potvaliant, potulent, overcome, whittled, screwed, tight, primed, oiled, corned, sewed up, lushy, nappy, muzzy, bosky, obfuscated, crapulous and drunk as David's sow; but I daresay you and I could nevertheless add a couple of dozen more! Mr. Ivor Brown quotes two very fine ones in his book *Say The Word*: "nimtopsical," which he confesses he does not understand,—nor do I—and "bosko absoluto," which is lordly.

"Gluttony," in the *Thesaurus*, is shown to be a subject twice as rich in words as "fasting"; and against 9 adjectives implying purity there are 63 having an impure connotation. Nor was Mr. Roget widely versed in such matters, I imagine; once again we could add a few more to his collection. So the wicked words flourish like the green bay tree; and recognising this Dr. Trench personalised them in his mind until he saw them no longer as mere reflections of man's sinfulness, but as things culpable in themselves. In such terms he proceeded to give them a well-deserved wigging:

"What a multitude of words, originally harmless, have assumed an harmful or a secondary meaning; how many worthy have acquired an unworthy."

He went on to point out that "knave" once meant no more than "lad," a "villain" was a peasant, a "churl" a sturdy fellow, "crafty" meant versed in a craft, and "cunning" implied only honest skill. When words change their meaning it is generally for the worse, according to Dr. Trench, who quotes more than a dozen formidable examples to

prove it—words which, says he, "bear the slime on them of the serpent's trail."

Nor is it relevant to the argument if we dare to point out that serpents are not slimy, and do not leave one.

WE NEED NOT share Dr. Trench's stern view of morals to recognise that
words in their changing meanings do sometimes reflect a fault in ourselves, a lowering of standards, a cheapening of outlook, a decline in
taste. For instance it is clear that literature and learning are not held
in very high esteem by people who describe shiny magazines as "books."
The word "charity," which Saint Paul used so beautifully, equating it
with love but not with half-hundredweights of coal and bowls of soup,
fell into disrepute during the last century and got itself an almost
contemptuous significance. "I'll not accept charity, thank you!" It may
never recover from the cold practicality of Victorian almswomen, at
whose hands it might well have been said "Charity suffereth long."

"Respectability" used to imply a way of life and behaviour which
was really respected. The smug, hypocritical, narrow attitude of mid-
dle-class "respectable" people brought it into disrepute a long time
ago. I don't suppose Walt Whitman was the first to employ it in a
disparaging sense:

> I think I could turn and live with animals, they
>   are so placid and self-contain'd . . .
> They do not lie awake in the dark and weep for
>   their sins,
> They do not make me sick discussing their duty to God,
> Not one is dissatisfied, not one is demented with the
>   mania of owning things,
> Not one kneels to another, nor to his kind that lived
>   thousands of years ago,
> Not one is respectable or unhappy over the whole earth.[1]

Sometimes over the shops of old-fashioned butchers and country
tradesmen you see the word "purveyor," which used to be a rather
proud description of himself by one who "purveyed" his goods, taking
them in the smart float behind the well-groomed pony, to the owners
of the big houses round about. Such "purveying" has become a casualty

[1] *Song of Myself.*

of a changing society, and the word is going out of use save in one respect: it survives in common speech as "a purveyor of gossip." The
altered meaning of "egregious" suggests a more serious criticism of the
modern outlook. The word comes, of course, from Latin—*grex, gregis*,
a flock, whence *egregius*, "apart from the flock or herd." Therefore it
meant distinguished, outstanding, not one of the sheep, but an individual who towered above them. When Marlowe in *Tamburlaine*
wrote of

Egregious viceroys of these eastern parts

he did not mean that the viceroys were fools. But that, alas, is what
we should intend by a similar sentence today. An egregious person is
asinine, egregious behaviour is outrageous. This perhaps reflects our
herd-instinct, our fear of being different, our mistrust and disapproval
of the individualist who does not go along with the herd.

People who behave alike tend to think alike. Heresy is anathema
to them. Yet the original meaning of "heresy" (from Greek *hairesis*, a
taking-for-oneself, a choosing, hence a sect or school of thought) was
simply "a private opinion." The Church altered all that, laying down
that it was sinful to hold private opinions about theological matters.
This term could include almost anything, for theology concerned itself not only with God but with the nature of the universe, the whole
field of natural science, and the whole gamut of personal morality.
Private opinion went up in flames, between 1231 and the end of the
16th century, over the whole of civilized Europe; and the word
"heresy" still carries an echo of the screams of the racked and a stench
of burnt flesh about it. In general we nowadays use it for any opinion
which we do not happen to hold ourselves. "They that approve a
private opinion, call it opinion; but they that dislike it, heresy," wrote
Thomas Hobbes; [1] or as Bishop Warburton neatly put it: "Orthodoxy
is my doxy; heterodoxy is another man's doxy." [2]

ALTHOUGH HERETICS are not burned nowadays, they are sometimes
"liquidated." Totalitarianism took over this word from the lawyers and
accountants. To liquidate a business is "to wind up its affairs." When

[1] *Leviathan.*
[2] A remark which he is said to have made to that Earl of Sandwich after whom
the snacks were named.

the Communists liquidate a person, they likewise wind up his affairs; but more quickly. They are curiously reluctant ever to use the word "kill." Hand in hand with their ruthlessness goes an inconsistent tortuousness of mind. They speak and write by circumlocution always. In common with their foes the Fascists, they look upon words rather as instruments of propaganda than as the means for exchanging ideas. " 'When I use a word,' Humpty-Dumpty said, in rather a scornful tone, 'it means just what I choose it to mean, neither more nor less.' " [1] For example "comrade" in their mouths no longer means a close companion, a mate; it merely signifies a member of the Party, a Communist. So a warm-hearted word expressing a human relationship is turned into a political tag, a label. Such words as truth, peace, warmonger, democracy are given meanings which they have never borne before and which are often quite contrary to their generally accepted sense. "Peace-loving" in Communist jargon acquires a meaning akin to "acquiescent"; and a "warmonger" is anybody who advocates opposition to the Communist point of view.

In this Wonderland of language, certain words become sacred and not-to-be-laughed-at, as happens under extreme religious intolerance, whether of Church or witch-doctory. "People" is one of them. Anything cheap, shoddy or second-rate is at once lifted out of the range of criticism when you attach this word to it,—the People's house, washing machine, fridge, above all the People's Will, which is supposed to possess an overriding authority simply by virtue of this sacred word. Indeed I have heard it spoken in the tone which superstitious tribesmen might use when speaking of the ghosts of their ancestors.

> *Holy State or Holy King—*
> *Or Holy People's Will—*
> *Have no truck with the senseless thing.*
> *Order the guns and kill!* [2]

wrote Kipling with bluff common sense. And indeed once a word becomes "holy" it becomes dangerous. We do not need to go to the vocabulary of totalitarianism for an example of this. Ordinary, decent, tolerant and sane Englishmen were turned into quite different people

[1] *Through the Looking-Glass.*
[2] *MacDonough's Song.*

during the First World War by the emotive power of two simple words which became mysteriously sanctified. The words were "cold steel." I do not know who first used this phrase instead of the word "bayonet," nor why the adjective "cold" had such a powerful effect on people, why it was supposedly worse to have your guts ripped out by *cold* steel rather than by hot iron in the form of a splinter of shrapnel. The fact remains that the two words acted in some way upon a rather unpleasant aspect of English patriotism, with the consequence that old blimps and home-front shirkers, who would themselves have run like rabbits at the sight of a fixed bayonet, boasted in pubs and even in print (for they often wrote "Letters to the Editor") *"The Huns won't face cold steel."* Dear old ladies became unnaturally excited by the words. They never thought of bayonets ripping into British bellies,—or anybody's, perhaps, since the Germans would turn and run, and receive their wounds in the unmentionable backsides!

But why all this nastiness and irrationality should have been provoked by the juxtaposition of those two quite ordinary words "cold" and "steel" I shall never understand. Perhaps the phrase was originally intended as a euphemism: its inventor used it because he did not want to evoke too vivid a picture of a bayonet in action (as the Communists employ the euphemism "liquidate" because they don't want to imagine the firing-squad, the volley, the pool of blood). But in the case of "cold steel" something mysterious happened in the minds of millions of people; and the substitute turned out to be more horror-evoking than the original word.

EUPHEMISM, OF COURSE, is very often the reason for words changing their meanings, going up or down in the world of fashion, flourishing or dying out.

It springs generally from shame. If the totalitarians had not been ashamed of murder, they would not have tried to make it respectable by calling it liquidation. A bookie calls himself a commission agent or a turf accountant because he is ashamed of being a bookmaker—itself perhaps a euphemistic word, "making a book" seeming politer than "laying the odds." But more often than not at the root of euphemism lies some sexual shame, shyness or embarrassment.

And the eyes of them both were opened, and they knew that they were naked; and they sewed fig-leaves together, and made themselves aprons.[1]

So runs the verse in King James' Bible; but Messrs. Whittingham, Gilbey and Samson, whose earlier Bible was published in 1579, were apparently much troubled by the thought of Adam and Eve going about with bare bottoms, so they substituted the word "breeches" for "aprons." Their edition is known in the book trade as the Breeches Bible, and you can buy a copy for five or ten pounds.

Now see by what a curious process taboo and euphemism go to work. Adam and Eve covered up their "shame" and probably blushed at the mere mention of it. When it had to be spoken of, various circumlocutions and synonyms were invented for it. The taboo was then taken a stage further. The covering garment, because of what it concealed, began to acquire prurient associations of its own; and so during a spell of exceptional primness trousers were "politely" described as "nether garments," and ultimately by a group of words so extravagant that they surely represent euphemism at its most ridiculous: unmentionables, inexpressibles, ineffables, indescribables, unspeakables and so on. Most of these were originally American, and amid the bleak puritanism of Massachusetts during the 19th century I daresay they may have been used quite seriously. But Dickens employed them only in fun; and as new ones were invented from time to time, their use in Victorian society became more and more jocular, until a series of fleeting fashions dictated that one should say "sit-upons," "unutterables," and at last "unwhisperables." I can hardly imagine even the primmest Victorian maiden using these expressions save with her tongue in her cheek; but the quirks of puritanism are very odd, and one can dismiss nothing in this line as entirely beyond belief. Lady Byron, for example, in her statements to the lawyers about the breakdown of her disastrous marriage, gave some truly outrageous instances of Byron's behaviour. She described things that would shock any girl today; but when it came to the allegation that he chaffed his half-sister with the words "Augusta, I *know* you wear drawers!"—they were optional garments then, and the jest was naturally a common one—then poor Lady

[1] *Genesis.*

Byron had to write the phrase in shorthand, deeming the word "drawers" too improper to be spelt! [1]

DICKENS WOULD HAVE heard of "inexpressibles" and "indescribables" during his visit to Boston, where he appeared at a dinner party wearing a fancy cravat and a vivid green waistcoat. Being asked by a lady which he thought was the most beautiful Englishwoman, Mrs. Caroline Norton or the Duchess of Sutherland, he is said to have replied as follows:

> Well, I don't quite know. Mrs. Norton is perhaps the most beautiful, but the Duchess to my mind is the most *kissable* person.

The effect of this remark must have been stunning; for Boston, where Cotton Mather once had thundered his denunciation of all the sins from witchcraft to womanising, had not entirely recovered from its puritan fever—indeed was in the early stages of a relapse. Its atmosphere has always been reckoned cold, aloof and superior: a Bostonian was defined as "the east wind made flesh," and there is a famous rhyme:

> *I come from the city of Boston,*
> *The home of the bean and the cod,*
> *Where the Cabots speak only to Lowells,*
> *And the Lowells speak only to God.*

When extreme puritanism got to work in this chilly medium the results were quite extraordinary; the bottled-up and sex-tormented ladies of the city became so obsessed with "wicked" thoughts about the human body, and especially its lower half, that they went to the length of speaking of the "limbs" of a piano, and described their own legs by the remarkable euphemism "benders." We are told that during the 1880's even the table-legs, in certain households, were thought to provide dangerous reminders of real legs, and consequently of "the demesnes that there adjacent lay"; so they were clothed in garments specially devised for the purpose, long white cotton pantaloons!

PANTALOONS, we may observe *en passant*, are so named after a character from the Venetian stage, a foolish old man wearing spectacles, slippers,

[1] Doris Langley Moore: *The Great Byron Adventure.*

and a special kind of trousers, probably in the nature of tights: Jacques' "lean and slipper'd pantaloon" in fact, Shakespeare having enthusiastically seized upon the word almost as soon as it arrived from Italy. It remained in the language, and Sir Thomas Browne used it sadly in a moment of disillusion: "In my warm blood and canicular days [1] I perceive I do anticipate the vices of age; the world to me is but a dream or mock show, and we all therein but pantaloons and antics." [2] The change of meaning, to trousers, did not occur until early in the 19th century, and the abbreviation to pants came much later—about 1880; but long before that the Americans had begun to use the word in the sense of trousers, though some thought it vulgar,—"a word," said Oliver Wendell Holmes snootily, "not made for gentlemen but 'gents.'" [3] All the same it stuck; and how happily at home it remains in American English you can judge from Mr. Ogden Nash's delightful quatrain addressed to a young lady:

> *Sure, deck your lower limbs in pants;*
> *Yours are the limbs, my sweeting.*
> *You look divine as you advance—*
> *Have you seen yourself retreating?*

CONTEMPORARY, I DARESAY, with the table-leg pantaloons of Boston was the currency of the word "he-biddy," which some inventive American substituted for the more usual name (so pregnant with implications) of the male domestic fowl. Puritan America was also responsible for one of the most remarkable of all recorded euphemisms, that which described a bull as a "gentleman cow." [4] Meanwhile in England Dr. Bowdler, a Cambridge vicar, had published his edition of Shakespeare "designed for reading in the family circle" from which all the words and phrases which he thought suggestive were cut out; and his friend and fellow clergyman, Mr. Plumtre, had "expurgated and improved" Shakespeare's songs, in which

[1] Dog-days.
[2] *Religio Medici.*
[3] *Rhymed Lessons*, 1846.
[4] We may smile; but "lady dog" for bitch was quite acceptable not long ago in suburban England.

> *Under the greenwood tree,*
> *Who loves to lie with me* [1]

became

> *Under the greenwood tree,*
> *Who loves to work with me.*

This new puritanism tightened its grip on England as the years went by; and the supersensitiveness about sex reached its climax during the middle years of Queen Victoria. By then most areas of the human body had become unmentionable even in the most innocent sense. For example, Dr. John Browne of Edinburgh published in 1864 an edition of the charming and precocious writings of little Marjory Fleming, who died before her ninth birthday, in 1811. One of her letters began "My dear Isa, I now sit down on my botom to answer . . ." Dr. Browne, without admitting he had made the cut, left "on my botom" out. This would be hardly worth mentioning, in the context of Victorian puritanism, but for a contrast which it highlights between the liberalism of Marjory's little world and the strictness of Dr. Browne's wider one only 50 years later. A short time before she died of measles, Marjory aged eight was reading the *Arabian Nights*, the *Newgate Calendar* ("very instructive and amusing"), and *Tom Jones* which she thought "excelent and much spoke of by both sex particularly by the men"!

THE WORD "BOTTOM" is still a source of embarrassment to the British, even of pain to those unfortunate families of whose names it forms an integral part,—Longbottom, Winterbottom, Ramsbottom, Higginbottom, and worst of all, if there really is such a name, Bottomwhetham. Who shall blame the Sidebottoms, say, if they change the spelling of their abhorred suffix to "botham," and hint to their friends that the correct pronunciation of the surname is Siddybotaam? Such a hint, it is said, was given by one of the clan when he was introduced to the late Horatio Bottomley.

"Siddybotaam?" repeated Horatio cheerfully. "How d'e do? I'm H. Bumley, Esquire."

Dr. Johnson, with a famous sentence, once quelled the giggles

[1] *As You Like It.*

which for various discomfortable reasons are provoked by the associations of the word. He had been speaking of an author who had married "a printer's devil"—that is to say, an errand-girl in a printer's office. Sir Joshua Reynolds was shocked; he thought a printer's devil was a creature in rags with a black face. "Yes," said Dr. Johnson, "but . . . she did not disgrace him; the woman had a bottom of good sense." "The word thus introduced," says Boswell, telling this story, "was so ludicrous . . . that most of us could not forbear tittering and laughing; though I recollect the Bishop of Killaloe kept his countenance . . . while Miss Hannah More slyly hid her face behind a lady's back." Dr. Johnson, however,

> glanced sternly around, and called out in a strong tone, "Where's the merriment?" Then collecting himself, and looking aweful, to make us feel how he could impose restraint, and as it were searching his mind for a still more ludicrous word, he slowly pronounced, "I say the *woman* was *fundamentally* sensible"; as if he had said, hear this now, and laugh if you dare. We all sat composed as at a funeral.

A hundred years later the word, in polite society, was absolutely taboo. Whereas its impact upon Johnson's listeners had been mainly "ludicrous," for the mixed-up Victorians it became deeply involved in the tormenting imagery of sexual "sin." A conspiracy of silence among the middle-classes kept up the pretence that British women simply did not possess that part of the anatomy in which the liberal Latins seemed to take such a frank and outrageous delight.

ALWAYS IN SEARCH of "polite" and "refined" equivalents for words which they regarded as unpleasant, embarrassing, vulgar or not quite nice, the Victorians seized gratefully upon "abattoir" for slaughterhouse, "lingerie" for the unmentionable undergarments, and "nude" as a substitute for naked. The last is a very old Anglo-Saxon word; it appeared in our language as long ago as 850. Nude [1] in the sense of unclothed was first used in English about 1850, when it acquired almost at once an odd kind of respectability. Nudes, such as Sir Edward Poynter's, were acceptable, because "artistic," at the Royal Academy Exhibitions; the ladies hastened past them, the gentlemen lingered be-

---

[1] From Latin *nudus*.

fore them if they dared. Yet "nakedness" was practically unmentionable; and there is a story of an artist's model who, being asked by an awe-stricken young man whether she really posed naked, blushed deeply and protested that she only did so in the nude. The word has its uses (e.g. "Nude Shows" and in popular journalism—being one letter shorter than naked it is handier for the headlines) but is always, it seems to me, ill-at-ease in the English language,—perhaps because we're not very good at pronouncing the long "u" sound. Compare Swinburne's lines to *Dolores*:

> *We shift and bedeck and bedrape us;*
> *Thou art noble and nude and antique—*

(three adjectives that look extremely silly when they are strung together) with the beautiful "nakedness," honest as the day, in Donne's *Epithalamion Made at Lincolnes Inne*, which I print in its original spelling because it looks so fine that way:

> *Thy virgins girdle now untie,*
> *And in thy nuptiall bed (loves altar) lye*
> *A pleasing sacrifice; now dispossesse*
> *Thee of these chaines and robes which were put on*
> *T'adorne the day, not thee; for thou, alone,*
> *Like vertue and truth, art best in nakednesse;*
> *This bed is onely to virginitie*
> *A grave, but, to a better state, a cradle . . .*

What a contrast, incidentally, with the whining and moping, so fashionable among the Victorians, over lost maidenheads! The line which ends the verse is a salutation:

> *Tonight put on perfection, and a woman's name!*

WE MUST NOT, however, lay all the puritanical evasions at the Victorians' door; we possess, and unaccountably cling to, some most displeasing examples ourselves. There is the word "convenience," beloved of Town Councils. Ultimately, of course, "lavatory," "toilet," the factual "W.C.," the suburban "powder-room" and the upper-class "loo" (? from *water*-closet), are all euphemisms too; but they are not so unattractive as "convenience." It is a fairly recent use of the word. To Smollett a convenience was a spittoon; [1] about the same period it was slang for a wife or a mistress. As a synonym for lavatory it is dying out; but in many towns we still see notices directing us to the "public conveniences." Surely "Ladies" and "Gentlemen" is a sensible and well-mannered compromise—though if one wishes to be priggishly egalitarian, like the B.B.C. and the Royal Shakespeare Theatre at Stratford, one can of course settle for "Men" and "Women."

Of all these euphemistic expressions, the most revolting I ever encountered was at a hotel which had been newly done up in Ye Olde Style, with oak panelling painted on the walls of its so called Dickensian Bar. A notice in black Gothic lettering, and a hand with pointing finger, showed the way to the "Little Boys' Room."

In South Africa, I am told, there is an extension, a second stage as it were, of this particular taboo. Instead of "W.C." the abbreviation used there is "P.K.," which stands for *picanin kyah*, in Kaffir "Little House."

BUT OF COURSE the most spectacular effect which social taboos have upon the language is in the matter of swearing. An oath is powerful in direct ratio to the strength of the taboo which is broken when a man utters it; and once any given taboo ceases to exist, the relevant swearword becomes pointless and goes into decline. The history of such a word as "bloody" therefore sheds a fascinating sidelight upon our ever-changing manners and morals.

We are apt to think of it as modern; but Swift was greatly addicted to it 250 years ago. Even in his *Journal to Stella* the good Dean would say that the weather was bloody hot or that he had a bloody cold. He caught a terrible one during the bitter Christmas season of 1712. It was so bad on Sunday the 28th December that he could not go to Church, though he ventured to dine at Lord Orkney's—"because I could cough & spitt there as I pleased." On the 31st the weather continued cruel, and so did his cold, and he wrote: "I have not the least Smelling." It was not until January 5th, 1713, that he began to recover, his rheum breaking as the frost broke, though with a shiver he declared: "It is still bloody cold."

[1] *Roderick Random.*

The word was considered ethically harmless in his day—and earlier it certainly had no offensive significance. (In *A Midsummer Night's Dream* "Whereat with blade, with bloody blameful blade, He bravely broach'd his boiling bloody breast" is but a harmless rusticity.) We have already noticed that favourite affectation of false scholarship, the assertion that this word represents a contraction of "By Our Lady." It does nothing of the kind, bears no supernatural implications, and its use as an interjection is defined by Partridge as "resulting naturally from the violence and viscosity of blood." Most people are dismayed by blood. "Who would have thought the old man had so much blood in him?" is one of the lines in *Macbeth* which chills us all. Blood is described or implied so often in that play that it seems almost obsessional. "I am in blood stept in so far . . ." "Blood-bolter'd Banquo" . . . "It will have blood, they say, blood will have blood" . . . "These hangman's hands" (a nasty reminder of what Elizabethan executions were like) and—most dreadful line of all—"Now he feels His secret murders sticking to his hands" . . .

That the word blood, with its associations of murder, war, pain and death should evoke horror and even fear in us is not surprising ("There's blood on the earth and blood on the foam And blood on the body when man goes home").[1] But it is difficult to understand why in "polite" society only the adjective should offend. I had a boisterous nautical friend who in my mother's hearing would exclaim "Buckets of blood!" without reproof; had he ever said "bloody" he would have been banished from her acquaintanceship. At worst the word is unpleasing. That it should ever have been "shocking"—and that Eliza's use of it in *Pygmalion* should have caused such a flutter in 1912—is a measure of the decline of invective in modern times.

The First World War removed it from the index of "taboo" words. Beatty at the Battle of Jutland complained "There's something wrong with our bloody ships today, Chatfield" which being quoted by Sir Winston Churchill in 1927 earned the Admiral a place in the *Oxford Dictionary of Quotations* which he would not otherwise have had. Meanwhile our troops, swearing terribly in Flanders, and the Australians, swearing still more terribly on the Gallipoli peninsula, had so

[1] G. K. Chesterton: *Who Goes Home?*

overworked the adjective that it became a starveling scarecrow of an oath, a figure of fun:

> A *sunburnt bloody stockman stood,*
> *And in a dismal bloody mood*
> *Apostrophized his bloody cuddy:*
> *"This bloody moke's no bloody good,*
> *He doesn't earn his bloody food.*
> *Bloody! Bloody! Bloody!"*

The anonymous satire is known as *The Australian Poem.* It goes on to tell how the bloody horse ran away with the stockman and came to a bloody creek:

> *He said: "This bloody steed must swim,*
> *The same for me as bloody him!"*
> *The creek was deep and bloody floody*
> *So ere they reached the bloody bank*
> *The bloody steed beneath him sank—*
> *The stockman's face a bloody study*
> *Ejaculating "Bloody! Bloody! Bloody!"*

In a sense swearwords are like germs. They will sometimes run through our speech and our writings like an infection, which reaches epidemic proportions before our natural defences come into play and we become immune. "Bloody," like the influenza after World War I, expended itself, lost its virulence, and became as mild as a mere sneeze, —so mild, indeed, that when *Pygmalion* was turned into a musical the word was cut out on the grounds that Eliza's use of it, in the curtain line which stunned and shocked our grandmothers, would today have the effect of anti-climax. So she says "Move your bloomin' arse," [1] instead.

The word is still with us, but lacks potency; we play conversational tricks with it, using it in quaint constructions, e.g. for emphasis: "He came round the corner on two bloody wheels" or, derisively, making a sandwich of it to express a cockney contempt for an overlong word or an established institution: "The prole-bloody-tariat" or "The 'Ouse of Bloody Commons."

[1] Lerner and Loewe: *My Fair Lady.*

IT IS INTERESTING to see how "whoreson" suffered an almost identical fate in Shakespeare's day to that of "bloody" in our own. Once upon a time it had been profoundly shocking; indeed in 1483 he who employed it was deemed worthy of the same punishment as one who swore by the awful mystic of the Host:

> Of what estate soever he be usying to swear customably by Goddes body . . . that they charge the Butler to give him no wyne at the meles . . . There was lyke motion to be made of the customable word of hoursen.[1]

The word probably lost its power through being applied not only to a person but to inanimate objects and abstract ideas. At last through repetition it became completely meaningless, and was used by vulgar fellows (such as the grave-digger in *Hamlet*) in exactly the same pointless fashion as "bloody" was used by the Australian stockman:

> 2nd CLOWN: Your water is a sore decayer of your whoreson dead
> 		body. Here's a skull now . . .
> HAMLET: 	Whose was it?
> 2nd CLOWN: A whoreson mad fellow's it was . . .

The word could still reinforce a flow of invective; but one needed imagination to use it so. The Earl of Kent in *King Lear* possessed the right kind of imagination, and having expended a fortune in epithets upon the miserable Oswald, he thought at the last moment of this outworn one, and turned it skilfully to his purposes:

> Thou whoreson zed! thou unnecessary letter!

But the power of the oath had faded; indeed, Doll Tearsheet was already using it as a term of endearment. She said to Falstaff:

> Thou whoreson little tidy Bartholomew boar-pig, when wilt thou leave fighting o' days and foining o' nights, and begin to patch up thine old body for heaven?[2]

Falstaff's answer is too good to leave out: "Peace, good Doll! do not speak like a Death's-head."

[1] *Liber Niger* in *Household Ordinances* quoted in the O.E.D.
[2] *King Henry IV, Part 2.*

WHEREAS "WHORESON" HAS altogether died out of the language "whore" remains very much alive, the most violent and offensive of all the nouns of feminine wantonness, which include trollop, harlot, tart, strumpet, prostitute. Incidentally there is a fascinating contrast between the derivations of those last two words. "Prostitute" comes from the Latin verb *prostituere*, "to place forward," therefore to expose oneself for sale. "Strumpet," on the other hand, is said to be akin to Mediaeval Dutch *strompen*, to stride or to stalk; so the strumpet, Mr. Partridge suggests, may be "a stalker of men." This brings to my mind a marvellous verse in *Isaiah*:

> The daughters of Zion are haughty, and walk with stretched forth necks and wanton eyes, walking and mincing as they go, and making a tinkling with their feet.
> (Wherefore, the Lord said: "It shall come to pass that instead of sweet smell there shall be stink; and instead of a girdle a rent; and instead of well set hair [1] baldness; and instead of a stomacher a girdling of sackcloth; and burning instead of beauty.")

Whatever its original sense, "strumpet" nowadays has a kindlier connotation than either "whore" or "harlot" or the professional term "prostitute." It is countrified and almost jovial, and signifies a generally wanton attitude rather than a mercenary act. Thomas Hardy contemplated a "levelled churchyard" and reflected:

> *Here's not a modest maiden elf*
> *But dreads the final Trumpet*
> *Lest half of her should rise herself*
> *And half some sturdy strumpet!*

But in the vocabulary of wantonness, fashions come and go, words pass out of use and years later are brought back out of their obscurity to match some social whim, meanings and shades of meaning are ever changing as they reflect the mutable attitudes of society. The 18th century "demirep," a woman with half a reputation, was succeeded by the ironic phrase "a woman of easy virtue," for which in turn the Victorians substituted such expressions as "a fallen woman," "an unfortunate female" or "one of the frail sisterhood." We may

---

[1] "Set"—exactly as a girl uses the word today!

think such euphemisms laughable; but they surely represent a more charitable attitude than ours, when we label a person a common prostitute [1] and produce her in the police court with that label attached— as if we should charge a man as "Bill Sykes, *burglar*" when he is put on trial for breaking and entering.

"Trollop" and "trull" present a puzzle. They look as if they were different versions of the same word; but the philologists derive "trull" from "troll," the elf, giant or demon which inhabits caves in northern fables, whereas "trollop," they say, comes from the other "troll," meaning to turn, trundle, roll, wander. So the trollop is a stroller, as the strumpet is.

"Harlot" is another problem for the philologists. It wasn't applied to a woman until the 15th century; and then it meant a female juggler, dancing girl, ballet dancer or actress, for some time before it acquired the sense of prostitute. Nobody knows where it comes from; though some ingenious fellow made the wild suggestion that it derived from the name of Arlette or Harleta, who was the Mother of William the Conqueror! This would make more sense if its original use (from 1300 onwards) had not been as a masculine word. It meant a knave, a rascal, an itinerant jester, a buffoon, or simply a young fellow-me-lad.

"Bitch" has also been used as a masculine epithet—"The Landlord is a vast comical bitch" (*Tom Jones*). But other than Fielding, the only writer I can think of who has so used the word is young Marjory Fleming, who recorded one day as she "sat on her botom" to write her *Journal*:

Today I pronounced a word which should never come out of a lady's lips it was that I called John an Impudent Bitch.

She, however, was a writer who did not take her genders very seriously, for she wrote the famous poem addressed:

> O lovely O most charming pug
> Thy graceful air and heavenly mug . . .
> His noses cast is of the roman
> He is a very pretty weoman
> I could not get a rhyme for roman
> And was oblidged to call it weoman.

[1] What is an uncommon one, incidentally?

"Bitch" has been applied to women since 1400; though the Elizabethans did not use it much in this sense,—Shakespeare never. The Thomas Hobbes, however, introduced it most surprisingly into his translation of the *Odyssey:*

> Ulysses looking sourly answered, You bitch.

Nowadays it seems to be especially popular in the U.S.A., and there is a quaint story of a professor there who was telling a young girl at a party about the fine litter of puppies to which his spaniel bitch had just given birth. Seeing the girl was blushing, he was both surprised and embarrassed; and she, suddenly aware of his concern, was thrown into still greater confusion. "It's quite all right," she said. "It's only that I'm not used to hearing that word applied to dogs."

"TART" BEGAN AS an endearment: the girl was sweet, like a jam-tart—compare the modern American "dish." Among Cockneys in the 1860's it was "a term of approval applied to a young woman." Little ones were called "tartlets." In Australia it meant a sweetheart, and is still among some classes there applied to any girl,—I am told they call prostitutes "tizzies." "Tart" got its bad meaning in England about 1900; but it has never, I think, had the force and damaging quality of "whore," which as epithet or accusation is generally a deliberate insult and an invitation to a row. I like the story of the Thames tugmaster who collided with a pleasure-boat and was accused by the superior young gentleman who had been rowing it of breaking an oar; he leaned over his rail and answered cheerfully:

> "Ow, did I, Charley? And talking of oars, 'aeow's your sister?"

It certainly isn't a pretty word, though one of the 18th century rakes wrote endearingly in a poem of the "small Whores and Play'rs" which during his young manhood had constituted his "only cares." But at least it's honest, straightforward and down-to-earth: "The woman's a whore and there's an end o't" (Dr. Johnson of Lady Diana Beauclerk). —"By God! I never saw so many whores in all my life before." (The Duke of Wellington, after a fashionable party, according to Thomas Hardy in *The Dynasts.*)

As a postscript to this discussion, here are three "nouns of assembly" which caught my fancy. The last, I understand, was invented by a well-known Divine:

A Fanfare of Strumpets
A Chapter of Trollops
An Anthology of Pros.

WE HAVE SEEN how the taboos and the consequent euphemisms associated with sex have resulted in all manner of word-making and word-
changing; but of course there are many other kinds of euphemism,
which have been equally prolific of words. For instance those who seek
to sell their goods or services to the public dress them up in the most
attractive words they can think of. That is the whole business of adver-
tising, which we are not concerned with here. But occasionally the
goods themselves possess such unattractive associations that they would
never sell under their true names; and so some minor genius invents
the term "rock salmon" for dog-fish, or "Alaskan sable" for the fur
of the skunk. As for "coney," it sounds much less common than rabbit-
fur except perhaps to readers of the Bible, where coney appears in the
sense of rabbit many times, and to country folk, for whom the Law pre-
serves it a little longer: poachers are still charged with "trespassing in
pursuit of coneys." Incidentally, the long "o" is comparatively recent;
until the middle of the last century the word was often rhymed with
money or honey, and generally pronounced so.

What about those who sell their *services?* Well, I recently read an
advertisement in a provincial paper which simply said: "FLUEOLOGIST"
followed by a telephone number. I can only assume he thought that
such a grand and Greek-sounding title would remove the stigma implied in Shakespeare's sad lines:

> *Golden lads and girls all must,*
> *As chimney-sweepers, come to dust.*[1]

A more familiar example is provided by the undertaker. That word has
had a series of different meanings; it has stood for "a helper or assistant"; for one who "undertook" to influence the voting in Parliament
(by cash, I fear, rather than argument) in the time of the Stuarts; for
a contractor; for a tax-collector; and even for a Lowland Scot dedicated
to the aim of colonising the Isle of Lewis! In the sense of "funeral
furnisher" it offends me less than the pseudo-classical American "mor-
tician," which contrives to be displeasing without being euphemistic

[1] *Cymbeline.*

at all. It's surprising to learn that undertaker, in the funeral sense, was used as long ago as 1700. If I had made a guess I should have put it down as a piece of genuine late Victoriana, associated with Gothic lettering on gravestones, and the dismal phrase "passed away."

THAT "PASSED AWAY" is typical of what are surely the saddest euphemisms of all. You can read their history in any churchyard which is fairly old; for the tombstones of the last 150 years tell a tale of our growing fear of death and our desperate attempts to find some less dismaying word for it. I suspect that this process has coincided with the decline of real faith, as distinct from the outward show of churchgoing. When a man truly believed in the life everlasting he could afford to speak lightly of death. He could look it straight in the empty eye-sockets and almost pity its powerlessness to harm him:

> *Death be not proud, though some have calléd thee*
> *Mighty and dreadful, for thou art not so,*
> *For those whom thou thinks't thou dost overthrow*
> *Die not, poor death.*[1]

At a time when few people were troubled by doubts concerning the resurrection of the body, it was not inadmissible to jest about the grisly processes of corruption:

KING: Now, Hamlet, where's Polonius?
HAMLET: At supper.
KING: At supper! where?
HAMLET: Not where he eats, but where he is eaten: a certain convocation of politic worms are e'en at him.

This swashbuckling defiance was a particular property of the Elizabethans, and didn't long survive them. Their politer and less exuberant successors spoke of death with more respect, but still without quibbling or prevarication. A person "gave up the ghost": his spirit left him; or he simply "dyed." So say the tombstones of the 17th and 18th centuries, —plainly, even bleakly; and it is not until about 1800 that the mealy-mouthed evasions appear. In country churchyards it is later still, for the fashion lags behind there. In any case these early euphemisms for

[1] John Donne: *Holy Sonnets*.

death are often in the nature of graceful metaphors which in no way offend. "Went to his rest" is gentle and decent, and reminds one of the splendid phrase in *Ecclesiastes:* "Man goeth to his long home." Here is another simple one—I had to scrape away the lichen to read it, and when at last I could make out the name I discovered that it really did belong to a mute inglorious Milton, not John but George.

GE   GE   MILT N

CLOS D   A   LONG   LIFE

26th June 1815

aetat 85

It was engraved in a plain and beautiful style, the work I daresay of a man who had learned his craft in the 1760's. The lettering on memorials gets steadily worse during the 19th century; and at the same time the euphemisms for death become more evasive, more uncomfortable, more ridiculous, as if self-deception went hand in hand with the decline in taste: which it probably did, for the most embarrassing expressions of all are generally to be found in association with imported marble, leprous white angels, and artificial flowers under glass domes. Those whom they commemorate "fell asleep" or something of the kind; they hardly ever died. The trend nowadays is towards simpler memorials and honester inscriptions; but there are still plenty of people in England who seem to be as frightened as primitive African tribesmen to use a plain word for death. The dear departed have either "passed away" or "passed on." Both expressions are horrible; but "passed on" has the very slight excuse that it may represent a faint echo of Bunyan's valediction upon Mr. Valiant-for-Truth:

So he passed over: and all the trumpets sounded for him on the other side.[1]

FOR CONTRAST WITH these funereal euphemisms, here is a cheerful and amusing one, which flourished briefly just after World War II, and suddenly died out. It has a quaint history. In 1945, when the Allied forces were marching into Germany, there was an order forbidding *fraternisation* with enemy civilians. Soldiers being what they are, it wasn't very long before they were giving chocolate to the children,

[1] *Pilgrim's Progress.*

walking arm in arm with the girls, and playing football against the men. *Non-fraternisation*, a ghastly phrase but fitting for the exact opposite of Christian brotherhood, quickly broke down; and the troops then began to speak of "fratting." As you can imagine, the most obvious example of fratting was going out with a girl; and since the average soldier believes with John Donne:

> *Whoever loves, if he do not propose*
> *The right true end of love, he's one that goes*
> *To sea for nothing but to make him sick* [1]

then "fratting" became a synonym for the right true end, and "frat" came into use as an affectionate term for the girl whom one attained it with.

HOW ANGRY our friend Dr. Trench would have waxed at such a word! He inveighed sternly against what he called "words which seek to turn the edge of the divine threatenings against some sin by a jest; as when in France a subtle poison, by which impatient heirs delivered themselves from those who stood between them and the inheritance which they coveted, was called *poudre de succession*." [2] You might think, he went on, that such "clokes for sin" were to be met with only among "people in an advanced state of artificial cultivation." Not at all; for what about the Fiji Islanders who described as "long pig" a man "dressed and prepared for food," in order to "carry off with a jest the revolting character of the practices in which they indulged"?

Another wicked euphemism, he held, was that which "profanely" applied the phrase *eau de vie* to "a drink which the untutored savage with a truer instinct has named 'fire-water'; and which has proved . . . not 'water of life,' but the fruitful source of disease, crime and madness, bringing forth . . . death." He saw words as things capable of fearful impostures; taking on a sort of "ethical colouring" which was like the sheep's clothing of deceitful wolves. He therefore approved the plain Anglo-Saxon word "whore"—though he dared not actually print it in his book—because its coarseness served as a reminder of the "true vileness" of the occupation. How he would have deplored our phrase "street-walker"! He believed in using "ugly words for ugly things."

---

[1] *Love's Progress.*
[2] *On the Morality of Words.*

"What a source of mischief without end in our country parishes is the practice of calling a child born out of wedlock a 'love-child' [1] instead of a bastard."

However much we dislike that sentiment, and Dr. Trench too for his cruel puritanism, we cannot deny that our moral attitudes are inevitably reflected in our choice of words; and for my part I can even raise a cheer for this uncompromising Victorian when he directs his stern glance towards the employers who advertise for so many "hands."
"A man could never have shrunk into a 'hand' in the eyes of his fellow man unless this latter had forgotten that annexed to those hands . . . were also heads and hearts."

"AS POLITENESS INCREASES," wrote Dr. Johnson in the preface to his Dictionary, "some expressions will be considered as too gross and vulgar for the delicate, others as too formal and ceremonious for the gay and airy; new phrases are therefore adopted, which must, for the same reasons, be in time dismissed." Words have their ups and downs, and are the subjects of fashion and foible. There was a time when the word "scent" seemed "too vulgar for the delicate," who substituted the more poetic and rarefied "perfume"; the M.F.H. could have "scent" for his sole use, to describe the rank fox-smell. But to-day it is "perfume" which is regarded as a suburban vulgarity, and a deb. buys what she calls scent from a shop-assistant who persists in using the out-of-fashion word. "Pudding" sounded so gross to our grandfathers that they described even a jam-roll as a "sweet"; but Miss Nancy Mitford would be as shocked if you offered her a "sweet" at dinner as she would be if you called a looking-glass a mirror, which she holds to be a mark of the badly brought-up. How she describes her car's driving mirror I do not know.

"Serviette," I'm astonished to learn, has been in English since the 15th century; but it completely disappeared for a time, and was reintroduced as a new word from France in the days of Queen Victoria. Its Parisian air appealed to the "delicate," who immediately branded "napkin" as intolerably vulgar. But by 1910 or so the position was reversed: and a book on etiquette called *Points Worth Noting* pleaded urgently with its readers *Except when in France do not call a table-napkin a*

---

[1] Old people in my part of the country call it an "oos-bird," I don't know why.

serviette. Elsewhere in this fascinating work its author declares that "There are social verbal solecisms which betray the speaker in a moment." (To say "Granted" when someone begged your pardon was one of them.) So this business of "U and Non-U" is no new phenomenon, and however silly it may seem, if we are interested in the history of words we have got to acknowledge its relevance. It has nothing to do with what is linguistically "correct," for the most indisputably U of our grandmothers said "ain't" and pronounced Calais as Callis. It is simply a matter of fashion in the fluctuating social scene. An uprising Middle Class, socially ambitious, takes its cue from "society" and overworks certain fashionable words. Society, considering the use by Mrs. Suburban-Jones of, say, "doily" or "preserve" (instead of jam) as an upstart affectation, an aping of its betters, then promptly brands both words as vulgarisms. It proceeds to make fun of the uprising class for its ignorance in continuing to use them:

> *Are the requisites all in the toilet?*
> *The frills round the cutlets can wait*
> *Till the girl has replenished the cruets*
> *And switched on the logs in the grate.*

> *It's ever so close in the lounge dear,*
> *But the vestibule's comfy for tea*
> *And Howard is out riding on horseback*
> *So do come and take some with me.*[1]

IT IS NOT only fashionable society that takes up words and makes a great fuss of them, merely to drop them like hot cakes when they become a bore. The professions, the civil servants, the gossip-writers, the journalists all have their favourites from time to time, and often create a kind of vogue for a particular word or set of words,—so that a person seems old-fashioned and out of touch if he doesn't use them. "Global" and "blueprint" had a marvellous vogue among the politicians and civil servants a few years ago. Both of these, I am glad to say, seem to be on the decline.

Our journalists are very apt to copy the American magazines, especially the New York weekly *Time*. A few years ago they seized with joy

[1] John Betjeman: *How to Get On in Society*.

upon the word "balding" and used it to describe any man in the news who had not got a spectacular thatch of hair. They seem at last to have grown tired of it. "Monolithic" is their present fad, to which they give every conceivable meaning other than its true one of "formed of a single block of stone." Another word which appears to be suffering at the hands of its friends is "ethical," a favourite of certain woolly-minded do-gooders, especially in America. They are in the process of changing its meaning from "pertaining to morality" into "proper" or "right." The psychiatrists, at the moment when I write this, are still inordinately fond of "maladjustment" and "imbalance"; and the literary critics of "pejorative," "commitment" and "off-beat." But by the time this book is published the vogue-words will be quite different, I daresay, and those I have quoted will have gone back, a bit the worse for wear, into the humble obscurity which of old was theirs, if indeed they had ever been previously heard of.

Now and then, however, a word which is the subject of a craze survives the inevitable reaction against it, and continues usefully in the language when the craze is done. "Gimmick" looks like being one of these. It has no real synonym, and so fills a gap. We may have grown very tired of it; but I do not think we can do without it altogether.

We got this word from the U.S.A.; it had been current over there, and in Canada, since the 1920's. "Brash" is another from across the Atlantic which has had a vogue lately, especially among journalists. But this is a word which the Americans borrowed from us, and which we have now taken back complete with the new meaning which it acquired while in America. In English it used to mean an attack or assault, also a boat, a sharp storm of rain, a heap of rubble, and hedge-clippings or dry twigs, in which sense it is still commonly employed in the English countryside. Emigrants took it to the U.S.A., where it somehow got the sense of hasty, rash, rough or pushing; but because it doesn't mean *exactly* any one of those things, but perhaps a combination of any two or three, it serves a useful purpose, and we are glad to have it back again.

Sometimes words come back to us after a long absence. I think "smog" may be one of these, for H. L. Mencken says it was of English origin. The inhabitants of Los Angeles seized upon it as an apt word to express their sufferings from smoke and fog in combination; while in the country of its birth it was clean forgotten. Its return, however, was dramatic. On 5th December, 1952, a vast, acrid, sulphurous fog descended upon London, and choked to death not only a number of old or bronchitic citizens, but many of the beasts which were gathered together at Smithfield for the Fat Stock Show. (Many others were saved by the enterprise of Scottish herdsmen, who gave them draughts of whisky proportionate to their size.) Next day these events made headlines in all the newspapers; and SMOG came back to England in thick black letters, an inch tall.

As long ago as 1500 we were calling a cotton material "jean" be-cause it was manufactured in *Genoa*. The word became an emigrant, and only recently has returned from the United States in the shape of "jeans," the trousers made of blue denim. "Fall," short for the season of leaf-fall, was used in a poem by Sir Walter Raleigh; also by John Evelyn in *Sylva*. But for the past 250 years most Englishmen have used the Latin name "autumn," [1] whereas almost all Americans have said "fall." Both words have given loveliness to prose and poetry; and our language has room for them both. So I am glad that lately we have taken to using "fall" again, not only in literature but in journalism and in the fashion advertisements. Fall has come home to stay.

WE ARE OFTEN told that our English language is becoming "American-ised," with the implication that this is something to be deplored. For my part I am astonished that the American influence is not much greater, seeing that we share our books, plays, films, songs, recordings and TV serials, besides having fought side by side in two recent wars. (And wars are great begetters, not only of babies, but of words.) In any case I suggest that we could do with more and more "American-ising," if by this we mean the accession of American vigour to our talk and our writing, American daring in the making of new words, and American toughness in rough-riding over some of the sanctified and stultifying conventions of grammatical correctitude. I certainly do not want to see the language that Shakespeare used (and himself boldly altered, adapted and improvised without much regard for the rules)

---

[1] A grim jest of the criminal classes reminds us that the old word was not en-tirely forgotten. During the 1850s their slang word for a hanging was autumn. The drop had superseded the old gallows, and the implication behind "autumn" was "a fall."

turned into a museum-piece, its words which were bright as butterflies and quick as serpents become like dried set specimens, or flaccid corpses preserved in formalin.

New ideas demand new words to express them; and new words can only evolve out of old ones, that is to say from a living language in the mouths of an inventive and creative people. So although I am all for taking words when we need them from any other language under the sun, I should much rather we made the new words for ourselves. American English is proliferating all the time; and though perhaps out of every 100 terms to which it gives birth only one proves viable, what matter if the sole survivor turns out to be as live-and-kicking an infant as, say, "Gobbledegook"?

How many of these new American words survive the Atlantic crossing, establish a good beachhead, extend it at last into our journalism and slang, and intrude into our common speech? Fewer, I think, than one would suppose. Half a dozen or so spring readily to mind: viewpoint, frame-up, caucus, teenager, chain-store, southpaw (that odd word for a left-handed boxer) and jeep. Probably you will think of many more. One which has an amusing history is "filibuster," a much-travelled word which came from Holland to England in the 16th century as *vrijbuiter*, and was translated literally into freebooter,—free + booty, hence a plunderer. The word went to France and came back into English as *flibustier*. Then the Spaniards adopted it as a term for certain piratical adventurers and as *filibustero* it sailed to the Caribbean and the states of Central America. Thence it went to the United States and became filibuster, with the new meaning of "one who practises obstruction in a legislative assembly." In such a sense it has re-crossed the Atlantic and come back to us. The Americans, I understand, have just invented a new word for a filibuster, in which a member of Congress or Senate speaks for hours in order to hold up a bill—the record is over a hundred. On the analogy, I suppose, of "marathon" they have rechristened this a "talkathon," a hideous bastard indeed. But the Americans, who pretend to be so modern, have a fatal weakness for words from old Greek and Latin, which they sometimes use horribly. We caught "logistics" from them in the late war, and it looks as if we have got it for good. It comes from Greek *logistikos* ("concerned with accountancy and finance") and it contrives to mean everything connected with the supply of armies, including packing and distributing and even dealing with the "rats, rats, as big as bloody cats" in the Quartermaster's Stores.

MOST OF THE words which arrive here from America do so by way of slang; a very small percentage survives for more than a year or two. Slang is a prodigal use of language; its bright bubbles effervesce out of man's invention, they take our fancy with their shimmer and sheen, but they are unstable, and very soon the changeable winds of fashion blow them away. The prigs and pedants who from time to time deplore some current piece of slang are wasting their breath; it is odds on any given word being forgotten in a season. But should a slang word by chance escape the common fate, then woe betide the pedant, for it will live to mock his memory. So do the words "bamboozle," "banter," "sham," "mob" and "bully" take their long revenge upon Dean Swift, who was so unwise as to describe them in 1710 as "Certain Words invented by some Pretty Fellows . . . now struggling for vogue," [1] and to attribute to such words the "Continual Corruption of the English tongue." Bamboozle is a fine word, I think, and I am surprised that Swift could not see it was destined for immortality. Nothing is known of its origin, but it probably comes from thieves' cant, which with the slang of soldiers and sailors, "low" Cockney speech, Romany, and the secret tongues of tramps and vagabonds, has long served as a livener-up of the language. We have got a lot of useful words from these sources,—humbug, bosh, swindler, for instance. Even the word "prig," which I used earlier, is said to derive from the underworld term for a thief! Such introductions from low life give a fillip to the language which might otherwise have lost its vitality,—in the same way as an interbred aristocratic community is given what the geneticists call "heterosis vigour" by the introduction of fresh strains from the classes beneath it.

FOR ANOTHER and quite a different reason we should take cheer from the very existence of slang. It is a token of man's lively spirit ever at work in unexpected places: even in the prison-cell, the doss-house and the dug-out. It is a perennial reminder that *Homo sapiens* in the mass, however unwise, is at any rate not the dunce and oaf which in

[1] *The Tatler*

our darker moments we may believe him to be. For slang, after all, is a kind of metaphor, and metaphor, we have agreed, is a kind of poetry; you might say indeed that slang is a poor-man's poetry. I know it has lifted my heart again and again,—during the war, for instance, when some grim-gay popular saying, some catchword which seemed bred by laughter out of despair, gave me fresh proof that the jesting imagination was still unquenched.

Yet how weird and how remote that war-time slang seems in retrospect: the odd schoolboy-talk of young naval officers ("It was harry flatters when we brought the pongos back from France"); the unflagging irony of those pongos or brown jobs, who termed the remarkable array of ribbons seen upon some allied breasts "Liquorice Allsorts," and their own—in 1942—solitary medal a "Naafi gong"; above all, the shoulder-shrugging laconics of the R.A.F., a language devised by men who were half-children and half-cynics and wholly fatalists to imply the things they dared not express—"Gone for a Burton . . . poor old Prune . . . pressed the tit and nothing happened . . . kissed the Spit good-bye and baled out into the drink . . . no future in it, no future at all."

How many of those war-time words and phrases are viable today? "Natter," perhaps? "Prune," an inept, clumsy young ass?—I doubt it. "Popsy"? "Mae West," for as long as people wear inflatable lifejackets? "Duff gen"? [1]—forgotten already. "Chad," the inexplicable name of the character who complained "WOT, NO—?" from barracks walls? Dead as a doornail. "Prang"? There is some life in it perhaps, though it seems to be out of favour at the moment; it remains for airmen the perfect echoic expression of a crash. Most of the others would vanish into limbo were it not for the industrious lexicographers, whose job it is to collect *every* word that has had a vogue in journalism or literature, whether it is current, obsolescent or obsolete. So is the historical record of the language well-kept and preserved. All the words I have mentioned are sure to be in Mr. Eric Partridge's *Dictionary of Slang* already; and without doubt almost every English word that did service in the war will be called on parade again in the next *Supplement* to the O.E.D.; for its editors are argus-eyed.

HOW VIGILANT and ever-wakeful they are, we shall learn if we turn

---

[1] Unreliable or useless information.

over the pages of the previous *Supplement*, published in 1933. The new words coined in the preceding fifty years, with the new usages of old ones, are comprised in its 866 large pages. Here we shall find "pelmanism," "puff-billiards" and "psychoanalysis" given dictionary status for the first time. "Willies" are described as "a nervous feeling of discomfort; the creeps" and we are shown that the word was apparently first used in 1900. And here is "whoopee" (also from the U.S.A.) which made its début in a popular song in 1928—the "harmless drudge" doesn't miss much!

> *Another bride, another June*
> *Another sunny honeymoon,*
> *Another season, another reason for making whoopee!* [1]

"To rejoice noisily," says the *O.E.D.* concisely, "to have a good time."

We find "caterpillar tractor," which in the next *Supplement* will be abbreviated to "cat," and "hike" ("of obscure origin, to walk or march laboriously or vigorously, to tramp") which will doubtless be joined in due course by "hitch." "Hula" is here ("a Hawaiian women's dance") and "hula-hula" is not forgotten. The "he-man" ("particularly virile or masterful") strides into the English language, and the "Gollywog" arrives, having been spied in a children's tale. "Tom Collins," whoever he was, is immortalized by a gin-drink. "Jodhpurs" arrive (1899) from India. "Fanatic" [2] is abbreviated to "fan," and fills a long-standing want, giving us an English equivalent of the indispensable Spanish word *aficionado*. And what's this odd-looking word?—None other than Rudyard Kipling's "camelious," described as a "jocund" invention:

> We get the hump—Camelious hump—the hump that is black and blue! [3]

What's more, the dictionary shows that Ian Hay borrowed "camelious," hump and all, in his book *A Man's Man*, 1909.

You get the impression that no published piece of writing, however trivial or frivolous, escapes this committee or coven of dedicated

[1] Gus Kahn.
[2] *Fanaticus* in Latin means "in a frenzy of religious fervour, possessed by a deity or demon" and comes from *fanum*, a temple.
[3] *Just So Stories.*

dictionary-makers. One of them has discovered that there is a new
sauce called Hollandaise (1907). Another has noticed that "aerie"—
the eagle's nest—has unaccountably changed its spelling to "eyrie." A
third has spotted, in *Truth* for 18th May, 1905, the agreeable phrase
"frou-frouing femininities," and caps this with a quotation from a
woman novelist whose heroine "found herself floating and frou-frouing" up some "monastic" stairs. How catholic is the reading of these
learned persons! For we find the word "swiz(z)"—"origin unascer-
tained"—observed for the first time in a novel bearing the promising
title *Mistress*; and, next below it, an early use of "swizzle," recorded
from the *Knickerbocker Magazine* in America.

A word which only just missed inclusion—it was "in being but not
fully established" when the *Supplement* went to press—was "usher-
ette." It will doubtless find its place in the next volume, illustrated with
the following quotation from an account of a court case in 1927:

> Mr. E. Smith, a male attendant, told Mr. Hawke that 3s. 6d. ticket
> holders were shown to their seats by an "usherette." Mr. Justice
> Hewart: Would not the feminine of usher be usheress? (Laugh-
> ter).[1]

LOGIC AND COMMONSENSE were certainly on the side of the future Lord
Chief Justice, but those unpredictable "people," who so determinedly
choose for themselves the words which they speak and write, care
nothing for logic and observe no hard and fast rules. The processes by
which they select and reject are not known, and the course of their
future word-making is always incalculable. If you would prove this to
yourself, think of a few familiar expressions which have come recently
into the language; and try to imagine what impact they would have
made on you if you could have had a preview of them, with their appropriate definitions, ten or twenty years ago. Surely most of them
would have seemed wildly improbable, mystifying or utterly absurd.
"Teddy-boy," for instance; "spiv"; "snorkel"; "shell-egg" (by which
term we distinguished the real thing from the powdered substitute
which was our chief source of what Falstaff called pullets' sperm, dur-

[1] *Daily Mail* 8th July, 1927, quoted by Mr. R. W. Burchfield, Editor of the
O.E.D. Supplement, New Edition, in an article in *The Periodical*, Summer 1958.

ing World War II). "Bulldoze": [1] by what means did such a word as that bash and barge its way into English? And what deep-rooted obstinate defiance of all grammarians preserved for us "layby" against the fury of the purists who wrote indignant letters to *The Times?*

Certainly we can be sure that the devoted lexicographers have observed and recorded the emergence, the struggle for survival, and the subsequent fortunes of these and all the thousands of other words lately created; and the enlarging O.E.D.[2] will continue to reflect, more accurately than most historians, each fad and fashion, trial and tribulation, diversion and discovery of the English-speaking people.

But concerning the ultimate why and wherefore of our word-making—the subtle and secret workings of the myriad-minded force which shapes the course of the language—the dictionary cannot help us, and the most learned of the word-books have little or nothing to say. And truly I think the scientists will have rifled the secrets of the moon and of Mars, long before they can tell us any more about the mystery of man's imagination than the poet did when he wrote

> *The mind of the people is like mud*
> *From which arise strange and beautiful things.*[3]

[1] It originally meant "to flog" in the U.S.A.
[2] Its next *Supplement* is promised for 1967.
[3] W. J. Turner: *Talking With Soldiers.*

Index of Words Discussed

Index of Names and Titles